United in Love

United in Love

Essays on Justice, Art, and Liturgy

Nicholas P. Wolterstorff

EDITED BY
Joshua Cockayne
AND
Jonathan C. Rutledge

FOREWORD BY
Alan J. Torrance

Analyzing Theology Series

 CASCADE *Books* · Eugene, Oregon

UNITED IN LOVE
Essays on Justice, Art, and Liturgy

Analyzing Theology Series

Copyright © 2021 Nicholas P. Wolterstorff. All rights reserved. Except for brief quotations in critical publications or reviews, no part of this book may be reproduced in any manner without prior written permission from the publisher. Write: Permissions, Wipf and Stock Publishers, 199 W. 8th Ave., Suite 3, Eugene, OR 97401.

Cascade Books
An Imprint of Wipf and Stock Publishers
199 W. 8th Ave., Suite 3
Eugene, OR 97401

www.wipfandstock.com

PAPERBACK ISBN: 978-1-6667-1559-0
HARDCOVER ISBN: 978-1-6667-1560-6
EBOOK ISBN: 978-1-6667-1561-3

Cataloguing-in-Publication data:

Names: Wolterstorff, Nicholas, author. | Cockayne, Joshua, editor. | Rutledge, Jonathan C., editor. | Torrance, Alan J, foreword.

Title: United in love : essays on justice, art, and liturgy / by Nicholas P. Wolterstorff ; edited by Joshua Cockayne and Jonathan C. Rutledge ; foreword by Alan J. Torrance.

Description: Eugene, OR: Cascade Books, 2021 | Series: Analyzing Theology | Includes bibliographical references and index.

Identifiers: ISBN 978-1-6667-1559-0 (paperback) | ISBN 978-1-6667-1560-6 (hardcover) | ISBN 978-1-6667-1561-3 (ebook)

Subjects: LCSH: Love—Religious aspects | Love—Philosophy | Christianity and justice | Justice (Philosophy) | Social ethics | Christian ethics | Christianity and the arts | Liturgics | Ritual | Worship

Classification: BV4639 W65 2021 (print) | BV4639 (ebook)

09/30/21

Chapter 2 was originally printed in *The Future of Creation Order, Volume 2*, edited by Govert J. Buijs and Annette K. Mosher, 143–151. New York: Springer, 2018. Reprinted with permission.

Chapter 3 was originally printed in *Love and Justice*, edited by Ingolf U. Dalferth and Trevor W. Kimball, 161–74. Tubingen: Mohr Siebeck, 2019. Reprinted with permission.

Chapter 5 was originally printed in *The Concept of Social Justice*, edited by Christopher Wolfe, 143–51. South Bend, IN: St. Augustine's Press, 2019.

Chapter 6 was originally printed in *Abraham's Children: Liberty and Tolerance in an Age of Religious Conflict,* edited by Kelly James Clark, 141–59. New Haven: Yale University Press, 2012. Reprinted with permission.

Chapter 7 was originally printed in *Christianity and Human Rights*, edited by John Witte and Frank Alexander, 153–72. Cambridge: Cambridge University Press, 2010. Reprinted with permission.

Chapter 8 was originally printed in *Envisioning the Good Life: Essays on God, Christ, and Human Flourishing in Honor of Miroslav Volf*, edited by Matthew Crossman, Zoran Grozdanov, and Ryan McNally Linz (Eugene OR: Cascade Books, 2017), pp.163–180. Reprinted with permission.

Chapter 12 was originally printed in *Christ the Sacramental Word*, edited by David Brown and Ann Loades, 103–22. London: SPCK, 1996. Reprinted with permission.

Chapter 13 was originally printed in *What Is Jesus Doing? God's Activity in the Life and Work of the Church,* edited by Edwin Van Driel, 247–69. Downers Grove, IL: InterVarsity Press, 2020. Reprinted with permission.

Contents

Analyzing Theology Series Introduction | ix
Foreword, by Alan J. Torrance | xi
Acknowledgements | xvii

United in Love
1. The Underlying Unity of Love, Justice, Art, and Liturgy | 3

Justice
2. Love and Justice | 25
3. What Makes Gratuitous Generosity Sometimes Unjust? | 36
4. The Just Limits of Love; or Why an Ethic of Pure Benevolence Is Not Sufficient for Morality | 51
5. All Justice Is Social, but Not All Justice Is Social Justice | 64
6. Religious Intolerance and the Wounds of God | 79
7. Modern Protestant Developments in Human Rights | 99

Art
8. Human Flourishing and Art That Enhances the Ordinary | 119
9. What Sort of Worth Do Works of Art Have? | 136
10. Art and the Formation of Just Persons | 148
11. Social Protest Art and the Graphic Art of Georges Rouault | 159

Liturgy
12. Sacrament as Action, Not Presence | 177
13. Preaching the Word of God | 196

14. Knowing God by Liturgically Addressing God | 214
15. Art and Liturgy | 240

Afterword | 252

Bibliography | 257
Index | 261

Analyzing Theology

The 1980s witnessed a sea change in the academic, philosophical study of Christian doctrines on the heels of a renewal in philosophy of religion initiated by such prominent figures as Alvin Plantinga, Marilyn McCord Adams, William P. Alston, Eleonore Stump, and Nicholas Wolterstorff. At the turn of the second millennium, interest in the analysis of Christian doctrine only grew more profound as analytic philosophers and systematic theologians began to interact in more substantive ways. These interactions eventuated in the rise of Analytic Theology, an explicitly constructive theological program equipped with the tools and methods of analytic philosophy.

Despite its significant promise for driving theology forward in both the academy and the church, much of analytic theology remains outside the grasp of non-specialists. One of the fundamental goals of this series is to broaden analytic theology's audience and influence.

Analyzing Theology is a series of books in Christian theology that showcases cutting edge work in analytic and systematic theology. Monographs in the series are aimed at: (i) introducing cutting-edge analytic and systematic theology, (ii) providing a platform for original contributions in analytic and systematic theology, and, (iii) connecting questions of theoretical significance to theology with the practices of actual theological communities.

Analytic Theology is an emerging methodology that draws from the tools and methods of contemporary analytic philosophy to serve the ends of constructive systematic theology. Those methods make use of contemporary logical and conceptual analysis, emphasize the virtues of clarity and concision (as employed within the analytic philosophical tradition), and typically include a commitment to the objectivity of truth, goodness, justice, and rationality.

The monographs in the series span a range of Christian traditions and encompass a range of subject matter. This includes discussions of the method of analytic theology, exploring its engagements with other theological disciplines (such as biblical studies), as well as exemplifying this method by addressing underexplored theological topics from an analytic perspective.

Series Editors:

Joshua Cockayne, Honorary Lecturer in Analytic and Exegetical Theology in the School of Divinity at the University of St Andrews and City Centre Mission Lead, Diocese of Leeds

Jonathan C. Rutledge, researcher at the The Logos Institute for Analytic and Exegetical Theology, University of St Andrews and Research Fellow at the Center for Philosophy of Religion, University of Notre Dame

Editorial Board:

Amy Peeler, Associate Professor of New Testament at Wheaton College.

Patrick Smith, Associate Research Professor of Theological Ethics and Bioethics; Senior Fellow, Kenan Institute for Ethics, Duke University

Eleonore Stump, Robert J. Henle, S.J., Professor of Philosophy, Saint Louis University

Helen de Cruz, Professor of Philosophy Danforth Chair in the Humanities Department of Philosophy, Saint Louis University

Alan Torrance, Professor Emeritus of Systematic Theology, University of St Andrews

Mark Wynn, Nolloth Professor of the Philosophy of the Christian Religion, Oxford University

William J. Abraham, Director of the Wesley House of Studies, George Truett Seminary, Baylor University

Linda Zagzebski, George Lynn Cross Research Professor, Kingfisher College Chair of the Philosophy of Religion and Ethics, University of Oklahoma

Foreword

Nicholas Wolterstorff is one of the foremost philosophical theologians of the last hundred years. Together with Alvin Plantinga, he was key to what has amounted to a sea-change in attitudes toward theism amongst academic philosophers, transforming attitudes towards the epistemic status of theism. His "Introduction" to the first volume of *Inquiring about God* opens with the observation, "the past several decades have seen an extraordinary flourishing of philosophy of religion within the analytic tradition of philosophy." What should be added is that his own contribution to this has been immense. One feature of his research, however, sets him apart from the rest of his peers. The range of his numerous monographs and other publications is unparalleled in the field, covering metaphysics, epistemology, theological ethics, political theology, aesthetics, and, more recently, liturgy.

The focus of his earliest research was in ontology and his first monograph on universals was inspired, in part, by his Harvard supervisor, D. C. Williams. This was followed by influential work in epistemology. He and Alvin Plantinga established what has come to be known as "Reformed Epistemology," which holds that religious belief can be rational without any appeal to evidence or arguments. Consequently, they opposed the widely held assumption that for theistic beliefs to be deemed rational they had to be shown to be grounded in other more foundational beliefs. The effect of their collaborative work has generated extensive research and numerous publications in the field over the last four decades. This, in turn, has inspired a root and branch rethink of how we approach the justification of Christian belief. In 1995, he published an influential monograph on the theological grounds of such belief, analyzing what is involved in the claim that God speaks.

Since 1980, he has published extensively in three fields of research that form the backdrop to the essays in this volume.

The first of these has been in the field of aesthetics. His first monograph in the field was entitled *Works and Worlds of Art* (Clarendon, 1980).

Over the four decades since, he has continued to publish extensively in this area, the most recent of his monographs being *Art Rethought: The Social Practices of Art* (Oxford, 2017).

The second focus of his research over the last four decades has concerned the overlapping issues in social ethics, political theology, and the nature of justice. This has also found expression in the publication of an extensive series of monographs. The first of these grew out of the Kuyper Lectures given in the Free University of Amsterdam in 1981 and was entitled *Until Justice and Peace Embrace*. There then followed six further monographs, the most recent of which appeared in 2015 and was entitled *Justice in Love*.

The third field of expertise represented in this volume concerns liturgy. This research interest has come to the fore during the last decade and includes *The God We Worship: An Exploration of Liturgical Theology* (Eerdmans, 2015), which was adapted from his 2013 Kantzer Lectures in Revealed Theology (TEDS) and, most recently *Acting Liturgically: Philosophical Reflections on Religious Practice* (Oxford, 2018).

A notable feature of his work has been his ongoing interest in the history of ideas. This is evident in his extensive engagement with the works of John Locke and Thomas Reid.[1] Together with William Alston and Alvin Plantinga, Wolterstorff did a great deal to revitalize interest in Thomas Reid, whose ideas were influential in their establishment of Reformed Epistemology.

A long-standing feature of the Reformed tradition, which harks back to the Puritans, has been a commitment to education. This tradition has also found expression in Wolterstorff's pedagogical interests. His commitment to communication is apparent from the lucidity and clarity of his writing style, but it is made explicit in the topics of three of his other monographs, namely, *Educating for Responsible Action* (1980), *Educating for Life: Reflections on Christian Teaching and Learning* (2002), and *Educating for Shalom: Essays on Christian Higher Education* (2004).

The book of his that has been most widely read, however, is not an academic book at all, namely, his diary of profoundly moving reflections written after the loss of his twenty-five-year-old son, Eric, who died in 1983 in a climbing accident. *Lament for a Son*, which belongs to a similar genre to C. S. Lewis' *A Grief Observed*, has proved a source of support and inspiration to a generation of people struggling with the loss of a loved one.

---

1. Reid was the "earliest and fiercest critic" of David Hume, his contemporary and fellow Scot. Cf. Bartholomew and Goheen, *Christian Philosophy*, 138.

Wolterstorff's academic standing in the field—across several fields, indeed—is evident not only in his many monographs but also in the prestigious endowed lectureships he has given. These include the Kuyper Lectures (Free University of Amsterdam), the Wilde Lectures (Oxford), the Gifford Lectures (St Andrews), the Stone Lectures (Princeton), and the Taylor Lectures (Yale).[2]

This book is a launch volume in a new and ambitious series in analytic theology. It is indicative of Professor Wolterstorff's perception of the importance of this series that he should have chosen this series in which to publish this key volume of essays. It is also a vote of confidence in its editors who, like him, are also analytic theologians with doctorates in analytic philosophy and who, it should be added, have impressive publication records in their own right.

Now to the volume itself. There are several features of this volume that make it particularly important. First, these are Professor Wolterstorff's culminating reflections on topics that have been the focus of his research over the last four decades, namely, justice, art, and liturgy. Half of its essays are new and, as yet, unpublished. All the essays, bar two, are the results of recent research. The second feature that makes it so important is that it provides unique insight into how he understands the relationship between justice, art, and liturgy.

The volume opens by discussing the "deep affinity" that unites justice, art, and liturgy and the distinctive way in which each of the three embodies that affinity. The springboard for his discussion is an analysis of five distinct forms of "love." This provides the setting for his account of the mutual relations between the three fields.

The central essay of the section on "Justice" opens with an analysis of social justice and the nature of rights. This leads into an analysis of the widespread unease with the notion of social justice. If, as he argues, social injustice is "injustice perpetrated on members of society by laws and public social practices," why would anyone speak out against a concern for social justice? First published in 2013, his analysis of attitudes is remarkably prescient of contemporary challenges confronting society at large and

---

2. It might be added that he has held visiting professorships in Harvard, Princeton, Yale, Oxford, Notre Dame, Texas, and Virginia and has served as president of the American Philosophical Association (Central Division) and of the Society of Christian Philosophers.

its conclusions could not be more pertinent. This chapter alone should be prescribed reading!

A preceding essay considers how far gratuitous generosity is compatible with the requirements of justice—a question that is relevant to the theology of divine mercy. Wolterstorff's analysis of the parable of the laborers in the vineyard serves to illustrate how a natural inclination to interpret gratuitous acts of mercy as unjust can be ill-conceived.

The next essay raises further questions on the relationship between love and benevolence on the one hand and justice on the other. What does justice bring to the table of morality that love as benevolence does not? For Wolsterstorff, "benevolence aims to enhance the quality of a person's life, justice pays due respect to a person's worth." The distinctions he makes are illustrated with reference to the former apartheid regime in South Africa where, he argues, Afrikaners were at times happy to talk about *their* moral status, their acting *benevolently*, while side-stepping recognition of the moral condition of the so-called blacks and coloreds and the fact that they were *being wronged*. What this demonstrates, he argues, is that "an ethic of pure benevolence is not sufficient for morality and can lead its adherents to perpetrate injustice."

The essay on religious intolerance develops further his interpretation of justice in terms of respect for a person's worth. No matter how much one may happen to dislike another person's religious beliefs, to be intolerant is to wrong that person and, given that she is beloved of God, to wrong her is to wrong God. In other words, there is a *theological* imperative to be tolerant towards those of other religious views. The section on justice concludes with a detailed and in-depth discussion of human rights and, indeed, "natural human rights." A person's rights are grounded not in some natural capacity that they possess but, rather, in the fact that "God loves redemptively all who bear the *imago Dei*—loves them equally and loves them perpetually. It is the worth we have on account of being so honored by God that grounds natural human rights." This is an approach that can affirm without qualification the rights and dignity of those who are not responsible for their actions due, for example, to advanced Alzheimer's or severe mental impairment.

At the heart of the second section on "Art" is Wolterstorff's argument that art contributes to our flourishing by enhancing our ordinary activities. Singing while working enhances the work; singing our praise and thanksgiving enhances our praise and thanksgiving. In this way, moreover, singing contributes to the shalom of those who participate in worship and musical liturgy.

The second essay focuses on the nature of music as art. In particular, it explores the implications of rejecting an instrumentalist view of art and music. For Wolterstorff, works of music have intrinsic, non-instrumental worth. So what does this mean for the relationship between the worth of works of music and our attentive listening to them? If music has intrinsic value, its worth does not lie in the satisfaction of the hearer in response to its being heard sonically. It can be enjoyed by a person reading a score and not "hearing" it physically at all.

The final two essays bring the discussion of art into relation with the discussion of justice and liturgy. When we appropriate the words of the Psalms in our worship, he argues, we are shaped and formed by those words to become lovers of justice. That is, music enhances our orientation towards God's just purposes for this world. Social protest art can be interpreted similarly, and Wolterstorff argues that Rouault's prints of nasty, arrogant, and self-satisfied human beings generate in us a sense of revulsion. The effect of protest art can be an enhancement of our sense and, indeed, recognition of injustice. In sum, when we view a visual expression of injustice in society, we find ourselves newly sensitized to such injustice.

The final section on liturgy uses speech-action theory to interpret Calvin's account of the sacraments and contrast it with that of Aquinas. The emphasis on God-action as opposed to sign-action opens the door to the recognition that, as he puts it, "to enter the liturgy, as Calvin understands it, is to enter the sphere not just of divine presence but of divine action." Here, "God is less a presence to be apprehended in the liturgy than an agent to be engaged." This raises the question as to the nature of divine agency in the reading of Scripture and the preaching of the Word of God. What exactly is meant by the acclamation in the liturgy, "This is the Word of the Lord?" Addressing this gives rise to a fascinating discussion of Karl Barth's views on the topic and what Wolterstorff perceives to be a tension between two different kinds of statements that Barth makes—a discussion that raises again the question of divine agency in and through the liturgy. In the next chapter, the focus moves from God's action in the liturgy to our participation in it. Liturgical address facilitates our knowledge of God in that it is a means of becoming attuned to the divine reality that we yearn to know.

So how precisely is the relationship between art and liturgy to be understood? For Wolterstorff, liturgical art is an *interpretation* of the liturgy where artistic interpretations of it actually change the liturgy itself, as well as our ways of understanding and experiencing the liturgy. When an architect designs a church building for a congregation, she does so in a manner that respects the congregation's understanding of the liturgy. At the same time, however, the building will have an impact upon the congregation's understanding of the liturgy. This requires us, he suggests, to adopt an interactionist model for thinking about liturgical art. What this suggests is that Christian liturgy and the practices of the arts interact with each other, engaging one another. In this engagement, he argues, each practice must honor the authentic norms and values of the other. This concept of mutual honor paves the way for the concluding essay of the volume.

The themes of enhancement, mutual respect, and affirming and upholding the dignity of the other are key to Wolterstorff's exploration of each of the three fields represented in this volume. They are also key to the way in which he understands the interrelationship between them. It is appropriate therefore, that the volume should conclude with an essay on honouring the other. Those created in the image of God are created to honor others in the recognition that they too are created in the image of God and bear God's image. This means that we are called in every form of interaction and debate to recognize that and witness to it. He concludes by quoting the author of First Peter, who addresses his readers as a "chosen race, a royal priesthood, a holy nation, God's own people called out of darkness into the light" (1 Pet 2:9) and concludes with the exhortation that we honor one another. This is key to understanding God's relation to the world and purposes for it. It is also key to understanding not only the nature and significance of justice, liturgy, and art but also the interrelationship between them.

This tightly coherent and profoundly insightful volume of essays is the outcome of a lifetime of academic research and reflection by one of the finest Christian intellectuals of our day. The topics it addresses, moreover, are of the utmost relevance not only to our flourishing as individuals but also to the well-being of our society, our culture, and the Christian church.

Alan J. Torrance, 2021

Acknowledgements

The editors would like to thank those who have made this volume possible: To Michael Thomson at Wipf & Stock for his enthusiasm for the series and for this project. Thanks to D. T. Everhart for his diligence in helping to edit the volume and to Alan J. Torrance for his splendid foreword.

We would also like to thank our colleagues at Logos Institute for Analytic and Exegetical Theology at the University of St Andrews for their ongoing support. This volume exemplifies all that the Logos Institute aims to promote and which Wolterstorff's career has been characterized by: the very best minds in philosophical theology writing on issues of importance to the life of faith. We would also like to thank our families—Eleanor, Judah, and Emmeline, on the one hand, and Bethany, Caspian, and Theodore, on the other—for their love and encouragement throughout the editing process.

United in Love

1

The Underlying Unity of Love, Justice, Art, and Liturgy

I have written extensively about justice,[1] about art,[2] and about liturgy.[3] I was not motivated to write about these three dimensions of our existence by some philosophical system I had devised that required, for its completion, that I address these particular dimensions. In each case, my decision to reflect on that dimension of our existence was motivated by certain engagements with justice and injustice, with works of art, and with liturgies. My reflections were motivated from below, as it were, not from above—motivated by experience.

Yet, when I now look back on how I have come to understand justice, art, and liturgy, I see that there is, in fact, a deep affinity among them. I see that it would have been possible to articulate, as three parts of a system, the conclusions to which I have been led. I do not propose doing that, neither here nor elsewhere. What I propose doing in this essay is to bring to light the deep affinity that I now discern among them and the distinctive way in which each of them embodies that affinity.

I have also written about love—though nowhere near as extensively as about justice, art, and liturgy. The English word "love" is used to refer to a number of quite distinct phenomena. One of those has the same deep affinity to justice, art, and liturgy that those have to each other. I propose, in this essay, bringing to light that affinity as well and the distinctive way in which that form of love embodies that affinity. Let me begin with what I have written least about, namely, love.

---

1. See especially Wolterstorff, *Justice: Rights and Wrongs,* and Wolterstorff, *Justice in Love.*

2. See especially Wolterstorff, *Art in Action,* and Wolterstorff, *Art Rethought.*

3. See especially Wolterstorff, *Acting Liturgically.*

Distinct Forms of Love

One form of love is the love that seeks to promote or sustain what one judges to be the good of some person or animal, call it *love as benevolence*. The New Testament writers used the Greek term *agapē* to refer to this kind of love when its object was God or a human being. Another form of love is the love that consists of being drawn to someone or something on account of what one judges to be some intrinsic goodness of the person or thing, call it *love as attraction*. It is love as attraction that one has in mind when one says, for example, "I love Schubert's late sonatas" or "I loved last night's display of the northern lights." Such love was called *eros* by the ancient Greeks. Third, there is the love that consists of finding enjoyment in some activity: loving playing the piano, loving gardening, loving woodworking, and so forth. Call this form of love, *activity-love*. Fourth, there is the love that consists of being attached to someone or something: to one's children, to one's spouse, to one's pets, to one's house. Call this, *love as attachment*. And fifth, there is the love of friends for each other, call it *love as friendship*. Such love was called *philia* by the ancient Greeks and by the New Testament writers.[4]

Love as benevolence, love as attraction, and activity-love, are alike in being oriented toward what the agent judges to be some actual or prospective instance of goodness, some actual or prospective case of *embodied goodness*; they are distinct from each other in the nature or object of the orientation. The orientation of benevolence-love toward embodied goodness is that of the agent being committed to promoting or sustaining what she judges to be some good in the life of some person or animal. The orientation of attraction-love toward embodied goodness is that of the agent being drawn to someone or something on account of what she judges to be some intrinsic goodness that the person or thing already possesses. The orientation of activity-love toward embodied goodness is that of finding enjoyment in what one judges to be some intrinsic goodness of the activity one is performing or could perform.

Love as attachment is different from these and, to my mind, more mysterious; it does not consist of orientation toward what one judges to be embodied goodness. I find myself attached to my spouse, my children, my friends, our house, our cat. It was not my recognition of the excellence of the person or thing that caused my attachment. If I can manage to view the situation objectively I may concede that, if I were just going for excellence, I would not have fastened onto these children, this house, this cat. What

---

4. There are yet other forms of love, for example, *instrumental love*: prizing something on account of some benefit that it brings to oneself, for example, prizing one's dog for the companionship it provides one.

accounts for my attachment is that, in one way or another, I became bonded. I recognize that your cat is finer than mine. No matter. Mine is the one that I found huddled on my doorstep one cold winter morning meowing piteously. I took it in, cared for it, and became attached. This is the cat I love. Of course, attachment may open one's eyes to some intrinsic goodness, hitherto unnoticed, of that to which one is attached.

Love as friendship is likewise not characterized by a distinct orientation toward embodied goodness. What characterizes friendship-love is, instead, that it combines love as benevolence, love as attraction, and love as attachment. Friendship love is complex in a way that the other forms of love I have identified are not.

In identifying and naming these five forms of love and pointing to a similarity among three of them, I have assumed that the readers of this essay already have some understanding of these forms of love. If our topic were just love, and not love, justice, art, and liturgy, I would spend the remainder of this essay trying to deepen our understanding of these various forms of love. I will have to forego that endeavor on this occasion.

I have written a good deal about the relation between love and justice.[5] In everything I have written on the topic, it was love as benevolence that I had in mind. My question was always, how is benevolence-love related to justice? Most other discussions of the topic have likewise focused on the relation of benevolence-love to justice. I propose taking a different tack in this essay. I propose exploring the relation between attraction-love and justice. How is loving Schubert's late sonatas related to doing what justice requires?

Attraction-Love

Love as attraction, *eros*, consists of being drawn or attracted to someone or something on account of what one judges to be its intrinsic embodied goodness: drawn to God for God's goodness, to persons, to animals and plants, landscapes, works of art, institutions and groups, projects, ideals, whatever. We love persons and things for something about them that we find good, something praise-worthy. Often it is difficult, sometimes impossible, to put into words what that is. But whether describable or not, it is for some praiseworthy feature of mind, of character, of body, of commitment, of achievement, that we love the person: something about her makes her love-worthy in our eyes. Something about the tree makes it love-worthy, something about the institution makes it love-worthy. The love Plato had in

---

5. See Wolterstorff, *Justice in Love*.

mind in the *Symposium*, and the love Augustine had in mind when he spoke of our love of God, was attraction-love.

As I mentioned above, I will have to forego trying to deepen our understanding of the nature of love as attraction. I confine myself to expressing my disagreement with two well-known theses concerning the nature of such love, one propounded by Plato and one by Kierkegaard, and to calling attention to a distinct species of such love that is important for those of us who are scholars and teachers to take note of.

The situation in Plato's *Symposium* is that Socrates is summarizing the speeches given at a banquet where the participants agreed that they would offer eulogies of the god Love (*Eros*). Each speech proves more elevated than its predecessor. Finally we arrive at the speech Socrates himself gave. He began his eulogy with the declaration that love always has an object. That object, he said, is something the lover wants or desires but lacks:

> "And so," continued Socrates, "a man may be said to love a thing not yet provided or possessed . . ."
>
> "Certainly," said Agathon.
>
> "Then such a person, and in general all who feel desire, feel it for what is not provided or present; for something they have not or are not or lack; and that sort of thing is the object of desire and love?"
>
> "Assuredly," said Agathon.
>
> "Now then," said Socrates, "let us agree to what we have so far concluded. First, is not Love directed to certain things; of which, in the second place, he has a want?" (200E)[6]

Socrates then reported that, in the remainder of his speech, he rehearsed what he once heard a woman named Diotima say on the topic of love. Diotima urged an ascent from love of beautiful things to love of Beauty Itself. By "ever climbing aloft," the lover of beauty arrives at "the Beautiful Itself and that alone; so that in the end he comes to know the very essence of beauty" (212A).[7]

Eros, said Socrates, is desire for something one lacks. We should entertain the possibility that what Socrates (and Plato) had in mind by the term "*eros*" is not quite the same as what I am calling love as attraction. But if Platonic *eros* is understood as attraction-love, then what Socrates said seems to me not true. Attraction-love is not to be identified with desire for something one lacks.

---

6. *Plato* (trans. Lamb), 171.
7. *Plato* (trans. Lamb), 207.

Start with Socrates' identification of attraction-love (*eros*) with desire. Distinguish between *occurrent* desires and *dispositional* desires. Though I love Schubert's late piano sonatas, I do not now have the desire to listen to them; that is not among my present, occurrent, desires. I do, however, have the disposition to desire listening to them at some time in the future. So might my attraction-love of Schubert's late sonatas be identical with that dispositional desire? And in general, might attraction-love for someone or something be identical with the dispositional desire to be in some sort of gratifying contact with that person or thing? Socrates (Plato) did not distinguish between occurrent and dispositional desires; but if we understand him as having had dispositional desires in mind, is his thesis true, that attraction-love (*eros*) for something is identical with the dispositional desire to be in some gratifying relation with that thing?

I think not. I have twice seen Frank Lloyd Wright's famous Fallingwater house in western Pennsylvania. I love it. But I am not disposed to desire to see it again. Twice is enough. I love it without being disposed to desire at some time in the future to see it.

Neither is Socrates (Plato) correct in holding that the object of attraction-love (*eros*) is always something one lacks. If that were true, then Socrates' lover of beauty would, ironically, no longer love beauty when she finally apprehends The Beautiful Itself. Whatever may be true of Socrates' lover of beauty, my attraction-love for Schubert's late sonatas does not disappear when I am actually listening to them. I love them both when I am listening to them and when I am not.

In *Works of Love*, Kierkegaard argues that every form of love other than agapic love is a form of self-love; in particular, erotic love and friendship-love. This was obscured from the ancients, he says, by their failure to recognize agapic love, that is, "love for the neighbor." They contrasted erotic love and friendship with self-love, which they found "abhorrent." "But Christianity, which has made manifest [agapic love], divides otherwise: self-love [and erotic and friendship] love are essentially the same, but love for the neighbor—that is love."[8] I must refrain from fleshing out Kierkegaard's argument for this claim.

Perhaps what Kierkegaard had in mind by "erotic love" is not quite the same as what I call "attraction-love." But it makes no difference, since his thesis is that every form of love other than agapic love is, at bottom, a form of self-love. That thesis seems to me clearly false. My attraction-love of Schubert's late sonatas has those sonatas as its object, not myself. My

---

8. Kierkegaard, *Works of Love*, 53.

attraction-love of last night's display of the *aurora borealis* had that flashing display in the northern sky as its object, not myself.

If one identifies attraction-love (erotic love) with desire, then there is some plausibility in regarding attraction-love as a form of self-love, since, on that understanding, attraction-love is for the gratification of one of one's desires; and that might plausibly be regarded as a case of self-love. But as we saw above, attraction-love is not to be identified with desire. It may be accompanied by desire for gratifying contact of some sort with the thing loved; but it is not identical with any such desire, since the desire may cease while the love remains.

As I mentioned in my introductory remarks, I want to call attention to a form of attraction-love that is especially important for those of us who are scholars and teachers to take note of, namely, love of learning. It would distract from the flow of my argument to do so here, however. So let me conclude my essay with that discussion, and turn here to justice.

Treating One's Fellows as Justice Requires

Justice, as Aristotle already recognized, comes in two main forms; let me call them *first-order justice* and *second-order justice*. First-order justice consists of justice in our ordinary interactions with each other: teachers and students treating each other justly, merchants and customers treating each other justly, receptionists and applicants treating each other justly, etc. Second-order justice becomes relevant when there has been a violation of first-order justice, when someone has wronged someone. It consists of responding to a violation of first-order justice with punishment, reprimands, reparations, fines, and the like. If the receptionist violates first-order justice by insulting an applicant, then second-order justice in the form of a reprimand becomes relevant.

Following Aristotle, these two forms of justice have commonly been called *distributive* justice and *corrective* or *rectifying* justice.[9] None of the terms seems to me apropos. First-order justice does often consist of the just distribution of benefits and/or burdens, but not always. If someone invades my privacy for prurient reasons, I have not been treated as justice requires; I have been wronged. But if I never learn about it, and if it has no effect on how he and others treat me, there has been no distribution of benefits and/or burdens, and hence no mal-distribution. And as for second-order justice:

---

9. These latter two terms are the terms that W. D. Ross uses to translate Aristotle's Greek terms in his translation of Aristotle's *Nicomachean Ethics* in Barnes, *The Complete Works of Aristotle*.

though some of it does consist of correcting or rectifying what was done, it doesn't all consist of that. A reprimand is not plausibly thought of as correcting or rectifying what was done.

Second-order justice has also often been called *retributive* justice. But that too seems to me not apropos. Retribution is pay-back: answering harm with harm. A reprimand is not plausibly thought of as pay-back, nor is punishment aimed at reform of the wrongdoer plausibly thought of as pay-back.

When I claim that there is a deep affinity between justice, on the one hand, and attraction-love, art, and liturgy on the other hand, it is especially first-order justice that I have in mind.

In the Western tradition, two ways of understanding first-order justice are dominant. One comes from Aristotle. Justice, said Aristotle, consists of equity in the distribution of benefits and/or burdens. The other understanding comes from Ulpian, a jurist of late-Roman antiquity (ca. 170–223). Justice (*iustitia*), said Ulpian, is a steady and enduring will to render to each person his or her *ius*, that is, his or her right or due (*suum ius cuique tribuere*). That's a definition of the *virtue* of being a just person. The definition implies that the *action* of treating someone justly consists of rendering to that person his or her right or due, and it implies that the *property* or *quality* of justice characterizes our social relationships insofar as we each render to others their right or due.

It will be evident from what I said above that I do not regard Aristotle's definition as satisfactory. Not all cases of justice are cases of some distribution of benefits and/or burdens, and so, of course, not all are cases of an equitable distribution. Ulpian seems to me to have gotten it right. All cases of treating someone justly are cases of rendering to them what is their right or due; and all cases of treating someone unjustly are cases of failing to render to them what is their right or due.

But this, by itself, doesn't tell us much. Now we have to know how to think about rights. What are rights? And what accounts for our having the rights we do have? As all readers of this essay will know, the answers to these questions are matters of deep controversy among philosophers. To the best of my knowledge, all parties agree that a right is a morally legitimate claim to something. A right is an entitlement. Beyond that, however, there is little agreement. Here I must confine myself to presenting my own account; I cannot engage alternative accounts.[10]

Begin with the fact that that to which one has a right always is, or implies, a way of being treated. My purchase of a ticket gives me the right to a seat on the plane; and that, obviously, is not a way of being treated. However,

---

10. In my *Justice: Rights and Wrongs*, I do deal at length with alternative accounts.

what is implied by my right to a seat on the plane is that I have a right to the airline officials allowing me to take a seat on the plane; and that is a way of being treated. Throughout our discussion, "being treated" should be understood as including *being permitted.* The right to the free exercise of one's religion is the right to be *permitted* to exercise one's religion freely.

A way of being treated to which one has a right is always a good in one's life, never an evil, never a harm. Rights are, in that way, intrinsically connected to goods. I do not have a right to someone's breaking my leg, period. In case I am in a car accident, I might have a right to someone's breaking my leg in order to extricate me from the wreckage. But then it is to that complex good, of which breaking my leg is a component, that I have a right.

Though that to which one has a right always is, or implies, some life-good of being treated a certain way, the converse is not the case: there are many ways of being treated that would be a good in one's life to which one does not have a right. A whimsical example that I have given in some of my writings is this: it would be a great good in my life if the Rijksmuseum in Amsterdam gave me Rembrandt's great painting, *The Jewish Bride,* to hang on my living room wall, along with a security force to stand guard. But I don't have a right to the life-good of the museum treating me that way; I am not wronged by their not giving me Rembrandt's painting.

So what accounts for the fact that one has a right to some ways of being treated that would be a good in one's life whereas, to other such ways, one does not have a right?

Some of our rights have been conferred, by law or social practice, on all those of a certain standing. I have a right to receiving a monthly Social Security check from the U.S. government because the U.S. Social Security legislation confers that right on all who have the standing of being U.S. citizens, of being sixty-five or over, etc. Such rights have traditionally been called *positive* rights.

By no means are all rights positive rights, however. Our department secretary has a right to being treated courteously by faculty and students. That right has not been conferred on her by law or social practice; it is not a positive right. We have some of our rights just by being the sort of creatures that we are and by standing in the sort of relations in which we do stand. It is such rights that are commonly called *natural* rights.

So what accounts for our non-positive, natural, rights? To explain the difference between those good ways of being treated to which one has a natural right and those to which one does not, we have to bring into the picture two fundamental facts about human beings.

One is the fact that every human being has worth, dignity, goodness, excellence in certain respects and to certain degrees; every human being is praiseworthy in certain respects, estimable. Not only is it the case that our *lives* are praiseworthy or regret-worthy in certain respects and to various degrees; *we ourselves* are praiseworthy in certain respects and to various degrees on account of some achievement on our part, some capacity that we have, some property we possess, some relationship in which we stand. The most fundamental of these relationships is that each and every one of us has the worth of bearing the image of God and of having the honor of being someone whom God wants as friend. This worth is ineradicable. And like much, if not most of our excellence, it is intrinsic, non-instrumental. We human beings are not just tools—though all too often some human beings have regarded others as nothing but tools and have treated them accordingly.

The other fact about human beings that has to be brought into the picture is that we can treat others in ways that befit their worth and in ways that do not befit their worth. If you are a student in a course I am teaching and you have the worth of having done topnotch work, then what befits your worth is that I give you an A for the course; what does not befit your worth is that I give you a C.

Using these ideas, I can now explain how I understand rights. You have a right to the good of my treating you a certain way just in case, if I did not treat you that way, I would not be treating you as befits your worth; I would not be treating you with due respect for your praiseworthiness. Rights are what respect for worth requires. If you are a student who has the worth of having done topnotch work in my course, then you have a *right* to the good of my giving you an A; if I give you anything less, I am not treating you as you have a right to be treated. And that is true even if some substantial good could be achieved by giving you a C rather than an A.

Here is a weightier example of the point: we each have a right not to be tortured as a means of punishment, because being tortured as a means of punishment does not befit the ineradicable worth that each of has on account of bearing the image of God and of being someone whom God wants as friend. I would not be treating you as befits your worth if I tortured you.

Essential to this way of thinking about rights is the distinction between the goodness or praiseworthiness of states and events in one's life—such as having friends, being employed, and having good health—and the praiseworthiness of the person herself—such as being considerate, being consistently just in how she treats others, and having done top-notch work in a course.

The affinity of treating others as justice requires with having attraction-love for someone or something, is now obvious: these are two modes of acknowledging embodied goodness.

Absorbed Attention to Some Work of the Arts

In the spring of 2007, the distinguished American poet Donald Hall paid a two-day visit to the University of Virginia. On the afternoon of the first day he read some of his own poetry to a large appreciative audience; the next morning he led a small seminar for students aspiring to be poets. Though I was neither a student nor an aspiring poet, I was invited to attend as an observer.

In the seminar, Hall frequently illustrated some point he was making by referring to changes he had made in some of his own poems between earlier drafts and the final version. One of his examples was this: in an earlier draft of one of his poems he had spoken of a dog wagging its tail; in the final version, he spoke instead of the dog *swinging* its tail.

A student asked why he made the change. He replied, "because it made it a better poem." Since all of Hall's poems are lyric poems, I assume he meant that it made it a better *lyric* poem. He did not explain why the change made it a better poem. The student who asked the question did not ask him to explain.

It would not be implausible, for those who were not present at the seminar, to interpret Hall's remark as a brush-off. But the remark came near the end of an hour in which he had been talking and fielding questions; and, given what I had discerned of his character in this hour, it never crossed my mind that he had given the student a brush-off. He meant no more and no less than what he said: he changed the line because it made it a better poem. My guess is that everyone in the room felt that *of course* it made it a better poem. It is a cliché to describe a dog as wagging its tail; it is not a cliché to describe a dog as swinging its tail. Lyric poems are better, in general, for not containing clichés. That is why the change made it a better poem. Might the sound of "swinging" as opposed to "wagging" also have contributed to making it a better poem? I don't know.

I was probably the only person in the room sufficiently struck by Hall's remark to remember it. Let me explain why it struck me. The dominant view in present-day philosophy of art as to what gives worth to a work of the arts is that the act of engaging it as an object of absorbed attention is a gratifying aesthetic experience. Gratifying aesthetic experiences are assumed to be *intrinsically* good. Certain works of the arts, when appropriately engaged, are *instrumental* to such intrinsically good experiences; that is what gives them their worth as works of art. Their worth is like the worth of a tool. Hammers are tools for driving nails. If you want to find out whether a certain hammer is a good hammer, try swinging it in the right way at some nails and take note of whether it is effective for driving nails; if it is, it is a good hammer. Works of the arts are for gratifying aesthetic experiences. If you want to find out whether some work of the arts is a good work of the arts, try engaging it as an object of absorbed attention and take note of whether it is effective for making one's attention a gratifying aesthetic experience; if it is, it is a good work of the arts. That is the dominant idea.

Now return to Hall's comment. He did not say that he made the change because he judged that readers would find reading the changed line a more gratifying aesthetic experience than reading the original line. He made no reference whatsoever to what he anticipated would be the experience of readers. His explanation was of a different order altogether. He said he made the change because it made it a better *poem*, that is, a better *lyric poem*. He implicitly identified the genre of his work, namely, lyric poem; and he said that the change made it a better example of its genre. Often, when we evaluate something, we have a certain genre in mind and we evaluate it as an example of that genre. That is what Hall was doing, the genre in his case being a literary genre. Instead of referring to anticipated reader experience, he implicitly brought the literary genre *lyric poem* into the picture.

I suggest that what Hall described himself as having done is typical of artists in general. They don't just make something and then afterwards classify it as a lyric poem, a symphony, or whatever. They have some artistic genre in mind and aim to make an excellent new example of the genre. Associated with each artistic genre is the social practice of creating and engaging works of that genre; and intrinsic within each such social practice are criteria for evaluating works of that genre. These criteria change over time; criteria that were once commonly employed fall into disuse, new criteria emerge to take their place. And, typically, some of the criteria are contested. Poet or critic *A* holds that *X* is a better poem than *Y* because it has a feature ø that *Y* lacks; poet or critic *B* disagrees that that makes it a better poem.

Attached to some artistic genres are criteria for excellence that make reference to audience response. That is true, for example, of the genre *music for easy listening*. The excellence of examples of the genre is determined, in part, by whether most of those who listen have a gratifying easy-listening experience. Possibly some of the criteria attached to the literary genre *lyric poem* also make reference to some sort of audience response. But suppose that Hall did in fact change the line because he wanted to avoid clichés. The property of containing no clichés is not a functional property.

That suggests this question: was Hall implicitly regarding his poem as having, at least in part, *intrinsic* goodness? Do lyric poems have intrinsic, non-instrumental, goodness? If so, then, by the same token, sonatas, symphonies, sonnets, short stories, abstract sculptures, and the like have intrinsic goodness.

Before we draw the conclusion that lyric poems, along with examples of these other artistic genres, do have intrinsic goodness, we should take note of the following. Though in his explanation of why he changed the line as he did, Hall made no reference to anticipated reader response, we can nonetheless assume that he had composed his poem *to be* engaged by the public in a certain way; he composed it *for* a certain public function, namely, absorbed attentive reading by the literary public. And we can assume that he hoped or expected that the literary public would find it gratifying to engage his poem in this way. If they did not find it gratifying, they would not give it a second reading, and no poet is content with that as the fate of his or her work.

Let me note, parenthetically, that the activity I am calling *absorbed attention* has customarily been called, by philosophers of art, *disinterested contemplation*. That term came into common usage in the eighteenth century when writers were trying to identify the way of engaging works of the arts that had recently become prominent and to praise and recommend that mode of engagement. The term "contemplation" carries connotations of passivity, the term "attention" does not. That is why I prefer the latter term "attention"; reading a novel, to take just one example, is not a passive act of contemplation. And as to the term "disinterested," often among the reasons one has for reading a novel is that one expects to be presented with insight into human nature; many novelists want their work to be read in that way. But to read a novel thus is not to read it disinterestedly, that is, for the sake of the activity itself of reading; it is to read it for the sake of one's interest in something that the activity causes, namely, insight. Such reading, though not disinterested, is nonetheless reading with absorbed attention. That is why I prefer the term "absorbed" to the term "disinterested."

End of parenthesis. If Hall wrote his poem with the aim that the literary public would engage it as an object of absorbed attention, and in the hope that a significant number of them would find it gratifying to engage in that way, would that aim and that hope not have guided his evaluations and choices? And if so, would he not implicitly have been taking the excellence of his poem to be grounded in its being instrumental to the public's gratifying experience of reading the poem with absorbed attention? But then, what are we to make of his claim that he changed the line because it made it a better lyric poem—a better thing of its kind? Didn't he *really* change it because he thought readers would like it better than way?

Let me propose an answer to this puzzle. Suppose that Hall's poem is in fact an excellent lyric poem; and suppose that a good many members of the literary public find reading the poem with absorbed attention a rewarding experience. The poem is not an excellent lyric poem because members of the literary public find reading it with absorbed attention a rewarding experience; rather, members of the literary public find reading it with absorbed attention a rewarding experience because it is an excellent lyric poem. And it is an excellent lyric poem because it meets the standards for excellence associated with that genre. Readers revel in its excellence— or more precisely, they revel in those features of the poem that contribute to making it excellent, those features being mostly, if not entirely, nonfunctional features such as freshness of language.

My conclusion is that lyric poems do indeed have intrinsic goodness, and that reading such poems with absorbed attention is a mode of acknowledging that goodness. (It may also be a way of finding out whether they possess that goodness.) And now to generalize: not only lyric poems, but a great many other works of the arts, possess intrinsic goodness. The action of absorbed attention to such a work, on account of what one judges to be its goodness, is a way of acknowledging that goodness.[11]

The affinity of paying absorbed attention to some work of the arts on account of its intrinsic excellence with having attraction-love for someone or something and with treating someone justly is now obvious: these are all modes of acknowledging intrinsic embodied goodness.

Liturgy

Down through the ages, human beings have assembled to enact their religious rituals. They have done so for many different reasons. Sometimes they have thought that the gods were angry with them for what they had done and that the rituals, when done properly and well, would propitiate or appease the gods; the rituals would distract the gods from the people's wrongdoing or would compensate for their wrongdoing. Sometimes the thought was not that the gods are presently angry but that they might become angry. The rituals serve to forestall their anger; when done properly and well they serve to keep the gods well-disposed. Whether the rituals are performed to

---

11. A further generalization beckons: not only works of the arts but other things as well are the objects of absorbed attention on our part for the sake of what we judge to be their intrinsic excellence. Mathematical proofs come to mind, and scenes in nature.

appease the anger of the gods or to forestall their anger, the assumption is that the gods will find the rituals pleasing.

Reading between the lines of some of the prophetic denunciations recorded in the Hebrew Bible/Old Testament, the idea that the rituals are for pleasing God seems to have been common in ancient Israel. Recall the well-known passage in Amos. God is the speaker:

> I hate, I despise your festivals,
>> and I take no delight in your solemn assemblies.
>
> Even though you offer me your burnt offerings and grain offerings,
>> I will not accept them;
>
> and the offerings of well-being of your fatted animals
>> I will not look upon.
>
> Take away from me the noise of your songs;
>> I will not listen to the melody of your harps.
>
> But let justice roll down like waters,
>> and doing what is right like an everflowing stream.
>
> (Amos 5:21–24)

I share the common view that Christians enact their liturgies primarily not to please God, in the hope of thereby placating God or of keeping on God's good side, but to worship God. Not everything that Christians do when enacting their liturgies is, strictly speaking, worship—confession of sins, for example. But worship is the all-embracing context.

What is worship? My *Merriam-Webster's Collegiate Dictionary* (11th ed.) tells me that our word "worship" comes from the Middle English *worshipe*, meaning respect or reverence paid to a divine being. And it says that the Middle English *worshipe* came, in turn, from the Old English *weorthscipe*, meaning worthiness. To my ear, the term "worship" in present-day English remains true to its etymological origins. To worship someone is to pay respect to them for their worthiness. It is, in that way, like the core of what we saw to be treating someone justly.

It is distinctly different, however, from treating someone as justice requires. It is a distinct form of paying respect. What is distinct about it? In particular, what is distinct about worshipping God, as compared to other ways of paying due respect to God for God's excellence? Following God's directives in how one treats one's neighbors is a way of paying due respect to God. But that is not worshipping God. What is distinctive of worship?

One thing distinctive of worship is its *orientation*. In our lives in the everyday we are oriented toward our tasks, toward our neighbors, toward the natural world. When we assemble to worship God we turn around and orient ourselves toward God; we face God. In attending to the heavenly bodies we discern a manifestation of God's wisdom and power; in attending to our neighbor we discern the image of God. But in neither of such attendings do we *face* God. In worshipping God, we turn away from attending to the heavenly bodies and away from attending to our neighbor so as to attend directly to God. We position our bodies accordingly: we kneel, we bow, we stand with face and hands upraised. There is no creature before whom we are kneeling or bowing or standing with face and hands upraised; we are kneeling or bowing or standing with face and hands upraised before God.

We are close to identifying that species of paying respect to God for God's goodness that constitutes worship, but we're not quite there yet. In the course of a theological discourse about God, a scholar might describe various aspects of God's nature and activity and might argue that these ground God's unsurpassable excellence; in so doing, he or she would, of course, be oriented toward God. But talking *about* God and God's excellence is not an example of *worshipping* God. What is missing?

What is missing, I suggest, is a certain *attitudinal stance* of the person toward God. By the term "attitudinal stance" I do not mean a feeling or emotion. The stance may include a feeling or emotion; but it is not to be identified with either of those. An attitudinal stance toward someone is a way of regarding that person. Regarding someone with admiration is an attitudinal stance toward that person; regarding someone with disdain is another example of an attitudinal stance.

The term "adoration" seems to me to come closer than any other word in English to capturing the attitudinal stance of the worshipper toward God; worship of God is adoration of God. When we who are Christians assemble to enact the liturgy, we orient ourselves toward God in adoration of God for God's praiseworthiness, God's excellence—God's *unsurpassable* excellence, let me add.

Adoration has somewhat different content depending on the object of adoration and on how that object is understood by the adoring person. Adoration of a painting by Vincent van Gogh is different in its content from adoration of some mathematical proof. So let me say a bit about what I see as the distinct contours of Christian adoration of God.

A trait that the biblical writers over and over ascribe to God is *glory*; God is of unsurpassable glory. To this the appropriate response is *awe*; Christian adoration of God incorporates *awe*. In the Orthodox liturgy, after the bread and wine have been brought into the sanctuary and the Eucharist proper is about to begin, the priest says, "let us stand reverently, let us stand in awe."

The content of Christian adoration of God includes more than awe, however. One can be in awe of something without worshipping it. Recall the Bush administration's claim, when the invasion of Iraq was about to begin, that the bombing of Baghdad would produce shock and awe. Though the bombing did no doubt produce awe in some people, in no one did it evoke adoration. What has to be added? In our adoration of God, what more is there than awe? *Reverence.* "In reverence, let us stand before the Lord," said the psalmist. Reverence is not the same as awe; nobody revered the bombing of Baghdad. It is especially God's *holiness* that calls for reverence. There was nothing holy about the bombing of Baghdad.

Without now making any claim to exhaustiveness I suggest that the adoration definitive of Christian worship has yet a third component, namely, *gratitude*, gratitude being the response called for by God's *love*. Christian worship is awed, reverential, and grateful adoration of God for God's unsurpassable excellence.

Loving someone or something with the love of attraction, treating someone as justice requires, paying absorbed attention to some work of the arts for its intrinsic excellence, facing God in a stance of awed, reverential, and grateful adoration: these four components of our human existence bear to each other the deep affinity of each being, in its own distinctive way, *a mode of acknowledging something's goodness.*

In Conclusion: Love of Learning

In bringing this essay to a conclusion, let me return to attraction-love and draw attention to a form of such love that is especially important for those of us who are scholars and teachers to take note of, namely, love of learning. I have written about this form of love previously in an essay that I titled "*Fides Quaerens Intellectum.*"[12] On this occasion, I will be brief.

There are college and university professors who do not love learning—or do not love that particular branch of learning in which they find themselves. But that is not how it should be. How it should be is that those of us who are teachers and scholars are in it for the love of it. In my own case, from the first half hour of my first college philosophy course I found myself in love with philosophy. I remember saying to myself, after those first thirty minutes, that I had no idea whether I would be any good at this stuff, but if I would be, this is it. That first love of philosophy has never grown cold.

---

12. The essay is included in the collection edited by Crisp, Porter, and Elshof, *Christian Scholarship in the Twenty-First Century*, 1–17.

What sort of love was that love of philosophy that I experienced in that first half hour? What is love of learning? I suggest that love of learning comes in three main forms.

First, notice how often those of us engaged in scholarship use the language of *doing* and *making*. We speak of gathering evidence, of constructing theories, of developing arguments, of conducting research, of writing books—all highly activistic language. Love of learning, when it takes this form, is the love of producing something of worth—a well-crafted essay, a new theory. It is a species of what I call *activity-love*. It is like love of gardening, love of woodworking, and so forth.

This form of love was not the sort of love of learning that I experienced in that first half hour of philosophy, for the obvious reason that producing philosophical essays was still well in the future for me. Love of learning takes two forms in addition to the activity-love of producing worthy pieces of scholarship, namely, *the love of understanding* and *the love of arriving at understanding*.

Previously one was baffled, bewildered, perplexed, or just ignorant; now one understands. The love of understanding and the love of arriving at understanding are species of love as attraction. The examples of attraction-love that I have given thus far were all examples of love for something distinct from one's self: love of Schubert's late sonatas, love of a display of the *aurora borealis*. Love of understanding and love of arriving at understanding are different in that the former is attraction-love for a state of oneself and the latter is attraction-love for a process of the self. Love of understanding is attraction-love for that praiseworthy state of one's self that consists of understanding something: understanding something of God, of nature, of human beings, of human products and institutions. Love of arriving at understanding is attraction-love for that praiseworthy process of one's self that consists of achieving the state of understanding.

These two forms of love of learning, the attraction-love of understanding and the attraction-love of arriving at understanding, do not exist side-by-side with the activity-love of producing worthy pieces of scholarship. They are the point of the activity. Scholarly activity is for the sake of understanding and of arriving at understanding, both on our part and on the part of others. We produce works of scholarship in order to articulate, record, and communicate what we have understood. Love of understanding and of arriving at understanding are what keep scholarship alive. If those loves were extinguished, scholarship would die out. What would be the point? Intertwined with these two forms of attraction-love is benevolence-love, specifically, the desire to promote in others the life-goods of understanding and of arriving at understanding.

When I read what deconstructionists and postmodernists write, I get the impression that they never think in terms of gaining understanding; for them, the academic enterprise consists entirely of producing essays that others will find interesting and provocative. Some take the radical next step of insisting that there is nothing out there to be understood, production is all there ever is—though it is worth noting that even those who say this tend to get upset when they think that they themselves have been *mis*-understood! They do not want their own works to be treated simply as the occasion for a play of imagination.

Why do we human beings long for understanding when we don't have it? Why do we love and prize it when we do have it? Sometimes we love and prize understanding because what we have learned enables us to causally bring about certain things—enables us to change the world and ourselves in certain ways. But this reason, prominent though it is in the modern world, is not the only reason for loving and prizing understanding. It is not the reason some of us love and prize philosophical understanding; as the old saw has it, "philosophy bakes no bread." There are forms of understanding that are to be loved and prized wholly apart from what they enable us to bring about causally.

So why do some of us love and prize understanding that is of no use for changing things? The only way of answering this question that is available to the secularist is to identify or postulate some factor within the psychological makeup of human beings; Aristotle thought that it is characteristic of human beings to *wonder* about certain things, to wonder why projectiles fall to earth, for example. The Hebrew Bible offers an answer of a very different sort, not incompatible but different, an answer that points away from the make-up of the self to God's awesome creativity.

> "How great are your works, O LORD,"
> "your thoughts are very deep" (Ps 92).

> How manifold are your works!
> In wisdom you have made them all;
> the earth is full of your creatures. (Ps 104)

Over and over the theme is sounded. The cosmos in which we find ourselves is not just here somehow, nor are we just here; both we and the cosmos were *made*. We are *works*, works of God, made with wisdom.

The response of the psalmist to this vision of the cosmos and ourselves as works of God made with wisdom was to meditate reverentially on these awesome manifestations of divine wisdom and to praise the One by whose wisdom they were made.

On the glorious splendor of your majesty,
and on your wondrous works, I will meditate. (Ps 145)

I will sing to the Lord as long as I live,
I will sing praise to my God while I have being. (Ps 82)

Cell biology of the past fifty years is an extraordinary human achievement—admirable both for its intrinsic beauty and for its multi-facetted utility. Those who know it love it. But more than that, it has revealed to us some of the awesome intricacy of this part of God's creation. In coming to understand that intricacy, we get a glimpse of divine wisdom. In response to our apprehension of this magnificence, we stand in awe of the divine wisdom that cell biology has brought to light. We love it.

Justice

2

Love and Justice

Two concepts long prominent in the moral culture of the West are *love* and *justice*. One can imagine a society in which one or the other of these (or both) was absent; in such a society, nobody would think in terms of love or nobody would think in terms of justice. In our society many of us, probably most, think in terms of both.

The reason for this is that we are the inheritors of two comprehensive imperatives issued by the writers of antiquity that employ these concepts. The imperative to do justice comes to us from both the Athens-Rome strand of our heritage and the Jerusalem strand. "Do justice," said the Hebrew prophet Micah in a well-known passage (6:8). The ancient Roman jurist Ulpian said that we are to render to each what is his or her *right* or *due* (*ius* in Latin). The imperative to love comes to us only from the Jerusalem strand: love your neighbor as yourself, even if that neighbor is an enemy.

These two imperatives—do justice and love your neighbor as yourself—do not reveal on their face how they are related to each other. Thus it is that over and over the question has been raised in the writings of the West, in philosophy, in theology, in literature: how are these two imperatives related to each other?

The fact that it is only in our Jerusalem heritage that both of these imperatives are to be found, and not in our Athens-Rome heritage, has the implication that the topic of love and justice was not discussed by the ancient Greek and Roman writers. The ancient Stoic, Seneca, wrote a small book titled *de Clementia*. "Clemency," as used in present-day English, refers to foregoing the appropriate punishment for some crime out of mercy for the offender or his family, out of concern for the common good, or whatever. So one would expect Seneca's topic to be that sort of relation between love and justice. But that is not his topic. By "*clementia*" Seneca did not mean foregoing the appropriate punishment of some wrongdoer out of mercy; he meant choosing the lesser of the punishments specified in law for some crime.

Perhaps the most prominent theme in the literature on love and justice is the theme of tension or conflict. Sometimes this theme takes the form of writers arguing that it is impossible to follow the two imperatives simultaneously; it is argued that they are inherently conflictual. To act out of love is perforce not to act as one does because justice requires it; to treat someone as one does because justice requires it is perforce not to act out of love. At other times the theme of tension or conflict takes the weaker form of writers arguing that following the love-imperative will sometimes wreak injustice, or that following the justice-imperative will sometimes be unloving.

The examples offered of love wreaking injustice fall, for the most part, into three types. First, the way generosity is sometimes dispensed is unjust. This is the issue posed by Jesus' parable of the laborers in the vineyard (Matt 20:1–16). Second, the way in which benevolent paternalism is sometimes exercised is unjust. And third, a persistent charge against forgiveness, pardon, amnesty, commutation of sentence, and the like, is that in foregoing or diminishing punishment of the wrongdoer, justice is violated. This charge is at the center of the controversies swirling around truth and reconciliation commissions of the past thirty years or so. It is also the issue Anselm raised when he discussed the relation between God's love and God's justice in chapter IX of his *Proslogion*. Addressing God, Anselm asks, "How do you spare the wicked if you are all-just and supremely just?"[1]

There are both different kinds of justice and different kinds of love. So a question that comes to mind, once one has noted this theme of tension between love and justice, is what kind of justice and what kind of love do those writers have in mind who see tension between these two?

The major distinction within the field of justice is that between retributive or corrective justice and primary justice—meaning by *primary* justice, the sort of justice whose breakdown makes retributive or corrective justice relevant. So what kind of justice is thought to be in tension or conflict with love?

All kinds. Sometimes the justice that a writer has in mind is retributive or corrective justice; sometimes it is primary justice. And within primary justice, sometimes it is distributive justice, sometimes it is so-called commutative justice.

The situation with respect to the idea of love in these discussions is different. One thing that the English word "love" refers to is love as attraction: the love that consists of being drawn or attracted to something on account of its worth or excellence—as when one says, "I love Beethoven's late string quartets." A classic discussion of such love is Plato's *Symposium*.

---

1. Anselm, *Proslogion*, 125.

Another thing that the English word "love" refers to is love as gratuitous benevolence or generosity—the love that consists of seeking to advance the well-being of another as an end in itself, paying no attention to whether or not justice requires this.

To the best of my knowledge, whenever a writer talks about the tension or conflict between love and justice, it is always love as gratuitous benevolence that he has in mind. Writers don't usually say that this is the sort of love they have in mind; they just talk about love. But when one looks closely at what they say, it becomes clear that it is love as gratuitous benevolence that they have in mind. Perhaps justice sometimes comes into real or apparent conflict with love as attraction; but I know of no case in which it is love as attraction that the writer has in mind when he talks about real or apparent conflict between love and justice. Always it is love as benevolence, love as gratuitous generosity.

Cases of real or apparent conflict between justice and benevolence are often ethically important and intellectually intriguing, as are many of the proposals for resolution that writers have offered. But on this occasion I want to set such cases aside so as to raise a prior question: if love as gratuitous benevolence so often yields real or apparent conflict with justice, forcing the person either to choose between love and justice or to analyze the case in such a way that the conflict is only apparent and not real, may it be that we are misinterpreting our Jewish and Christian inheritance? May it be that when the Torah and Jesus issued the imperative to love our neighbor as ourselves, it was not gratuitous benevolence that they had in mind but some other form of love? And may it be that between justice and this other kind of love there is not tension but unity? May it be that we must re-think our understanding of love—and that some of us must also re-think our understanding of justice?

The Greek word that the New Testament writers used to report Jesus' injunction to love our neighbors as ourselves is *agapē*. The view that what Jesus meant by *agapē* was gratuitous self-sacrificing benevolence or generosity was never more thoroughly developed than it was by the members of the so-called agapist movement in late nineteenth- and twentieth-century Protestant ethics. Taking a brief look at what the modern-day agapists had to say will be a good way of identifying the fundamental issues.

Among the prominent members of the modern-day agapist movement were Søren Kierkegaard, Anders Nygren, Karl Barth, Emil Brunner, Reinhold Niebuhr, Paul Ramsey, and John Howard Yoder. I recently read *Free of Charge* by my former Yale colleague, Miroslav Volf. Volf takes it for granted in his book that the sort of love that Jesus and the New Testament writers had in mind is gratuitous generosity.

The two great documents of the modern-day movement are Kierkegaard's *Works of Love* and Anders Nygren's *Agape and Eros*. Let me on this occasion take Nygren rather than Kierkegaard as my main example of the movement—mostly because, though Kierkegaard was the more profound, Nygren was not only more influential but also more relentless in drawing out the implications of the agapist understanding of New Testament *agapē*.

Nygren saw three great motifs as locked in a struggle for dominance in Western thought. One motif is that of *eros*, *eros* being love as attraction. The motif of *eros* is dominant in the Platonic tradition; it's the topic of Plato's discussion in his *Symposium*. Nygren argues, implausibly in my view, that eros is at bottom a form of self-love. A second motif is that of *nomos*, law. Nygren associates *nomos* with justice; and he holds that the motif of *nomos* is dominant in the Old Testament. The third motif is *agapē*, understood as gratuitous self-sacrificial benevolence that pays no attention to what justice requires. The motif of *agapē*, so Nygren argues, is dominant in the New Testament; it is the love that Jesus attributes to God and enjoins on us in the second love command.

Nygren unhesitatingly affirmed the implications of this scheme, including the implication that in the New Testament, the Old Testament "motif" of justice has been supplanted by the New Testament "motif" of agapic love. He even goes so far as to say that, though Marcion may have gone to extremes, basically he got it right: the New Testament understanding of God is fundamentally different from the Old Testament understanding. The Old Testament God is a god of justice; the New Testament God is a god of love.

Jesus, says Nygren, "enters into fellowship with those who are not worthy of it." His doing so is directed "against every attempt to regulate fellowship with God by the principle of justice."[2] "That Jesus should take lost sinners to Himself was bound to appear, not only to the Pharisees, but to anyone brought up and rooted in Jewish legal righteousness, as a violation of the order established by God Himself and guaranteed by His justice."[3] For them it was "a violation not only of the human, but above all of the Divine, order of justice, and therefore of God's majesty."[4]

Nygren's point is unmistakable: the agapic love displayed and enjoined by Jesus does not incorporate or supplement justice but supersedes it. "'Motivated' justice must give place . . . to 'unmotivated' love."[5] We are not to love

---

2. Nygren, *Agape and Eros*, 86.
3. Nygren, *Agape and Eros*, 83.
4. Nygren, *Agape and Eros*, 70.
5. Nygren, *Agape and Eros*, 74.

the neighbor agapically *in addition to* treating her as justice requires; we are to love her *instead of* treating her as justice requires.

Why did Nygren see love as supplanting justice in the New Testament? Why not love *and* justice? Nygren's answer to this question was admirably clear. He held that the paradigmatic New Testament example of God's love, the example that should shape all our thinking, both about God's love and about our love of neighbor, is God's forgiving and covenanting love of the sinner. God's forgiveness is not a case of doing what justice requires; the wrongdoer cannot claim that justice requires that God forgive him. From this Nygren concluded that the love that Jesus and the New Testament writers had in mind expels any note of doing what justice requires. New Testament love is blind to justice and injustice. New Testament love is an utterly gratuitous self-sacrificing concern for the wellbeing of the other. Here is how Emil Brunner puts the point in his *Justice and the Social Order*: love "does not render to the other what is his due, what belongs to him 'by right,' but gives of its own, gives precisely that to which the other has no right."[6]

Nygren took the argument a step farther. In its blindness to justice and injustice, agapic love may perpetrate injustice. Nygren regarded that as the point of Jesus' parable of the laborers in the vineyard. The landlord, on Nygren's interpretation, acknowledges that when he paid the late-comers the same amount as those who worked all day in the heat, he was being unfair and unjust to the early workers. But the landowner dismisses their complaint with the remark that he has a right to be generous as he wishes. Nygren drew the lesson that we must expect that agapic love—gratuitous self-giving generosity—will sometimes wreak injustice. No matter. The follower of Jesus is called to remain faithful to love and say farewell to justice if that proves necessary.

After Nygren, the figure in the modern-day agapist tradition who thought most deeply about the relation of New Testament love to justice was Reinhold Niebuhr. Niebuhr joined Nygren in interpreting New Testament love as gratuitous self-giving generosity that pays no attention to what justice requires; and he agreed with Nygren that such love might perpetrate injustice. But Niebuhr thought that Nygren's response to the possibility of conflict was glib and naïve. Stick with love, said Nygren. Niebuhr thought that as a social and political policy agapic love was a calamity. Try responding to Hitler with agapic love! A major part of Niebuhr's lifelong opposition to liberal American Christianity was his opposition to what he saw as its naïve assumption that if Christians just loved people enough, people would respond in kind and love would rule the world. In this present age, said Niebuhr, we must expect that

---

6. Brunner, *Justice and the Social Order*, 17.

love will not evoke love but will both perpetrate or abet injustice and get run over. The life of Jesus ended on the cross.

So what to do? Niebuhr thought that it was deeply irresponsible to be content with abetting or perpetrating injustice. Yet as a Christian theologian and ethicist he could not give up on love. His solution was to argue that justice is for this present fallen world of conflicting interests whereas agapic love is for the eschaton of "frictionless harmony," as he called it. To this he added the qualification that here and now, in small-scale situations where conflict is absent, agapic love can be practiced without aiding and abetting injustice.

I judge that Nygren's line of thought is untenable—and Niebuhr's as well, for somewhat different reasons. On this occasion let me focus on Nygren.

First, Nygren's line of thought is exegetically untenable. Justice is not supplanted by love in the NT. Even a casual reading of the New Testament will reveal that, rather than being supplanted in the New Testament, justice is at the heart of the New Testament. I argue this point in detail in *Justice: Rights and Wrongs*;[7] here is not the place to repeat that argument. Let me instead confine myself to noting that Nygren has misinterpreted the parable of the laborers in the vineyard—this being his main textual basis for saying that New Testament love may conflict with justice and that, when they do, the Christian must remain faithful to love and say goodbye to justice.

The landowner in the parable does not say to the complaining all-day workers what Nygren interprets him as saying, namely, it's true that I have treated you unjustly but I have a right to dispense my generosity as I wish. Let me quote what the landowner does say: "Friend, I am doing you no wrong; did you not agree with me for the usual daily wage? . . . I choose to give to these last the same as I give to you. Am I not allowed to do what I choose with what belongs to me?" (Matt 20:13–15, NRSV). The Greek word translated here as "wrong" is *adikos*. I am not treating you unjustly, says the landowner to the complainers. Rather than agreeing with the complainers that he has treated them unjustly, but then insisting that this is an acceptable consequence of his generosity, the landowner contests their understanding of justice.

Not only is Nygren's line of thought exegetically untenable; it is also systematically incoherent. We are always to think of love on the model of God's forgiveness of the sinner, says Nygren. But reflect for a moment on the nature of forgiveness. One cannot just spread forgiveness hither and yon. One can only forgive someone if he has wronged one, and only *for* the

---

7. Wolterstorff, *Justice: Rights and Wrongs*.

wrong he did one. But to wrong someone is to treat that person unjustly, to deprive him of what he has a right to. So forgiveness cannot be blind to justice and injustice. To the contrary: forgiveness presupposes attentiveness to injustice.

The reply may be forthcoming that though it's true that forgiveness cannot be inattentive to injustice—Nygren was mistaken about that—nonetheless it remains the case that forgiveness is not *motivated* by what justice requires. True. But now take note of another and deeper incoherence in Nygren's position, that it is acceptable to perpetrate injustice out of agapic love.

If in loving someone agapically I treat him unjustly, then I violate his right not to be so treated; I wrong him. And if he has a right not to be so treated by me, then I *ought not* to treat him that way. In general, it's the case that if someone has a right against me to my not treating him that way, then I have a correlative obligation toward him not to treat him that way. And if I have an obligation not to treat him that way, then I am not permitted to treat him that way. Nygren's position implies that I am sometimes permitted to do out of love what I ought not to do; sometimes it is even the case that I *should* do out of love what I ought not to do. But that is incoherent. If I ought not to do it, then not only is it the case that I *should* not do it; I am not *permitted* to do it.

Let us now back up, and rather than just assuming that what Jesus meant by *agapē* was justice-blind gratuitous self-sacrificial benevolence, let us look for clues in the biblical text as to what he did mean.

All three of the Synoptic Gospels report the episode in which Jesus presented the two love commands (Matt 22:34–40; Mark 12:28–34; Luke 10:25–37). The episode is described a bit differently in the three Gospels. But in their report of the two commands themselves, there are only slight rhetorical differences—with two exceptions. Mark reports Jesus as introducing the first command with the Shema: "Hear O Israel, the Lord our God, the Lord is one." And Matthew reports Jesus as saying that the second command is like the first.

So consider the two commands. The first says that we are to love God with our whole being. Nygren saw this as posing a difficulty for his interpretation of love as gratuitous generosity. Treating God with gratuitous generosity seemed to him impossible. So with the courage of his convictions he concluded that Jesus and the New Testament writers were speaking loosely when they said that we are to love God. What they meant, strictly speaking, was that we are to have faith in God. In the first command Jesus was enjoining us to have faith in God with our whole being.

What then are we to make of Jesus' statement, in Matthew, that the second command is like the first? Given Nygren's interpretation of the first commandment, the second is quite *unlike* the first. I am not aware that Nygren ever took note of this problem.

Now consider the second command: love your neighbor as yourself. The rhetorical structure of this command is the familiar *just as . . . so also* structure. Just as you love yourself, so also, love your neighbor. You love yourself, right? Love your neighbor as well. The second command presupposes the legitimacy of self-love and enjoins us to love not only ourselves but our neighbors as well. But love of self is obviously not self-sacrificial gratuitous benevolence. Karl Barth often described *agapē* as "being for the other." But love of oneself is not being *for the* other; it is being *for oneself.*

In this case, Nygren does not resort to saying that Jesus must have been speaking loosely. Instead, he emphatically declares in various passages that Christianity is opposed to all forms of self-love. I am not aware of any place in which he asks how this position can be squared with the fact that the second love command takes for granted the legitimacy of self-love.

Now for a point that is more important for our purposes here than either of the preceding two points. The two love commands are not just statements of the essence or heart of Torah. They are quotations from the Torah. The first is a quotation from Deuteronomy 6; the second, a quotation from Leviticus 19. So suppose we look at the context in which these two commandments occur in the Torah in the hope that the context will illuminate their meaning in the Torah. Context doesn't always illuminate meaning, but often it does. Suppose that in this case it does. I submit that it would have been likely that Jesus and his interrogators understood the commands with the same meaning that they had in the Torah. It's possible that they understood them differently; but the burden of proof lies on the person who holds that they did understand them differently.

On this occasion, let's confine ourselves to looking at the context in which the second commandment occurs in the Torah. The situation is Moses is delivering the divine law code to Israel. The context extends over several chapters. It will be sufficient for our purposes here to quote just a few of the immediately preceding verses.

> You shall not oppress your neighbor or rob him. The wages of a hired servant shall not remain with you all night until morning. . . . You shall do no injustice in judgment; you shall not be partial to the poor or defer to the great, but in righteousness shall you judge your neighbor. You shall not go up and down as a slanderer against your people, and you shall not stand forth

against the life of your neighbor. . . . You shall not hate your brother in your heart, but you shall reason with your neighbor, lest you bear sin because of him. You shall not take vengeance or bear any grudge against the sons of your own people, but you shall love your neighbor as yourself. I am the LORD your God. (Lev 19:13–18, RSV)

What we have here is a number of more or less detailed injunctions concluding with the love command.

A question that comes to mind is whether that final command, love your neighbor as yourself, should be interpreted as just one injunction among the many. That is not how Jesus and his interrogators regarded it; it was for them the heart of the Torah. And that is not how the Jewish tradition to this day understands it. The love command is *the generalized summation* of what has preceded. We are to read it as if it were prefaced with the words, "in short." "In short, love your neighbor as yourself."

And now for the point relevant to our present concerns. In this passage from Leviticus, love is not pitted against justice. To the contrary: treating one's neighbor justly is cited as among various ways of loving one's neighbor. Justice is an example of love.

My conclusion is that the love that Jesus enjoins on us for our neighbors is not to be understood as sheer gratuitous benevolence that pays no attention to whether or not it wreaks injustice. We have to re-think love so that love incorporates justice. We have to understand love in such a way that treating the neighbor justly is an example of loving the neighbor.

How do we do that? Begin with this question: why is it that gratuitous benevolence sometimes wreaks injustice? What is it that love as benevolence does not take account of in such a case? To answer that question I must explain, all too briefly, how I understand justice.

I hold that justice is grounded in rights; justice is present in society insofar as the individual and social members of society enjoy what they have a right to. In turn, I hold that to understand what a right is we must distinguish between, on the one hand, how well or poorly a person's life is going—her wellbeing—and, on the other hand, the worth or value of that person herself. A truly admirable person may find that her life is going poorly; these are the Jobs of the world. Conversely, a person whose life is going very nicely may not be an admirable person; this gives rise to the ancient complaint, why do the wicked prosper? The complaint presupposes a distinction between the worth or admirability of the *person* and the worth or admirability of her *life*.

Rights, as I understand them, are an interweaving of these two phenomena, the phenomenon of how well or poorly a person's life is going (her wellbeing), and the phenomenon of the worth or dignity of the person herself. That to which one has a right is some life-good of being treated a certain way. Specifically, one has a right to the life-good of being treated a certain way just in case not being treated that way would constitute being treated in a way that does not befit one's worth. In other words: to deprive a person of her right to the life-good of being treated a certain way is to treat that person with under-respect. An ethical framework, such as classical utilitarianism, that works only with the idea of life-goods, and not also with the idea of the worth or dignity of persons, cannot give an adequate account of rights, and hence not an adequate account of justice.

Here then is my suggestion as to how the love that Jesus attributes to God and enjoins on us should be understood. Such love for the other or for oneself seeks to advance the good of the other or of oneself. But the good of the other and of oneself has two dimensions: the dimension of the wellbeing of the person, of how well or ill the person's life is going, and the dimension of respect for the person's worth. Love attends to both dimensions—not just to the former. Love does indeed seek to promote the wellbeing of the person; but love also sees to it that the worth of the person is honored, that the person is treated with due respect. The rule to be followed is this: never seek the wellbeing of someone at the cost of treating that person or anyone else in a way that does not befit their worth or dignity.

The English word "care" is commonly used to express exactly this understanding of love—not caring *for* but caring *about*. When one cares about someone, one not only seeks to advance their wellbeing; one also seeks to insure that they are treated with due respect for their worth—that they are not demeaned, not treated with under-respect. Love that seeks to promote someone's wellbeing but at the cost of wronging that person or some other may be an exemplary case of benevolence, but it is a malformed instance of care. I suggest that the love Jesus enjoined on us is not love as self-sacrificial gratuitous benevolence that pays no attention to justice and injustice; the love that Jesus enjoined on us is *love as care*.

Many lines of exploration now beg for attention. For one thing, we will want to go back and look once again at the cases of tension that I mentioned at the beginning—unjust paternalism, unjust distribution of goods, etc. Now we will look at them differently, however. Rather than analyzing them as cases of conflict between justice, on the one hand, and love as benevolence, on the other, we will analyze them as cases of malformed care; and the practical goal of our analysis will be to see if we can form some generalizations as to how to prevent love as care from being malformed in such a way as to wreak injustice. But that's for another occasion.[8]

Let me close by re-stating my main point: we should re-think love—and if necessary, also re-think justice—so that we no longer think of love and justice as in tension with each other. When love is well-formed care, there is no conflict. Care often goes beyond what justice requires; but well-formed care always does *at least* what justice requires.

---

8. I have in fact done this in my recent *Justice in Love*.

3

What Makes Gratuitous Generosity Sometimes Unjust?

Sometimes one's bestowal of a good on someone other than oneself, or one's distribution of some good among a number of persons, is morally required of one; it is one's duty. On other occasions it is not out of duty but out of generosity that one bestows or distributes some good. Such generosity sometimes perpetrates injustice. Though one would wrong no one if one did not bestow or distribute the good, in bestowing or distributing the good as one does, one wrongs someone. I'm not sure whether it is ever correct to apply the term "generosity" to the distribution of some good when that distribution is morally required. But to make clear that it is distributions that are not morally required that I have in mind, I will often speak of such distributions as "gratuitous generosity." The question whose answer I want to pursue is, what makes gratuitous generosity sometimes unjust?[1]

The Parable of the Laborers in the Vineyard

Two of the most famous examples in world literature of gratuitous generosity that some people in the story found unjust, but that the narrator clearly did not, are Jesus' parable of the prodigal son (Luke 15) and his parable of the laborers in the vineyard (Matt 20). The former has captured the artistic imagination of the West far more than the latter. Because most readers find the generosity exhibited in the parable of the laborers in the vineyard more problematic than that exhibited in the parable of the prodigal son, and because it is less well-known, let me remind the reader of how the parable goes.

---

1. This present essay is a substantial revision of Wolterstorff, "What Makes Generosity Sometimes Unjust?" (2019).

The owner of a vineyard hired some day laborers early in the morning, saying that he would pay them the going daily wage. He hired others at nine o'clock, telling them that he would pay them whatever was just (*dikaios*). He hired an additional group around noon, another around three o'clock, and a final group around five o'clock. When the working day was over, he instructed his manager to pay the workers, beginning with those hired last and ending with those hired first.

Those hired last were given the going daily wage. Those hired first took note, and expected considerably more. But everybody was paid the same. So those hired first grumbled. Whereas they had worked long hours through the heat of the day, the five o'clockers had worked only one hour when the heat was moderating. It wasn't fair to give equal pay for such unequal work. It was an in-your-face injustice.

"Friend," said the landowner to one of the grumblers, "I am doing you no wrong [*adikeō*, doing you no injustice]; did you not agree with me for the usual daily wage? Take what belongs to you and go; I choose to give to this last the same as I give to you. Am I not allowed to do what I choose with what belongs to me? Or are you envious because I am generous?"[2]

Jesus obviously approved of the action of the landowner. My guess is that most people who do not simply accept what Jesus said because he said it believe the grumblers had a case. The landowner was not obligated to be charitable to anyone; his obligation was to pay the workers what was due them for the work they had done. But if he was going to go beyond his obligations and be gratuitously generous, then he was obligated to be just in his generosity. And the policy that he settled on seems patently unjust: a big dollop of charity to those who worked only one hour and none to those who worked all day. The response of the landowner to the grumblers ignores this point. "Is he not allowed to be generous?" he asks. Of course he is allowed to be generous; nobody said he was not. But he is not permitted to be unjust in his generosity.

It is not hard to imagine a scenario in which the charge of injustice would be somewhat mitigated. Suppose the landowner was aware of the fact that these workers all had families dependent on them, and that the going daily wage was just enough to support a family. That is what led him to act as he did; he cared about the families of these workers. This interpretation fits the point about the kingdom of God that Jesus was using the parable to make. It is important to everyone that they have a place in the kingdom. That is why God treats the late-coming gentiles the same way as the Jews who have labored long and faithfully in the vineyards of Torah.

2. I am using the New Revised Standard Version.

The early workers have an obvious response. If all along it was the landowner's intention to give everybody an amount equal to the going daily wage, whether they had earned it or not, then why didn't he announce that to everybody at the beginning? Then everybody could freely decide how much work he wanted to put in.

The landowner was no fool; he knew that if he openly presented this option to all the day-laborers at the beginning of the day, nobody would show up for work until five o'clock. So he manipulated the situation, in order both to get the work done and to be generous. The result of his curious combination of earned pay to some with generosity to others was that he wronged the early workers; he perpetrated injustice.

Though Christian commentators agree with Jesus in his positive estimation of the landowner, they are all over the place in stating just what it was in the behavior of the landowner that was admirable. Some take the landowner at his word, that he did the early workers no injustice, though I know of no one who explains just why that is. Others say that the grumblers were right, they were treated unjustly, but love trumps justice. Let me quote a few sentences from Anders Nygren's interpretation:

> If it were really a question of merit and worthiness, then the labourers who complained were undoubtedly in the right. It is impossible to make a simple addition of the exercise of kindness and the non-infringement of justice. . . . The principle of justice requires a due proportion between work and wages. . . . It is futile to try to eliminate from this Parable that which is offensive in it from a juridical point of view. The offence only ceases when the principle of justice itself is eliminated as inapplicable to the religious relationship . . . Where spontaneous love and generosity are found, the order of justice is obsolete and invalidated.[3]

Nygren does not explain how he interprets the insistence of the landowner that he is not treating the early workers unjustly (*adikeō*).

Emil Brunner's interpretation is essentially the same. Having spent several chapters in *Justice and the Social Order* affirming the importance of our natural sense of justice, he says that this

> natural sense of justice is violated . . . by Christ's parable of the labourers in the vineyard. . . . [I]t is love, the incomprehensible gift, bound to no law of retributive justice and standing in absolute contrast to what we must call just in the things of this world, which is shown here as God's manner of action. . . . The substance of the parable is not the *justitia civilis* but the *justitia*

3. Nygren, *Agape and Eros*, 87–90.

evangelica which consists precisely in the cessation of all deserving, in the denial of all lawful claims, and is hence the antithesis of the law of worldly justice.[4]

I will come back to the parable at the end of my discussion.

Examples That Refute the Aristotelian Paradigm

Let me say again that my concern here is solely with those cases in which the distribution of some good to one or more parties is not required by justice but is an act of pure generosity—cases in which none of the recipients would have been treated unjustly had no distribution been made. Refusal to make the distribution might reflect poorly on the character of the person who declines the opportunity to be generous; but it would not constitute wronging anybody.

Anyone acquainted with the Western philosophical tradition will at this point immediately think of Aristotle's formula for justice in distributions: justice in distributions always takes the form of equality of a certain sort, and injustice, the form of inequality of the relevant sort. I judge that the statement of Aristotle's idea that Joel Feinberg gives in one of his articles is more illuminating of what Aristotle had in mind than are Aristotle's own formulations. When divisible goods are being distributed, says Feinberg, "the Aristotelian paradigm [is that] justice requires that relevantly similar cases be treated similarly and relevantly dissimilar cases be treated dissimilarly in direct proportion to the relevant differences between them."[5] Injustice in such cases consists in "arbitrary and invidious discrimination of one kind or another: a departure from the requisite form of equal treatment without good reason."[6]

There is a difference in how the Aristotelian paradigm is formulated in the two sentences quoted from Feinberg. The idea expressed in the first sentence is that justice in distributions consists of treating relevantly similar cases similarly and relevantly dissimilar cases dissimilarly. The idea expressed in the second sentence is that justice in distributions requires that similar cases be treated similarly unless one has a good reason for doing otherwise—or as Feinberg puts it in other places, unless one has a *morally relevant* reason for doing otherwise. The first sentence speaks of relevant similarities and dissimilarities. The second speaks of morally

---

4. Brunner, *Justice and the Social Order*, 111.
5. Feinberg, "Noncomparative Justice," 310.
6. Feinberg, "Noncomparative Justice," 299.

relevant reasons. According to the first formulation, dissimilarity in one's assignment of goods has to be justified by pointing to some relevant dissimilarity among the potential recipients; otherwise the assignment is unjust. According to the second definition, dissimilarity in one's assignment of goods among potential recipients has to be justified by some morally relevant reason; otherwise the assignment is unjust.

The difference is only skin deep. The idea behind both formulations is the following. Suppose that one has some good that one wishes to distribute, and suppose that there are a number of persons for whom it would be a good. Then justice requires that one distribute it equally and proportionately among those persons unless one has some morally relevant reason for excluding some or giving some less; and a morally relevant reason will always consist of some morally relevant difference between the included and the excluded. What makes a distribution unjust is that it is a departure from equality or proper proportionality that cannot point to a morally relevant difference. Either there is no reason or the distribution is arbitrary. Or the reason is not a morally relevant reason; for example, one withholds the benefit from certain people because one doesn't like the color of their skin.

Is the Aristotelian paradigm, as formulated by Feinberg, correct? Does it pinpoint what it is that makes generosity sometimes unjust? Does the Aristotelian paradigm explain why it is that, in some gratuitous distributions, one or more persons are not receiving what is due them—why it is that one or more persons are wronged?

A preliminary point is that if the Aristotelian principle is to have any plausibility whatsoever, one has to be exceedingly lax and generous in what one is willing to count as a morally relevant dissimilarity. Often the relevant dissimilarity will not be the excluded person's lack of some property or feature that recipients possess but the fact that the excluded person is not related to the distributor in a way that the recipients are.

For example: come Christmas, I give gifts to those to whom I am especially attached, family and friends. The children on my block aren't much different from my own children; nonetheless, I don't give them gifts. And my neighbor isn't much different from my friend; but I don't give him a gift either. We all agree that there is nothing unjust in this sort of partiality. So if the Aristotelian principle is to hold for such cases, we have to regard the possession and lack of the relational property of *being someone to whom I am attached* as constituting a morally relevant similarity and dissimilarity. This is just one of many examples of the point.

The example can be used to make another preliminary point. When selecting Christmas gifts for my children, my attention is focused entirely on doing my best to insure that they will more or less equally prize the gifts I give them; that will insure that I am being fair to each of them. The thought that I am giving gifts only to my own children and not to the children on my block never crosses my mind. But in applying the Aristotelian principle, one has to attend not only to relevant similarities and dissimilarities within the distribution class on which one is focused but also to relevant similarities and dissimilarities between those within that class and those outside. It is especially when one attends to the latter similarities and dissimilarities that one comes to realize how lax and generous the idea of a morally relevant reason has to be if the Aristotelian principle is to come out true. Of course, if the good that one is distributing is non-divisible, then the distinction between these two sets of similarities and dissimilarities disappears; in such cases, there are no similarities and dissimilarities among the members of the distribution class, since the class has only one member.

Enough by way of preliminaries. Does the Aristotelian paradigm explain what makes some exercises of gratuitous generosity just and others unjust? Well, suppose that I am seated at my desk, getting ready to write checks for my end-of-the-year charitable contributions. Over the course of the year I have sorted out the appeals for funds that came my way, filing those from organizations that seemed to me to serve a worthy cause and to be needy of funds, and tossing the others into the wastebasket. Now I open my file and find that I have collected appeals from thirty organizations, to none of which I feel any particular attachment.

As I am wondering how to proceed, the Aristotelian paradigm comes to mind. I conclude that what it tells me to do is rank these organizations in terms of some combination of worthiness and need, and then proportion my contributions accordingly. But as I am reflecting further on whether to employ the paradigm, so understood, as my guide, it occurs to me that I have been almost entirely passive up to this point. I have made no attempt to search out needy and worthy organizations. I have simply taken the appeals that arrived in the mail and sorted them into two categories. But surely there are many needy and worthy organizations that happen not to have had me on their mailing list. Is that a morally relevant reason for treating them differently from those that did have me on their list? I'm not sure; I find that I don't have a very good grip on the concept of a morally relevant reason. But it doesn't seem like a morally relevant reason. It is hard to see why one would think it was, other than that one wants to keep the Aristotelian paradigm from coming out false for this case.

I dismiss these unsettling thoughts and return to asking myself whether I should follow the Aristotelian paradigm, as I understand it, for the organizations whose appeals I have kept. Should I rank them in terms of some combination of worthiness and need, and then proportion my contributions accordingly? For no particular reason, I decide that this year I don't want to spread my charity thin in the way that this would require. I will select just a few, four or five perhaps, and concentrate my charity on them.

Now I have to select those few. I carefully read once again the brochures in my file, this time looking for anything I can seize on as a morally relevant reason for tipping my decision one way or the other. After several hours of this, I find myself paralyzed; I cannot choose. So in desperation I assign numbers to the various organizations and make my choice by rolling dice. Or perhaps I hit on graphic design as the deciding factor and give my money to the five organizations whose brochures strike me as the most attractive. Or perhaps I notice that a few of these organizations list the members of their boards of directors; I find this apparent openness appealing and decide to give my money to them. Or I notice that four of them have their home offices in my state; that tips me toward them. Or I recall that I visited Africa in the course of the year and found myself very moved by what I experienced there; so I decide to give all my money this year to organizations that work in Africa. It is easy to go on in this vein and imagine other ways of making my decision.

So far as I can see, none of the ways mentioned constitutes treating any organization unjustly. If those I pass over become aware that I have passed them over, they will regret my doing so; but they cannot claim to have been wronged. Yet the Aristotelian paradigm has surely not been satisfied. In no case did I have a morally relevant reason for choosing as I did; in no case was my departure from equal treatment based on morally relevant similarities and dissimilarities among the organizations. In each case my choice was more or less whimsical and arbitrary. How is the location of an organization's home office relevant? How is the aesthetic quality of its brochure relevant?

Or if one declares that the fact that an organization came up with a winning number on a roll of the dice is a morally relevant reason for including it within my benefactions, then surely the idea of a morally relevant reason is no longer doing any work; it is not explaining anything. One's only reason for calling such a fact morally relevant would be that one wants to prevent the Aristotelian paradigm from implying that the form my generosity took in this case was unjust.

Feinberg suggests that we are offended by arbitrary discriminations and find them unjust because they are "offensive to reason." "The principle that relevantly similar cases should be treated in similar ways, put in just that general way, is a principle of reason, in much the same way as Aristotle's principles of identity, contradiction, and excluded middle are 'laws of thought.' It is *absurd* to treat relevantly similar cases in dissimilar ways."[7] We do, of course, find many arbitrary discriminations unjust, and we are rightly offended by them. But as for myself, the examples of arbitrary discrimination that I have given seem to me not at all unjust and offensive; they do not violate some principle of reason. And they represent just the tip of the iceberg.

Suppose someone offers to fund a scholarship at his alma mater and insists that the criteria for eligibility include the requirement that the candidate have been born in the same small Minnesota village that the donor came from. The university authorities will try to talk him out of such a quirky stipulation; but in doing so, they cannot claim that it would be unjust. Or suppose some millionaire decides to dispose of some of his wealth by tossing $100 bills out of the window of his Manhattan condo; is anybody wronged by this erratic behavior? Or suppose the Gates Foundation decides to concentrate its AIDS endeavors on Africa because the first person suffering from AIDS that Bill Gates met was born in Africa. Hardly a morally relevant reason; but is anybody wronged?

And then there are all the cases of arbitrary random assignment of indivisible goods. Suppose I decide to bequeath my automobile to one of my children. After trying and failing to find some "rational" way of deciding to whom to give it, I resort to chance. I have my children pull straws, throw dice, or whatever. Those who lose in the draw will naturally be regretful; but they can't claim to have been wronged.

So far as I can see, the Aristotelian formula is patently mistaken. Its grip on Western thought is not because of its truth but in spite of its falsehood.

Some Factors That Make Gratuitous Generosity Unjust

My conclusion thus far is negative. The Aristotelian paradigm was offered as an explanation of why certain exercises of gratuitous generosity are just and why others are unjust. The paradigm says that what makes a selective exercise of generosity *just* is the presence of a morally relevant similarity among the persons included in one's benefaction and the lack of that similarity in those excluded. We have found cases of just generosity whose justice the paradigm does not illuminate; the paradigm mistakenly implies that those cases are unjust. It would be desirable if we could get beyond this negative conclusion and gain some insight into why some benefactions are just and some are unjust. And let us keep in mind that it is possible that though the Aristotelian paradigm does not explain all cases, it does explain some.

7. Feinberg, "Noncomparative Justice," 319.

Let us approach the matter from the side of injustice. Let us look at some examples of unjust generosity in the hope of discerning what makes them unjust.

Suppose that I have promised to bequeath the art prints that I own to my children; and suppose further that, after considerable discussion in the family, we have agreed on a distribution that makes all the children equally happy. Then in the course of a party that I throw for my neighbors one evening, one of the neighbors admires one of my prints and I, pleased by his admiration, impulsively say, "here, it is yours." Flush with good feelings and a bit too much wine, I then grandly announce that everybody is free to select a print and take it home with them. When everybody is gone, I have none left. Only next morning do I remember, to my horror, that I had promised them to my children.

My generosity is clearly a violation of justice. But being flush with good feelings for my neighbors seems a morally relevant difference between them and everybody else. Had I not made the promise to my children, my generosity to my neighbors would not have been unjust; and a defender of the Aristotelian paradigm would have pointed to my good feelings for my neighbors as the relevant similarity among them and the relevant dissimilarity between them and everybody else.

What this example shows is that having a morally relevant reason of the Aristotelian sort for making one's distribution as one did proves not sufficient for justice. I did have a morally relevant reason of the Aristotelian sort for being generous in the way that I was. Nonetheless, my generosity was unjust. What made it unjust was my breaking of a promise.

Consider the following example. Sam is a widower who likes to offer candy every now and then to children on the block. None of the children on the block has a right to receive candy from Sam; giving out candy is gratuitous generosity on his part. And let us agree that he is not wronging the children in the next block by giving candy only to those who live on his block—though for the Aristotelian, it is a nice question why living on this rather than that block constitutes a morally relevant principle of discrimination.

But Sam has taken a strong dislike to one of the children on the block, Roger. Why he dislikes Roger is not clear to him. He has no reason to think that Roger has a bad character, Roger has always treated him politely; and Sam has never seen Roger being mean to other children. But there is something about the look on Roger's face that turns Sam off; perhaps it is because of some episode buried deep in his memory. In any case, whenever Sam distributes candy, he sees to it that Roger gets none.

Sam's charity is patently unjust; in making his distribution as he does, he wrongs Roger. Why? Why is his exclusion of Roger from his benefactions unjust whereas his exclusion of the children on the neighboring block is not unjust? Suppose Sam had tossed all the candy up into the air and that, in the ensuing scramble, everybody managed to get some except Roger. Add that Roger is as agile as any of the other children. This outcome would be unfortunate; one hopes that some of the children would take pity on Roger and give him some of theirs. But it would not be unjust.

Sam's exclusion of Roger from his generosity was unjust because his exclusion of Roger was motivated by inexcusable ill-will. No such ill-will motivated his exclusion of the children in the neighboring block from his largesse; and no such ill-will would account for Roger winding up with no candy had Sam tossed it all up into the air.

Consider, next, a case Feinberg presents that is more or less of the opposite sort. Imagine a father who is making out bequests to his two sons, A and B. "let us suppose," says Feinberg, "that A and B are roughly of the same age, size, health, appearance, abilities, beliefs, and ideals, that each has the same basic financial needs and that the bequests more than fulfill them in each case." And now suppose "that the father leaves everything else after those basic needs have been met—say, one million unsuspected dollars—to A simply because he likes A better."[8] Feinberg thinks that this would be a case of injustice. I agree; I think son B is wronged by such treatment.[9]

Why? If B's needs are adequately met by the bequest from his father, why is he wronged? Isn't the father permitted to dispose of that extra million dollars as he wishes? Suppose he had donated all of it to some charitable organization. Then B would not have been wronged. So why is he wronged if the father gives the million dollars to B's brother?

It is the father's favoritism that is the culprit. The bestowal of the million dollars on son A is an act of favoritism on the father's part; B is wronged by that favoritism. Parents sometimes like one of their children more than another; perhaps they usually do. I dare say that ideally they would like all their children equally. The fact that often they don't is not as such, however, a blot on their moral character. But when a parent's liking of one child more than another takes the form of favoritism in the distribution of goods, then the disfavored child is wronged. An important normative component in the role of parent in our society—it may be different in other societies—is that parents are to do their best to be even-handed

---

8. Feinberg, "Noncomparative Justice," 315.

9. Feinberg takes the example from A. D. Woozley, who thinks it would not be a case of injustice.

in promoting the flourishing and respecting the worth of their children. Favoritism is a violation of this role-obligation.

One way of interpreting Jesus' parable of the prodigal son is that the elder son is accusing the father of favoritism for his scoundrel brother. Though he doesn't actually say that the father's favoring of the younger son is an injustice to him, clearly that is the idea. As the elder son is coming in from the fields, he hears the noise of a party in the family home. He inquires from someone what is going on, and learns that a party is being thrown to celebrate the return of his dissolute younger brother. The elder brother is very angry and refuses to join the party. The father goes out and pleads with him to join the festivities. The elder son responds, "Listen! For all these years I have been working like a slave for you, and I have never disobeyed your commands; yet you have never given me even a young goat so that I might celebrate with my friends. But when this son of yours came back, who has devoured your property with prostitutes, you killed the fatted calf for him!"[10]

The father does not concede the charge of favoritism and then go on to contend that, nonetheless, no injustice was done. Instead, he contests the charge; the elder son is misinterpreting the situation. It is not favoritism that led the father to throw the party. Remember, he says, "all that is mine is yours. But we have to celebrate and rejoice because this brother of yours was dead and has come to life, he was lost and has been found."[11]

Finally, consider the following example. A small manufacturing company is holding its annual Christmas party. Since the company has been unusually profitable this year, the owner has decided to share the wealth and give out bonuses; he has never done that before. So at a certain point in the festivities he stops the music, says that he has a surprise announcement, and declares that he will now hand out bonuses. He explains that for some time he contemplated proportioning the size of a person's bonus to their position in the company, the quality of their work, and so forth; but eventually he decided that things were getting too complicated. Give everybody a $2,000 bonus, he decided. So he calls the workers forward one by one, in alphabetical order. But he fails to call out Joseph's name, Joseph being the only person of color working for the firm. Some of the workers notice the omission and call it to the attention of the owner. The owner blandly replies, "You're right; I did skip Joseph." Whereupon he sits down.

---

10. Luke 15:29–30.

11. Luke 15:31–32. There is a fascinating and pointed contrast between the elder son referring to the one who returned as "this son of yours" and the father referring to him as "this brother of yours."

Joseph rightly feels hurt and angry. I would say that he has been wronged; the way in which the owner dispensed his generosity was unjust. But why? Neither Joseph nor anyone else had a bonus coming; nobody would have been wronged had the owner not given any bonuses. So why is Joseph wronged by not receiving a bonus? The answer, once again, is obvious. Joseph has been demeaned and humiliated on account of the color of his skin; there is no other way to read the situation. The owner might have chosen some random procedure for distributing bonuses to only some of the people in the firm; those who didn't win a bonus in the lottery would be regretful, but they could not claim that they had been wronged. It was the owner's demeaning of Joseph in how he distributed his generosity that made his distribution unjust.

Let me pull things together. Feinberg interprets the Aristotelian paradigm as declaring that injustice, in the sorts of cases we are considering, consists of "departure from the requisite form of equal treatment without good reason," a good reason always consisting of some morally relevant dissimilarity between those included in one's generosity and those excluded. If one has a good reason of this sort for departing from equality in the distribution of one's generosity, one's distribution is just; if one does not have a good reason of this sort, one's distribution is unjust. The implicit assumption is that the default option in the exercise of generosity is that everybody who can benefit is to be treated equally.

We have seen that, even if we expand the notion of a morally relevant reason so far that it no longer has any explanatory content, an unequal distribution may be just even though the benefactor does not have a reason of the Aristotelian-Feinberg sort for acting as he did; he may have employed quirky reasons, or he may have resorted to chance procedures. Conversely, we have seen that often it is not the absence of a morally relevant difference between recipients and non-recipients that accounts for the injustice of an unequal distribution but some other feature of the situation.

I submit that there is no one thing that explains the injustice of unjust generosity. Sometimes what makes a distribution unjust is that distributing the largesse to certain people breaks a prior obligation to distribute it to other people. Sometimes what makes a distribution unjust is that a nefarious reason is guiding the exclusion of someone from the distribution. Sometimes what makes a distribution unjust is that it is motivated by unacceptable favoritism. Sometimes what makes a distribution unjust is that it humiliates someone. No doubt if we continued looking at examples, we would find yet other sources of injustice in generosity.

On the theory of justice that I favor, to treat someone unjustly is *to treat them in a way that does not befit their worth*.[12] If that theory is correct, then what is common to all the examples of unjust generosity that I have offered is that someone is treated in a way that does not befit his or her worth. There are, of course, many different ways of treating someone in a way that does not befit his or her worth: breaking a promise is one way, favoritism is another way, humiliating the person is another way. What I have been looking for in this essay is some particular way of treating someone in a way that does not befit their worth that is common to all cases of unjust generosity. Our search has been unsuccessful. We have not discovered a replacement for the Aristotelian paradigm.

Generosity Not Made Unjust by the Violation of Rights That It Generates

An implication of the Aristotelian principle is that, where the good is divisible and nobody has a prior right to a share in the benefactor's generosity, the generosity generates in certain people a right to a share in the good. Once the benefactor begins his distribution, then he finds that he has generated, in those who are relevantly similar to the initial recipients, the right to a share that is equal or proportionate to the share that the initial recipients received. If any receive, then now all who are relevantly similar have a right to receive.

But if the conclusion that I drew just above is correct, this implication is mistaken. It is not in general true that generosity generates new rights and that it is the violation of those newly generated rights that accounts for injustice in generosity. Roger had a *prior* right not to be treated with culpable ill-will; it was Sam's violation of that prior right that accounted for the fact that Roger was wronged. Son *B* had a *prior* right not to be the victim of his father's favoritism; it was the violation of that prior right that accounted for the fact that *B* was wronged. Joseph had a *prior* right not to be demeaned and humiliated on account of the color of his skin; it was the violation of that prior right that accounted for the fact that he was wronged by the owner's omission of him in the distribution of bonuses. Generosity, to be just, must attend to the rights that we already have.

---

12. I develop and defend this theory in Wolterstorff, *Justice: Rights and Wrongs*.

Our Conclusions Hold for Generosity in the Form of Mercy

None of my examples has been an example of generosity in the form of mercy. Mercy comes in two forms. One form is mitigation of the severity of punishment; the other is alleviation of the plight of the unfortunate. Does mercy in either of these two forms require different conclusions from those I have drawn?

I think not. Start with mercy of the former sort, mitigation-mercy. Examples of this sort that come immediately to mind are pardons issued by government officials—in the United States, by the president of the country and by the governors of the states. We, the citizens of the United States, expect that the president, with the assistance of the Department of Justice, will be reasonably systematic in selecting the most worthy candidates for pardon. If the president departs from that expectation by tossing coins, or by allowing his choice to be determined by favoritism or prejudice of one kind and another, we are disturbed and regard the process as unfair and unjust. But suppose that in some kingdom there is the longstanding practice of the king employing a random procedure for selecting ten prisoners for release each New Year's Eve. So far as I can see, no one is wronged by such a procedure; justice is not violated.

Generosity in the form of alleviating the plight of the unfortunate is no different. Let it be noted that mercy in the form of alleviation of hardship is not always an exercise of gratuitous generosity; sometimes it is obligatory. The Samaritan in Jesus' parable of the good Samaritan was, I would say, obligated to come to the aid of the wounded man, as were the priest and the Levite. And I have a so-called *imperfect* duty to show mercy to some of the unfortunates who accost me with their pleas for aid as I walk about Manhattan. But not all such mercy is obligatory; some goes above and beyond the call of duty. A good deal of volunteer work is like that—volunteering to help out at the local soup kitchen, volunteering to help out in a near-by retirement home, and so forth. Does volunteering to help out on one occasion imply that if one fails to help out on all relevantly similar situations, one is acting unjustly? Of course not.

Was the Owner of the Vineyard Unjust?

Let's return to the story with which we began. Did the owner of the vineyard wrong anyone by the highly unusual way in which he combined earned pay to some with generosity to others? Everybody but the five o'clock workers disliked the owner's combination of earned pay with generosity; the early workers disliked it intensely. But was anyone wronged?

Jesus was walking a tightrope when he told the parable. His aim was to unsettle the convictions of those who thought that it would be unjust for God to extend the offer of salvation to everyone and not limit the offer to the Jews who had labored faithfully in the Lord's vineyard for many centuries; but he had to unsettle their customary ways of thinking about justice with an example that they would concede to be an example of justice.

I fail to see that anyone in the parable was wronged. The landowner did not act out of ill-will toward anyone, nor did he act out of favoritism. Did he perhaps demean and humiliate the early workers, treat them as of less worth than those who came at five o'clock? Not so far as I can see. Did he then perhaps break an agreement between himself and the early workers? Had he led them to believe that the only principle on which he would act was equal pay for equal work and unequal pay for unequal work? He had not. He was entirely forthcoming with the early workers as to the basis on which he would pay them, namely, the going daily wage for those who worked the full day, a just wage for those who arrived a bit later. He kept his word. Was there perhaps an implicit understanding in the society that workers would be paid what they earned, no more and no less? The owner's rhetorical question, "am I not allowed to be generous?" seems to me to indicate that there was no such implicit agreement.

The owner did not cite a morally relevant reason for the unusual way in which he dispensed his charity. In fact, he didn't cite any reason at all for the peculiar pattern of his largesse; he just declared that he was permitted to be generous. But as we have seen, selective generosity may be just even in the absence of any morally relevant reason for one's selection. The early workers strongly preferred that the owner pay each person what he had earned and then, if he wished to be generous, give everybody an equal-sized gift. Better yet would have been proportioning the size of the gift to the length and onerousness of the work. But the fact that they strongly preferred these arrangements does not establish that the landowner wronged them in not choosing one of those alternative arrangements.

And as to the religious import of the parable: *pace* Nygren and Brunner, God's generosity does not transcend justice by violating justice; God's generosity transcends justice by doing what justice requires and more. We are to do likewise.

4

The Just Limits of Love; or Why an Ethic of Pure Benevolence Is Not Sufficient for Morality

A common assumption in the Christian tradition, among laypeople and theologians alike, is that the Christian ethic is an ethic of love. Those who work in the natural law tradition might want to qualify that flat statement in one way or another, or even to dissent from it; but apart from those there is, I think, near-universal agreement that the Christian ethic is an ethic of love. I would say that the two writers who have most powerfully articulated this understanding are Søren Kierkegaard in *Works of Love* and Anders Nygren in *Agape and Eros*.

There is, of course, a reason for this near-universal agreement; it is not accidental. All three Synoptic Gospels report the episode in which Jesus, in response to the question from a hostile interrogator as to the greatest commandment in the Torah, says,

> "You shall love the Lord your God with all your heart, and with all your soul, and with all your mind." This is the greatest and first commandment. And a second is like it: "You shall love your neighbor as yourself." (Matt 22:37–39)

Whereas Jesus spoke Aramaic, the Gospels are written in Greek. The Greek word translated into English as "love" that the Synoptic Gospels use to report what Jesus said is *agapē*. Hence, in the literature on these matters the love that Jesus enjoined for God and neighbor is often called *agapic love*. The love that Jesus enjoined in the second commandment is often called, for obvious reasons, *neighbor love*.

There are a number of distinctly different phenomena called "love" in English. There is love as attraction, the sort of love that one expresses when one says, "I love Beethoven's late string quartets." (This is the *eros* of the ancient

Greeks.) There is love as attachment, the sort of love one has for one's children, for the family cat, for the house in which one has lived for thirty years, etc. There is love as friendship. And there is love as benevolence.

What sort of love was it that Jesus enjoined when he commanded us to love our neighbors are ourselves? Almost all Christian ethicists have understood the neighbor love that Jesus enjoined as benevolence.

And how have they understood benevolence? Benevolence, as they understand it, has both a characteristic aim and a characteristic motivation. As to aim, benevolence aims to enhance the goods in someone's life, the life-goods, and to diminish the non-goods. It aims to enhance his or her well-being. As to motivation, benevolence is spontaneous or gratuitous. In benevolence one aims to enhance someone's life-goods not because one expects some sort of return, not because one finds the other person attractive, not because it is in some way required of one—required by justice, for example—but out of sheer generosity.

Let me quote a few passages from Christian ethicists in which the benevolence interpretation of what Jesus meant is stated explicitly. In love, says Karl Barth, a person "gives himself to another with no expectation of a return, in a pure venture." He identifies "with [the other's] interests in utter independence of [the other's] attractiveness, of what [the other] has to offer."[1] In his book on Reinhold Niebuhr, Robin Lovin declares that love "is the disposition to seek the well-being of persons generally that theologians and moral philosophers have called 'benevolence.'"[2] And Gene Outka says that "agape is, in both its genesis and continuation, an active concern for the neighbor's well-being which is somehow independent of particular actions of the other."[3] The person who treats others with agape considers "the interests of others and not simply his own. Others are to be regarded for their own sakes, for what *they* may want or need, and not finally because they bring benefits to the agent."[4]

In the course of developing his understanding of Christian love Paul Ramsey mentions what he says is the other main interpretation "of the meaning of Christian love contending for acceptance in present-day theological discussion."[5] The main alternative, he says, is *mutual love*—that is, love that both loves and seeks to be loved. In mutual love, "self-referential motives . . .

---

1. Barth, *Church Dogmatics*, 745.
2. Lovin, *Reinhold Niebuhr and Christian Realism*, 199.
3. Outka, *Agape*, 260.
4. Outka, *Agape*, 8.
5. Ramsey, "Love and Law," 104.

are co-present with other-regarding motives."[6] Ramsey brusquely dismisses this alternative. "Surely," he says, "the benevolence interpretation is the more correct reading of Biblical and New Testament texts."[7]

An obvious question to raise at this point is: what about justice? If the Christian ethic is an ethic of love, if the love in question is benevolence, and if benevolence is purely gratuitous—not seeking the good of the other because it is required by justice or anything else but out of sheer generosity—what happens to justice?

Could it be that justice comes tag-along with love? Notice that love as benevolence is motivationally incompatible with justice: in acting out of benevolence, one is not doing what one does because justice requires it; and conversely, in doing what one does because justice requires it, one is not acting out of benevolence. But might it be that the demands of justice are automatically satisfied when one loves the neighbor with the love of benevolence? It is my impression that most writers on these matters assume that that is the case. It is commonly said that love often does more than justice but never less.

Love as Benevolence Sometimes Perpetrates Injustice

I want now to argue that that assumption, common though it is, is mistaken. Love as benevolence often perpetrates injustice. Let me begin with the episode in my own life in which that first became starkly clear to me. I have described the episode in print; perhaps some of you have read what I wrote. But I'm sure not all of you have.

In September 1975 I was sent by Calvin College, where I was a philosophy professor, to an international conference on Christian higher education at the University of Potchefstroom in South Africa. Potchefstroom is a small city located roughly an hour's drive from Johannesburg. At the time, only whites were admitted as students.

Most of the South Africans present at the conference were white Afrikaners; but there were a few so-called blacks and coloreds from South Africa as well. In addition, there were scholars from other parts of Africa, a sizable contingent from the Netherlands, a number of us from the US and Canada, and a few from Asia.

Though the conference was not about the South African system of apartheid—recall that 1975 was well before the revolution—apartheid was the dominant topic of conversation during coffee breaks and meals, and it

---

6. Ramsey, "Love and Law," 106.
7. Ramsey, "Love and Law," 106.

constantly threatened to intrude into the conference itself. Eventually the organizers of the conference consented to hold a special evening session on apartheid.

The discussion in that late night session was more intense than anything I had ever before experienced. The Dutch delegates were very well informed about South Africa and very angry about apartheid; they vented their anger at the Afrikaners. The Afrikaner defenders of apartheid in turn vented their anger at the Dutch. Later I would learn that Afrikaners fended off most critics of apartheid by telling them that they were misinformed. They could not plausibly charge the Dutch with being misinformed. Instead they charged them with being self-righteously judgmental.

Eventually the so-called black and colored scholars from South Africa began to speak up, more in tones of hurt than of anger—or so it seemed to me at the time. They described the daily indignities heaped upon them and the many ways in which they were demeaned; they spoke of being expelled from their homes and herded off into Bantustans; with great passion they cried out for justice. I was profoundly moved by this cry for justice coming from these victims of injustice.

The response by the Afrikaners at the conference who spoke up in defense of apartheid to this cry for justice took me completely aback. They did not contest the charge of injustice. Instead they insisted that justice was not a relevant category. Apartheid, they insisted, was an act of goodwill on the part of the ruling Afrikaners, an act of benevolence. In South Africa, they explained, there were some ten or eleven different nationalities. The system of apartheid was inspired by the ideal of each of these nationalities finding its own cultural identity. If that was to happen, they could not live mingled through each other; they would have to live separately, apart; hence, *apartheid*. To this visionary nationalism some added stories about their own individual acts of charity: clothes they gave to the "black" family living in the backyard that their own children had outgrown, trinkets that they gave to the children at Christmas, and so forth.

In short, the Afrikaners presented themselves as a benevolent people. And they complained that almost always their benevolence went unacknowledged; no gratitude was forthcoming. "Why can't we just love each other?" one of them asked plaintively of the so-called blacks and coloreds, "Why do you only criticize us?" They complained that critics of apartheid ignored the visionary beneficent ideal that motivated the project and only took note of the difficulties encountered in achieving the ideal.

What I saw, as never before, was benevolence being used as an instrument of oppression—*self-perceived* benevolence, of course. More specifically, what I saw was unjust paternalism. The scales had fallen from my eyes.

I returned home a changed person. I began to see unjust benevolence in the form of paternalism all around me. All too often charity demeans the recipient by treating her as an object of pity. The agent feels good about himself; he is a good and generous person. But the recipient has been humiliated. If she had the courage to say what she would like to say she would say, perhaps adding an expletive, "keep your charity."

Let me now identify, more briefly, a few of the other ways in which love as benevolence may perpetrate injustice. Sometimes it is the consequences of our benevolence or charity that makes it unjust. Not infrequently benevolence and charity, rather than enabling and encouraging the recipients to stand on their own feet, encourage in them a culture of dependency; all too often relief and developments projects aimed at relieving impoverishment perpetuate injustice by relieving the pressure on those who are causing the impoverishment rather than forcing them to stop what they are doing. Some of the speakers at this conference have developed these points powerfully in their writings. Let me present an example of a somewhat different sort that a friend described to me a few days before I composed this talk.

My friend is a member of an inner-city church in Grand Rapids, Michigan. A few years back the congregation decided to distribute food baskets at Thanksgiving to households in the neighborhood. After they had done this for two years in a row, the manager of a 7–11 store in the neighborhood came to them and respectfully asked them to stop the practice. He explained that he was just barely able to stay in business. The busiest days of the year for him were the days before Thanksgiving and before Christmas. This year and the year previous he had had almost no business before Thanksgiving; the charity of the church members was threatening to put him out of business. The church promised that in subsequent years they would purchase as much as possible of the food they distributed from his store.

Sometimes it is the selective way in which some good is distributed that makes benevolence or charity unjust. Suppose that one distributes a good of some sort out of pure generosity; justice does not require that one distribute the good. For no good reason one distributes the good in question to these people and not to those, this in spite of the fact that they are all in the same room, that they can all make good use of the good in question, and that one possesses more than enough of the good in question to distribute it to those others as well. I would say that those who received nothing have been wronged; they have been treated unjustly.

Let me offer an example of generosity that is unjust in how the goods are distributed; the example is rather quirky, and it is made up rather than real. Suppose that I have bequeathed the art prints that I own to my children; and suppose further that, after considerable discussion in the family, we have agreed on a distribution that makes all the children happy. Then in the course of a party that I throw for my neighbors one evening, one of the neighbors admires one of my prints and I, pleased by his admiration and conscious of the fact that I am of an age where I have to start de-acquisitioning things, impulsively say, "here, it is yours." Flush with good feelings and bit too much wine, I then grandly announce that everybody is free to select a print and take it home with them. When everybody is gone, I have none left. Only next morning do I remember, to my horror, that I had promised them to my children. I have wronged them, treated them unjustly.[8]

Last, let me mention the sort of case of benevolence perpetrating injustice that was prominent in the mind of Reinhold Niebuhr. It was characteristic of liberal Protestants in the early decades of the twentieth century to argue that love *of* the neighbor evokes love *from* the neighbor. If only Christians were more loving, the kingdom of God would appear on earth. Liberal Protestants, wrote Niebuhr, "approached the injustices and conflicts of this world with a gay and easy confidence. Men had been ignorantly selfish. They would now be taught the law of love. . . . Once . . . obscurantist theology had been brushed aside, the Church would be free to preach salvation to the world. Its word of salvation would be that all men ought to love one another. It was as simple as that."[9]

Niebuhr's response was emphatic dismissal. The second love command is not a prudential strategy for creating a community of loving people. Self-interest is much too deeply embedded in human beings for that. Only God's eschatological triumph will loosen the grip of sin on human beings; it is naïve and dangerous to think that Christians loving their neighbors will remake those neighbors into loving human beings. In situations of conflict—and life is full of conflict—benevolent neighbor love is more likely to perpetrate and perpetuate injustice and get run over than change people's hearts. This is the core of Niebuhr's so-called "realism." He writes:

> the divine love can have a counterpart in history only in a life which ends tragically, because it refuses to participate in the claims and counterclaims of historical existence. It portrays a love "which seeketh not its own." But a love which seeketh not its own is not able to maintain itself in historical society. Not only may it fall victim to excessive forms of the self-assertion of others; but even the most perfectly balanced system of justice in history is

---

8. An expanded version of this example can also be found in chapter 3.
9. Niebuhr, *The Nature and Destiny of Man*, 7.

a balance of competing wills and interests, and must therefore worst anyone who does not participate in the balance.[10]

Nygren on the Conflict between Love and Justice

I have identified four types of examples of benevolence-love perpetrating injustice; no doubt with a bit of thought and imagination we could identify other types of examples. There was nothing esoteric about the sorts of examples I identified; they are common and familiar to all of us. So why has it so often been assumed that love as benevolence carries justice in its wake—that such love will never do less than what justice requires but will often do more? I don't know. I have no explanation.

Anders Nygren, in *Agape and Eros,* saw clearly that benevolence-love may perpetrate injustice. He might have developed the point as I have, by pointing to ordinary examples. Instead he developed it by citing two parables of Jesus, the parable of the laborers in the vineyard (Matt 20:1–16), and the parable of the prodigal son (Luke 15:11–32). Let me not rehearse these parables but confine myself to quoting what Nygren says about the parable of the laborers in the vineyard.

> If it were really a question of merit and worthiness, then the labourers who complained were undoubtedly in the right. It is impossible to make a simple addition of the exercise of kindness and the non-infringement of justice. If the principle of merit and reward is laid down as finally decisive, then there is an "infringement of justice" when . . . the more deserving and the less deserving are treated in the same way. The principle of justice requires a due proportion between work and wages.[11]

So what are we to do when love and justice conflict in this way? Say farewell to justice and hold fast to love, said Nygren. "'Motivated' justice must give place . . . to 'unmotivated' love."[12] Nygren argued that the Old Testament is all about justice. In the New Testament, he says, justice is superseded by love. "Where spontaneous love and generosity are found, the order of justice is obsolete and invalidated."[13]

This position seems to me biblically indefensible. In Luke's report of the brief inaugural sermon that Jesus preached in the synagogue in

---

10. Niebuhr, *Nature and Destiny of Man.*
11. Nygren, *Agape and Eros,* 88.
12. Nygren, *Agape and Eros,* 74.
13. Nygren, *Agape and Eros,* 90.

Nazareth, Jesus declares that he has been anointed to inaugurate the reign of God's justice. This same Jesus would later issue the command to love one's neighbor. I dare say that most of you are familiar with the passage. But I think it is worth having it in front of us.

> Jesus stood up to read, and the scroll of the prophet Isaiah was given to him. He unrolled the scroll and found the place where it was written,
>
> "The Spirit of the Lord is upon me,
>
> because he had anointed me to bring good tidings to the poor.
>
> He has sent me to proclaim release to the captives
>
> and recovery of sight to the blind,
>
> to let the oppressed go free,
>
> to proclaim the year of the Lord's favor."
>
> And he rolled up the scroll, gave it back to the attendant, and sat down. The eyes of all in the synagogue were fixed on him. Then he began to say to them, "today this scripture has been fulfilled in your hearing." (Luke 4:16–30)

Though the word "justice" does not occur in what Luke quotes Jesus as reading, when one looks up the passage in Isaiah from which Jesus read, it is all about justice. Jesus' declaration that he has been anointed to inaugurate God's reign of justice is just one marker of the fact that justice has not been superseded by love in the New Testament.

Nygren's position also seems to me conceptually incoherent. Start with the fact that rights and duties are correlative: If Matilda has a right to be treated a certain way by Malchus, then Malchus has a duty to treat her that way, and conversely. Now if in my benevolent love for someone I treat that person or some other person unjustly, then I violate that person's right not to be so treated. I wrong them. And if that person has a right not to be so treated by me, then, by the principle of correlatives that I just enunciated, I ought not to treat him that way; I have a duty not to treat him that way. But Nygren says that I should always act out of benevolent love. So his position has the implication that I may find myself in a situation where I *should* treat a person lovingly even though in so doing, I violate someone's rights and thereby do what I *ought not* to do. But it is incoherent to claim that I should do what I ought not to do.

Nygren was implicitly claiming that an ethic of pure benevolence is sufficient for morality. I think the examples I have given force us to the conclusion that an ethic of pure benevolence is not sufficient for morality.

Morality cannot do without justice. Benevolence needs, as it were, the eyes and ears of justice to steer and guide it.

What Does Justice Contribute?

Before I consider what we are to make of the conclusion to which we have been led, namely, that an ethic of pure benevolence is not sufficient for morality, let me ask what it is that justice brings to the table of morality that benevolence and charity do not. Why is it that an ethic of pure benevolence is not sufficient for morality?

To answer this question, I have to explain how I think of justice. In the Western tradition there are basically two ways of thinking about justice, one that comes from Aristotle and one can comes from the ancient Roman jurist Ulpian. I prefer the way of thinking of justice that comes from Ulpian. Ulpian's well-known formula was this: justice consists of rendering to each person his or her right, what he or she has a right to—the Latin word is *jus*. It could also be translated as, rendering to each person his or her *due*.

The question this formula raises is obviously: what is it to have a right to being treated a certain way? A right to being treated a certain way is always a right to be treated in a way that would be a good in one's life—a life-good. I do not have a right to having my leg broken, unless, of course, breaking my leg is necessary for achieving some greater good. But though a right is always a right to being treated in a way that would be a good in one's life, the converse is not true; not all the ways of being treated that would be a good in one's life are ways of being treated that one has a right to. I think it would be a great good in my life if the Rijksmuseum in Amsterdam gave me one of their Rembrandt paintings to hang on my living room wall—along with a security force to stand guard. But I don't have a right to their doing that; I have not been wronged by the fact that they have not done that.

I hold that rights are connected with two basic facts about human beings. One is the fact that every human being has worth, worth of various sorts: the worth they have intrinsically as human beings, the worth they have on account of their possession of certain capacities, the worth they have on account of accomplishments on their part, and so forth.

The second fact is that each of us can be treated in ways that befit our worth and in ways that do not befit out worth. If you have written a top-notch paper in a philosophy class that I am teaching but I refuse to give you an A because I don't like your attitude, your skin color, or whatever, I have not treated you as befits the worth you have acquired of writing a top-notch philosophy paper.

So here is how I think of rights. You have a right to the good of my treating you a certain way when my treating you that way is required for treating you as befits your worth—or to put it negatively, when not treating you that way would not befit your worth. Why don't I have a right to the Rijksmuseum giving me one of their Rembrandt paintings? Because their not giving it to me does not mean that they are not treating me as befits my worth. Why does that student in my course have a right to an A on his record? Because if I don't give him an A, I am not treating him as befits the worth he has acquired of writing a top-notch philosophy paper.

Think of the moral order as having two fundamental dimensions: the agent-dimension and the patient-dimension, the actor-dimension and the recipient-dimension. On the one hand, there is the moral significance of what we do; on the other hand, there is the moral significance of how we are done unto.

The language of love, charity, benevolence, duty, etc., is all about what we do; such language brings the agent-dimension of the moral order to speech. The language of rights, and the companion language of being wronged, are for bringing the recipient-dimension of the moral order to speech, the dimension of how we are done-unto. Consider an abused spouse, and suppose that the only language available to her is the agent-language of love, duty, and the like. With such language she can call attention to the moral condition of her abusive husband: he is acting unlovingly, he is guilty of not acting as he ought to act, etc. What she cannot do is call attention to *her own* moral condition. Rights-talk enables her to do that. Her moral condition is that she has been wronged.

To think in terms of what justice requires of me, in terms of the right of the other person to being treated a certain way by me, is to be *decentered*. Rather than thinking in terms of *my* obligations, *my* goodness, etc., I think in terms of the demands placed on me by the worth of *the other*.

The Afrikaners at the conference were happy to talk about *their* moral status: they were *acting benevolently*. They did not want to talk about the moral condition of the so-called blacks and coloreds: they were *being wronged*.

So what does justice bring to the table of morality that love as benevolence does not? Recall the explanation I gave of the aim of benevolence. Benevolence, I said, aims to enhance the goods in someone's life, the life-goods, and to diminish the non-goods. It aims to enhance his or her well-being. Quite obviously one's life-goods, the states and events in one's life that contribute positively to one's well-being, are not to be identified with the worth that one has as a human being. These are two fundamentally different modes of goodness: the quality of one's life versus one's worth. Whereas benevolence aims to enhance the quality of a person's life, justice pays due respect to a person's worth. That is what justice brings to the table of morality.

The problem with the Afrikaners who spoke up in defense of apartheid at that conference was that they were so full of their self-perceived benevolence that they never opened themselves up to recognizing the worth and dignity of the so-called blacks and coloreds. That is why their benevolence took the form of oppressive paternalism.

Located in Grand Rapids is a large psychiatric hospital called Pine Rest—formerly known as Pine Rest Christian Psychiatric Hospital. It is now about a hundred years old. A few months ago I had lunch with its director, Mark Eastburg. He told me that recently they had begun thinking in terms of honoring the worth and dignity of their patients; previously they had thought only in terms of charity and benevolence. That was beginning to make a profound difference in how they treated their patients, he said; it was even beginning to make a difference in the architecture. I think it must be very easy to think of mental patients as objects of charity rather than as bearers of worth and dignity.

What to Make of Our Conclusion

Back to the question I posed: what are we to make of the conclusion to which we were led, namely, that an ethic of pure benevolence may lead its adherents to perpetrate injustice and is, for that reason, not sufficient for morality? Reinhold Niebuhr was also of this view. As I noted earlier, he thought that it was especially in situations of conflict that benevolence-love was likely to perpetrate injustice. But rather than following Nygren and saying that in such situations one should say farewell to justice and hold fast to love, he argued that in such situations it is not love that is called for but justice. As he saw it, morality for life in this present world requires two ethics, an ethic of pure benevolence and an ethic of justice, the former for situations of harmony, the latter for situations of conflict. "It is impossible to construct a social ethic out of the ideal of love in its pure form, because the ideal presupposes the resolution of the conflict of life with life, which is the concern of law [and justice] to mitigate and restrain. For this reason Christianity really had no social ethic until it appropriated the Stoic ethic."[14] In the eschaton there will be no conflict, only harmony. The ethic of love will then prevail; justice will then no longer be relevant.

I find this resolution of the issue we are considering unsatisfactory for several reasons. I find it biblically untenable. When Jesus declares, in

---

14. Niebuhr, *Love and Justice*, 149-50.

the inaugural sermon that I mentioned earlier, that he is inaugurating God's reign of justice, surely he is not saying that he is inaugurating God's reign of justice for this present world, but that justice will disappear in the eschaton. And note that he did not say, "love your friends and do justice to your enemies." He said, "love your enemy." Love the neighbor even when the neighbor is hostile to you.

I also find Niebuhr's proposal conceptually confused. If the understanding of justice that I sketched out above is correct, justice is not relevant only to situations of conflict. Justice pertains to how we treat each other whether or not we are in conflict. Both in conflict and not in conflict, we are to treat the other in a way that befits her worth.

So what then are we to make of the conclusion to which we were led, that an ethic of pure benevolence is not sufficient for morality? I suggest that what we have to do is re-visit the assumption that it was pure benevolence that Jesus had in mind when he said that we are to love the neighbor. Agape, in the context of Jesus' command, does not mean pure benevolence.

When Jesus replied to his hostile questioner by saying that we are to love God with all our being and our neighbor as ourselves, he was not just summarizing the Old Testament Torah; he was quoting. The second love command was a quotation of Leviticus 19:18: "you shall love your neighbor as yourself." In Leviticus, the command comes as the culmination of a large number of more specific "you shall's," for example, "you shall not hate in your heart any of your kin." The love command occurs in Leviticus as a summary of what has preceded. It is to be read like this: "in short, love your neighbor as yourself."

What's relevant for our purposes is the fact that, among the more specific commands of which the love command is a summary, there are commands to do justice: "you shall not render an unjust judgment;" "you shall not defraud your neighbor;" "with justice you shall judge your neighbor." I think the conclusion is irresistible. Treating one's neighbor justly is to be numbered among the ways in which one loves one's neighbor. Recall our discussion of benevolence: one is not acting out of benevolence if one acts as one does because justice requires. That cannot be the right interpretation of the love that Jesus had in mind. Treating one's neighbor as justice requires is an example of the love that Jesus enjoins.

Recall a point I made earlier, that a right to being treated a certain way is always a right to being treated in a way that would be a good in one's life. What we learn from Leviticus is that we are to aim to enhance some life-good of the neighbor both when justice requires of us that we do so and when justice does not require it.

So how then should we understand the love that Jesus had in mind when he said, "love your neighbor as yourself"? I suggest that we have to understand it as having a dual focus. Recall the distinction made earlier, between the quality of a person's life and the worth the person has, her praiseworthiness, on account of intrinsic features such as bearing the image of God, on account of accomplishments, on account of abilities, etc. The love Jesus had in mind takes account of both of these. It aims at enhancing the neighbor's life-goods; and it aims at doing so in such a way that the neighbor is treated with due respect for his or her worth.

Do we have a term in English for this dual focus kind of love? I think we do. It is the term "care about." When I care about someone, I both aim to enhance her well-being and I see to it that she is treated with due respect by myself and others. I suggest that the love Jesus had in mind was *love as care*.

Let me draw out an implication of my proposal. At any given time my attention will, of course, be focused on only some of my neighbors; but I have to keep all of them in mind. What this implies is that, when I am focused on caring about, say, Maria, I must not only see to it that I am doing so in such a way that I am not wronging her, not treating her in a way that does not befit her worth; I must see to it that I am doing so in such a way that I am not wronging anyone.

In the first part of this essay I argued that an ethic of pure benevolence is not sufficient for morality. What I now contend is that an ethic of care-love, as I have explained it, is sufficient for morality.

5

All Justice is Social, but Not All Justice Is Social Justice

I take social *in*justice to be injustice perpetrated on members of society by laws and public social practices. I take social justice to be the struggle to right social injustice. After explaining these ideas, I then address the question: why are so many people opposed to the very idea of social justice? I offer a number of explanations, among them, that to acknowledge that there is social injustice in one's society often requires considerable change on one's part.

The term "social justice" is a site of controversy. For some people it expresses their mission in life. For others it evokes images of busybody do-gooders and intrusive government. I want to explore why the term evokes resistance—and not only the term, but the thing itself, namely, social justice. Before we can do that, however, we'll have to identify the sort of justice that social justice is. And in order to do that, I will to have to explain what I take justice as such to be. My explanation of the nature of justice will be a brief exposition of the way of thinking about justice that I develop at length in my book, *Justice: Rights and Wrongs*.

What Is Justice?

A well-known formula for justice handed down to us from antiquity comes from the ancient Roman jurist Ulpian: justice is rendering to each his or her *ius*—that is, his or her right, his or her due. Ulpian's formula is a definition of just action. Justice itself is present in society insofar as each person is rendered that to which he or she has a right.

An important preliminary point is the following. Our English term "a right" is used to express two quite different ideas. We say, "I have a right to walk on the Charlottesville Mall," when what we mean is that one is *permitted* to walk on the Mall—such a right is a *permission-right*. But we also say, "I have a right to a monthly Social Security check from the government," when what we mean is that one has a legitimate claim to a monthly social security check—such a right is a *claim-right*. A permission-right is a right to do something. A claim-right is a right to be treated a certain way.

The fact that the same term, "a right," can be used to refer either to a permission-right or a claim-right, invites confusion. Worse yet, some sentences can be used to refer to either of these sorts of rights. When someone says, "I have a right to walk on the Charlottesville Mall," what he might mean is not that he is permitted to do so but that he has a legitimate claim to doing so *unhindered*.

It is claim-rights that Ulpian's definition has in view. My discussion in what follows will likewise focus on claim-rights. When I use the term "rights" without qualification, it is claim-rights to which I am referring.

Notice that Ulpian tacitly distinguishes between having or possessing a right, and being rendered that right—or as I will sometimes say, *enjoying* that right. Not being rendered one's right does not mean that one does not possess that right. It means that one is not enjoying a right that one possesses, that one is being deprived of it. If one has or possesses a certain right, then one may either be rendered that right or be deprived of it. In the former case, one enjoys that to which one has a right; in the latter case, one is wronged. Being wronged is the dark side of having a right, just as guilt is the dark side of obligation. The person who does not enjoy her right is wronged; the person who does not do what she ought to do is guilty.

To have or possess a right is not to stand in the relation of possession to some metaphysically mysterious entity called "a right." Having a right consists of having a right *to* something: it makes no sense to say that one has a certain right but that there is nothing to which one has that right. To have or possess a right is to stand to something that is not a right in the relation of *having a right to* it. The whole term, "having a right to," expresses the relation. The indefinite article "a" does no work—one might as well say, "having right to."

The relation is, of course, a normative relation. To stand to something in the relation of *having (a) right to* it is to stand to it in the relation of *having legitimate claim to* it. Or to express the same idea in yet a third way, it is to stand to it in the relation of its *being due* one. Let us first consider the sort of thing to which one can stand in this relationship, and then consider the nature of the relation itself.

That to which one can stand in the relation of having (a) right to it is, in the first place, some state or event in one's life that is or would be a good in one's life, a life-good.[1] Admittedly it is not always evident from how we speak about rights that this is true. We speak, for example, of having a right to a seat on the plane, but a seat on a plane is not a state or event in one's life. However, if we look beneath the words to the structure of the situation, we'll see that what I said is true. What we refer to as a right to a seat on the plane is more fully described as a right to *be allowed to take* a seat on the plane. And taking a seat on the plane is an event in one's life. More specifically, it is an event that is or would be a good in one's life. Of course, enjoying one's right to take a seat on the plane might have disastrous consequences—e.g., the plane might crash. In that case, although the whole package, taking a seat on the plane and the plane's crashing, is a bad thing in one's life, that doesn't make the thing itself to which one had a right, namely, taking a seat on the plane, a bad thing.

And now for an important step in the argument: those life-goods to which one has a claim-right are always *ways of being treated* that are or would be a good in one's life. That to which one has a right is always to the good of being treated a certain way. Normally it is to the good of being treated a certain way by others, but in the limiting case, it is to the good of being treated a certain way by oneself. It will simplify our discussion if we set that limiting case off to the side and say that that to which one has a right is always some good of being treated a certain way by others.[2]

Earlier I said that rights are normative relationships. What we can now add is that rights are normative *social* relationships: that to which one has a right is always to the good of being treated a certain way by one's fellows. It takes at least two to have a right—with the exception of those cases in which one has a right to being treated a certain way by oneself.

If Ulpian was right—and I think he was—that justice consists of being rendered that to which one has (a) right, then what can now be said is that justice is present in society insofar as the members of society stand

---

1. This statement requires a qualification that, on this occasion, I will not insert into the text. There are certain ways of depriving me of life such that I have the right against my fellow human beings to the good of their not depriving me of life in those ways. (This may be a prima facie right, not an ultima facie right, and it may be a right that one can forfeit.) So consider the good to which I have that right, the good of their not depriving me of life in those ways. This is obviously a good that *pertains to* my life, but it is not, strictly speaking, a good *in* my life. That is to say, it is not a state or event *in* my life that contributes positively to its estimability. It was a question put to me by Chris Eberle that led me to see the need for this qualification.

2. Third party rights constitute an exception to this principle: I may have a right against you to your treating Mary a certain way rather than to your treating me a certain way. This would be the case if you promised me that you would extend some benefit to Mary. Continually taking account of this sort of exception in the text would unnecessarily complicate the discussion.

to each other in the normative social relationship of being treated as they have a right to be treated.

We now face what I regard as the most challenging point for anyone trying to construct a theory of justice, namely, explaining the nature of the relation of *having a right to*. Though that to which one has a right is always a way of being treated by others that is or would be a good in one's life, the converse is not the case: there are many ways of being treated by others that would be a good in one's life to which one does not have a right. I think it would be a great good in my life were I to be given a Rembrandt painting by the Rijksmuseum in Amsterdam to hang on my living room wall, along with a security force to stand guard. But I don't have a right to that life-good—i.e., my not enjoying that good does not imply that I am being wronged by the museum. So what accounts for the fact that, of those ways of being treated by others that would be a good in one's life, one has a right to some and not to others?

Obviously some of our rights are bestowed on us by legislation or social practice, or generated in us by some such speech act as promising. I have a right to receive a monthly Social Security check from the U.S. government on account of the Social Security legislation passed in the 1930s—plus the fact that I possess the qualifications specified in the legislation. But not all my rights are like that. Some are *natural* rights. Wholly apart from legislation, social practices, and speech acts, I have a right to not being murdered, to not being tortured for the pleasure of the torturer, and to not being insulted or demeaned. So what accounts for the fact that, of those ways of being treated by others that would be a good in one's life, one has a *natural* right to some of those ways of being treated while, to others, one either has no right or only a socially bestowed or generated right?

The view on this point that is presently dominant in the literature is that natural rights are all either specifications of, or conditions for the enjoyment of, our fundamental natural right to autonomy—that is, our fundamental natural right to form for ourselves a plan of life and to enact that plan, revising it along the way as seems appropriate.

Popular though this theory is, however, I think it has to be rejected. One problem confronting the theory is explaining what is meant by "autonomy"—clearly no one has the right to do whatever he or she sees fit to do. I judge that no autonomy theorist has succeeded in giving a satisfactory explanation of what autonomy is. But suppose a satisfactory explanation were forthcoming. Then we need an explanation of how it comes about that we have that supposedly fundamental natural right to autonomy. The explanation offered for all other natural rights is that they are specifications of, or conditions for, the enjoyment of our fundamental natural right to autonomy. But what, then, accounts for *that* right?

Suppose these problems could be overcome. We then face what seem to me decisive counterexamples. Everybody reading this essay will agree that to torture imprisoned criminals as a way of punishing them is to wrong them: they have a right not to be punished by torture. To employ torture as a means of punishment is to treat them unjustly. But what makes it wrong is not that their autonomy is thereby impaired. Their autonomy is already impaired: they are locked up. What is wrong about torturing them, I would say, is that their dignity as human beings is violated. So too, what is wrong about rape is not that the autonomy of the victim is impaired, though it certainly is. What is wrong about rape is that the victim is treated as worth no more than an object to serve the rapist's pleasure or power. And in general, it is my view that natural rights are grounded in the worth, the dignity, of the rights-bearer. I have a right to the life-good of being treated a certain way by others just in case, were I not treated that way, I would be treated in a way that does not befit my worth, my dignity.

Rights, so understood, represent an interweaving of life-goods, on the one hand, and of the worth or dignity of the human beings whose life-goods those are, on the other hand. Any ethical theory that works only with life-goods, and not also with the worth or dignity of human beings, is incapable of giving an account of natural rights. Modern utilitarianism is one such theory; eudaimonism, currently enjoying a renaissance, is another. One does not get rights by piling up life-goods. The fact that having a Rembrandt painting hanging on my living room wall would be an enormous good in my life and in the lives of others does not bring it about that I have a right to that good.

One final point must be made here, namely, that rights have peremptory or trumping force. Let me develop the point in a slightly roundabout way that will prove useful later in our discussion.

Kant introduced the distinction between *perfect* and *imperfect* duties. A perfect duty is the duty to treat a specific person in such-and-such a way. An example would be my duty to give five dollars to the handicapped person sitting begging in front of my bank. An imperfect duty is the duty to treat someone or other in such-and-such a way without there being any person such that it is one's duty to treat *that* person in that way. An example would be my duty to give five dollars to one or another of the beggars on the Mall without there being any beggar such that it is my duty to give *him* five dollars.[3]

---

3. A duty can also be imperfect in that one has a duty to treat a particular person in

Now let us introduce, as the mirror image of this concept of an imperfect duty, the concept of an imperfect right. An imperfect right is the right to be treated in such-and-such a way by someone or other when there is no one such that one has the right to be treated in that way by *that* person. A beggar on the Mall may have the right to receive charity from one or another of the well-to-do people on the Mall without there being anyone such that he has a right to receive charity from *that* person.[4] If so, then his right to receive charity is an imperfect right.

Let us now set these ideas of imperfect duties and imperfect rights off to the side for the time being. We can then formulate the following *principle of correlatives* for the relation between perfect duties and perfect rights:

> A person A has a right against a person B to B's treating him in such-and-such a way if and only if B has a duty toward A to treat him in that way.

Hassan has a right against Randall to Randall's not torturing him if and only if Randall has a duty toward Hassan to refrain from torturing him. The principle holds for both prima facie duties and rights and ultima facie duties and rights.

Now suppose I have an ultima facie duty toward you to refrain from torturing you and that you have the correlative ultima facie right against me to my not torturing you. But suppose I can bring about a large number of goods in the lives of people by torturing you, goods to which no one has a right. What should I do, all things considered?

I should refrain from torturing you. I should refrain from torturing you because I *ought* to refrain from torturing you; it is my duty to refrain. And if I ought to refrain from torturing you, then it is morally impermissible for me not to refrain. Obligation trumps. And if obligation trumps, then rights trump—by virtue of the principle of correlatives. If Hassan has an ultima facie right to Randall's not torturing him, then not torturing him is what Randall ought to do—no matter how many goods Randall might bring about by torturing Hassan, goods to which no one has a right.

---

some way or other within a certain range, but not a duty to treat him in any particular way within that range. For example, I may have a duty to alleviate a particular person's poverty in some way or other, without having the duty to do so in any particular way.

4. A right can also be imperfect in that one has a right against a particular person that he treat one in some way or other within a certain range—to alleviate one's poverty in some way or other, for example—but not a right to his treating one in any particular way within that range.

What Is Social Justice?

That completes the presentation of my way of thinking about justice and rights. It is time to turn our attention to social justice.

What is social justice? As we go about trying to discover the answer to this question, let us keep in mind that we are dealing here with only a part of justice. It us an extremely important part; but it is not the whole.

The Old Testament prophets were the first great spokesmen for social justice in what has come to be the Western tradition. Taking a look at the structure of what they said will prove to be a good way of getting hold of the idea. Here, from Isaiah, is a typical passage:

> Woe to those who decree iniquitous decrees,
> and the writers who keep writing oppression,
> to turn aside the needy from justice
> and to rob the poor of my people of their right,
> that widows may be their spoil,
> and that they may make the fatherless their prey!
> What will you do on the day of punishment,
> in the storm which will come from afar?
> To whom will you turn for help,
> and where will you leave your wealth?
> (Isa 10:1–3)

Biting words. Even more biting are the following words, also from Isaiah:

> The Lord said:
>
> Because the daughters of Zion are haughty
> and walk with outstretched necks,
> glancing wantonly with their eyes,
> mincing along as they go,
> tinkling with their feet;
> the Lord will smite with a scab
> the heads of the daughters of Zion,
> and the Lord will lay bare their secret parts.
>
> In that day the Lord will take away the finery of the anklets, the headbands, and the crescents; the pendants, the bracelets, and the scarves; the headdresses, the armlets, the sashes, the perfume boxes, and the amulets; the signet rings and nose rings; the

festal robes, the mantles, the cloaks, and the handbags; the garments of gauze, the linen garments, the turbans, and the veils.

Instead of perfume there will be rottenness;
   and instead of a girdle, a rope;
and instead of well-set hair, baldness,
   and instead of a rich robe, a girding of sackcloth;
   instead of beauty, shame.
Your men shall fall by the sword
   and your mighty men in battle.
(Isa 3:16–25)

Notice, first, that Isaiah does not mention any particular episodes of injustice or any particular wrongdoers. He and the other prophets were not hesitant to point the finger when the occasion arose; recall the prophet Nathan confronting King David for his affair with Bathsheba with the accusing words, "you are the man" (2 Sam 12:7). The target of Isaiah's attack in these passages is not specific episodes of injustice and specific wrongdoers; his target is laws and public social practices whose effect is to turn aside widows, orphans, and the poor from justice and to rob them of their right.

I suggest that we are touching here on the central feature of that special form of injustice which is social injustice. Social injustice is the injustice that is wreaked on members of the community by its laws and public social practices. Of course, strictly speaking it is not the laws that wreak the injustice but those who pass and enforce the laws, and strictly speaking it is not the practices that wreak the injustice but those who engage in the practices.

To recognize social injustice one must be able to look beyond particular episodes of injustice, and beyond particular wrongdoers and victims, to recognize a certain pattern in a number of episodes. That done, one must then be able to look behind those patterns to discern what accounts for them, namely, certain laws and public social practices. This latter ability, the ability to discern the cause of the pattern of injustice, requires the ability to engage in a certain kind of abstraction. To determine whether someone is a participant in a public social practice that wreaks injustice one must be able to abstract from his intentions. A person may wrong someone without intending to do so. We'll be coming back to this point later.

Some people find it difficult, both in their own case and in the case of others, to perform the sort of abstraction required for recognizing social injustice. This is not how they normally think. Others find it not so much difficult to think this way as offensive to be told that they and their friends are perpetrating injustice. They are good people with the best of intentions: "if the prophet Isaiah thinks that Asher and Benjamin did something wrong to someone, then he should have the courage to name them and point his finger at them. He should not use a wide brush that tars good people with bad."

Given the understanding of social *in*-justice that I have just now spelled out, it is tempting to say that social justice is present in a society when there is no social *in*-justice in that society, that is, when no one is being treated unjustly by the laws and public social practices. But that is not how the term "social justice" is ordinarily used. It is ordinarily used to refer to the actions of speaking up in opposition to social injustice and struggling to undo it. Social justice organizations are organizations that oppose social injustice. So that is how I will use the term.[5] When it is the laws and public social practices of society that lead to members of the community being robbed of their rights, the struggle for justice requires more than speaking out against particular episodes of wronging and more than trying to forestall such episodes. It requires speaking out against, and trying to alter or eliminate, those laws and social practices. And that is social justice.

In focusing the fire of his critique on iniquitous laws and public social practices, the prophet assumes that things can be different. The extant laws and practices are not laws of nature ordained by God; neither do they express the ineluctable laws of the marketplace or the unalterable preconditions of social order. The prophets do not think of the widows, the orphans, and the impoverished as social unfortunates about whom there is nothing to be done. Instead, they think of them as the victims of laws and practices that can be changed. It is sometimes said that not until the early modern period did people in general believe that social structures and practices are human constructs that can be changed. It seems to me unmistakable that the Hebrew prophets already believed that.

Not only does the prophetic critique of social injustice assume that the laws and public social practices of society *can* be changed, it also assumes that they *ought to be* changed. The prophetic critique assumes that there is a moral standard outside those laws and practices by which they are to be judged, and it declares that they fail to meet that standard. The laws and practices are not a standard unto themselves. The fact that this is how we do things in our society does not make those things just. Justice transcends our laws and practices. The prophet attacks the laws and practices because they fall short of what is required by the justice that transcends them.

---

5. Social justice can also take the form of defending laws and public social practices that secure justice when those laws and practices are threatened.

The prophets say very little about how to get from here to there—very little about how to get from the social injustices of one's present society to a society in which those injustices are removed. They do not pinpoint the laws that must be changed in their society. They do not mention the political activities that must take place to get those laws changed. They provide very little advice to social activists. If the ancient Israelites were like us, this silence on the part of the prophets would have been a source of annoyance to many: "If you're so smart and think you know everything that is wrong about America, why don't you tell us how to fix things and yourself get down in the trenches and start fixing them instead of just lobbing grenades over the wall? Talk is cheap."

The prophet does not see it as his calling to get into the nitty-gritty of legal and social reform. He's doing what has to be done first. He's trying to open the eyes of those with power to the injustices they are perpetrating, trying to unstop their ears to the cries of those afflicted, trying to soften their hardened hearts so that they are moved.

Though the prophet does not give practical advice to reformers, what he does do, beyond launching his critique, is to imagine a society in which things are different. He employs social imagination. Some of the most lyrically visionary passages in all of Western literature are expressions of the social imagination of the Hebrew prophets. The prophet imagines a day when the bonds of wickedness are loosed and the thongs of the yoke are undone, when the oppressed are let free and every yoke is broken, when people share their bread with the hungry, take the homeless poor into their houses, clothe the naked, and do not avert their eyes from their own kin (Isa 58:6–7).

By turning to the Hebrew prophets to understand the nature of social justice I do not mean to suggest that opposition to social injustice must take the form of imitating the prophets. Often it should not. Often it should take the form of getting down into the trenches and trying to change things: trying to repeal the laws that oppress the weak and vulnerable, trying to replace those laws with laws that protect the weak and vulnerable, trying to get the government to enforce those laws, and so forth. And the rhetoric of those who speak up in opposition to social injustice need not always take the sharp accusatory form that it typically took in the prophets. Sometimes it should instead take the form of reasoning together.

Always, however, opposition to social injustice will have to aim at awakening people to what is happening, shaking them out of their slumber. And not infrequently that will require something other than reasoning together; not infrequently it will require sharp accusatory speeches, vivid presentations of the victims, and so forth. Much of the rhetoric of Martin Luther King, Jr. is an example of the point.

Why the Opposition to Social Justice Speech and Action?

I announced at the beginning of this essay that my topic is why so many people reject the idea of social justice. If social injustice is what I have suggested it is, namely, injustice perpetrated on members of society by laws and public social practices, and if social justice consists of speaking out against such injustice and doing what one reasonably can to undo it, then how could anybody be opposed to the idea of social justice? That is the question I want to address.

Some people are opposed to the idea of social justice because they are opposed to the idea of justice in general. They hold that we should be talking about people's responsibilities, not about their rights. Or that we should be talking about loving each other, not about doing what justice requires. Or, coming from the opposite end of the spectrum, that we should each be asking what is in it for us, and not busying ourselves with the rights of others. On this occasion I want to set off to the side those who are opposed to the idea of justice in general and consider only those who don't like the idea of social justice in particular. Before I do that, however, let me describe the form taken by opposition to justice-talk in general that I witnessed on the occasion of my first visit to South Africa.

It happened at a conference in Potchefstroom in 1975. Present at the conference were a sizable number of academics from South Africa—white, colored, and black, to use the categories employed at the time. Present were also people from other parts of Africa, a sizable contingent of people from the Netherlands, and a few of us from North America.

Apartheid was not the topic of the conference. Nonetheless, the Dutch, who were very well informed about apartheid and very angry about it, eventually managed to find a way to express their opposition to apartheid in public. The Afrikaners who spoke up in defense of apartheid responded by telling the Dutch in no uncertain terms that they were unfair, unloving, and morally arrogant. After several hours of this angry back and forth, the Dutch fell silent and the so-called blacks and coloreds from South Africa began to speak up. They described the indignities daily heaped upon them, and they cried out for justice.

I was taken aback by the response to this cry by the Afrikaner defenders of apartheid. They insisted that justice was not a relevant category; benevolence was the relevant category. Apartheid was motivated by benevolence. There were some eleven different nationalities in South Africa. Apartheid was aimed at the great social good of enabling each of these nationalities to find its own unique identity. For that good to be achieved, these diverse nationalities had to be separated from each other—hence, apartheid. It was unfortunate that attaining that great social good, of each nationality developing in its own unique way, required restricting the liberties of some people and creating misery in certain quarters. But it was all for the good.

I saw, as I had never seen before, why the idea of social justice is indispensable. Justice applies moral brakes to paternalistic benevolence. Social goods are not to be achieved at the cost of wronging people.

The Myopia of Some Social Justice Activists

One reason people are opposed to the idea of social justice is that they are turned off by the Mrs. Jellyby's and the Miss Ansell's of the world. Let me explain. Mrs. Jellyby is a character in Charles Dickens' novel, *Bleak House*, who neglects her own children in order to devote all her time and energy to some great cause of social justice in Africa. "Miss Ansell" is the name of an actual Mrs. Jellyby with whom I had the ill fortune to become acquainted.

Miss Ansell owned a large Victorian house on the outskirts of Cambridge, England. In the fall of 1956 my wife and I rented two rooms on the second floor of her house; a young Israeli couple rented the other rooms on the floor. It became clear to us that they were very poor. This was at the time of the Hungarian Revolution. Miss Ansell spent all day every day at her desk writing letters to world figures urging them to do something to stop the Russian invasion of Hungary. She wrote to the British prime minister offering to lay her body across the tracks of the trains transporting Russian soldiers into Hungary if the British government would pay for the cost of her travel to Hungary.

Miss Ansell had a large garden back of her house, with a number of apple trees in it. The trees were ripe with fruit; the apples were beginning to fall. The Israeli couple asked if they could pick some of the apples. Miss Ansell tartly replied that they were not to go into the garden; the garden was off limits to her renters.

The eyes of Mrs. Jellyby were so firmly fixed on social injustices in distant Africa that she never saw the wrong she was doing to her own children. The eyes of Miss Ansell were so firmly fixed on injustice in distant Hungary that she never saw the wrong she was doing to her renters. Such people give social justice a bad name. Their concern for social justice is combined with a mystifying and offensive oblivion or indifference to the injustice they are perpetrating at home. Not uncommonly they regard themselves as morally superior to those who are not similarly devoted to some great cause of social justice.

My response to those who oppose the idea of social justice because they are turned off by the Mrs. Jellyby's and the Miss Ansell's of the world is that they are right to be turned off by such people, but not right to let that turn them against the idea of social justice itself. What we see in Mrs. Jellyby and Miss Ansell is a perversion of the moral life. Speaking up against, and struggling against, social injustice need not come, and should not come, at the cost of being oblivious or indifferent to the injustices one is perpetrating at home.

Another reason people are opposed to the idea of social justice came up earlier in our discussion. Social justice requires being capable of a certain kind of pattern recognition: one has to look beyond particular episodes of injustice to discern regularities in those episodes. That done, one must then engage in a certain kind of social analysis; one must discern, as the cause of those regularities of injustice, laws and public social practices. This latter discernment requires the ability to make a certain kind of abstraction: one must be able to abstract the laws, the practices, and their effects on victims, from the attitudes toward the victims of those who institute or enforce the laws and of those who engage in the practices.

I mentioned that some people find this abstraction difficult. They don't think in terms of social practices. Rather, they are baffled by the charge that in acting as they do, they are perpetrating injustice. Others are not so much baffled as offended. How can their actions be tarred with perpetrating racial injustice when they don't have a racist bone in their bodies? How can their actions be tarred with wronging the poor when they give generously to the benevolence fund of their church or synagogue? Such people assume that to find out whether someone is perpetrating injustice, one looks to that person's *intentions*. Their own intentions are entirely good. They are good people. They contribute to charity. They teach Sunday School. They serve on vestry. They are members of the parish council.

This protest raises an important point. One's actions can wrong someone, deprive her of what she has a right to, treat her unjustly, treat her with under-respect for her worth, without one's being blamable for performing those actions. Perhaps one didn't know and couldn't be expected to know what one was doing to her. Or perhaps one did know but didn't realize, and couldn't be expected to realize, that one was treating her in a way that she had a right not to be treated. In each such case, one is not to be blamed but excused. Nonetheless, it remains the case that one wronged her, treated her with under-respect. Injustice does not track with culpability; one can unwittingly wrong someone.

It is my impression that resistance to the idea of social justice often has its source in confusion on his point—confusion on both sides, both in the minds of those engaged in social justice and in the minds of those opposed to the idea of social justice. The person opposed to the idea of social justice assumes that if he concedes that some social practice in which he participates victimizes certain people, then he must also concede that he bears a burden of guilt. He insists that he does not bear a burden of guilt; his intentions have always been pure.

The thing to be said in response is that he may be right about that last point: it is possible that he does not bear a burden of guilt. But from the fact that he is not culpable, it does not follow that he has not been wronging those affected by his actions. And let us not overlook the fact that his ignorance may be willful ignorance, in which case he is not to be excused.

A third reason for opposition to the idea of social justice is that some people hear the term "social justice" as a code word for the activities of those who favor an expansive welfare state. They have been led to believe that if they concede that the plight of the widows, the orphans, and the impoverished is not merely unfortunate but unjust, then they are committed to asking the state to dispense welfare to them or to introduce a large body of regulations. They regard an expansive regulatory and welfare state as an all-enveloping octopus. So they oppose the idea of social justice.

The assumption is false. Recognizing that something is a social injustice carries no implications whatsoever as to how that injustice should be remedied. In particular, it does not carry the implication that the state is the remedy of first resort. No Hebrew prophet said that the remedy for the social injustice of poverty was that the king hand out doles to the poor.

The state should seldom be the remedy of first resort for undoing social injustice. Indeed, it should almost always be the remedy of last resort. It would have been far better if the practitioners of slavery had acknowledged its injustice and stopped the practice, rather than insisting on perpetuating the practice and forcing the state to intervene. It would be far better if our capitalist economy provided work and a living wage to all adults who can work, rather than failing to do so and forcing the state to intervene by dispensing welfare so that people won't starve. It would be far better if our market economy made it possible for everyone to afford health insurance, rather than falling far short of that and forcing the state to intervene by regulating the health insurance industry. And so forth.

The concept of imperfect rights that we introduced earlier is relevant here. An objection sometimes lodged against the idea of social justice is that it cannot be true that to be the victim of impoverishment is to have one's rights violated, since there is no one to whom one can point such that it is against *that* person that one has these rights. The argument is fallacious. One can have a right to be treated a certain way by someone or other without there being someone such that it is against *that* person that one has the right. The rights of the widows, the orphans, and the impoverished are, in good measure, imperfect rights.

In Conclusion

My project in this essay has been to unearth and appraise the reasons people have for rejecting the idea of social justice. Some people reject the idea because they are put off by the Mrs. Jellyby's and the Miss Ansell's of the world. Others reject the idea because they find it either difficult or offensive to believe that good people like themselves could be guilty of inflicting injustice when they are simply doing business as business is done and contributing, out of the goodness of their hearts, to charitable organizations. Yet others reject the idea because they have been led to believe that to acknowledge something as a social injustice is to commit oneself to appealing to the state as the remedy of first resort, and they see this as leading to a state that is a menace to freedom.

Let me close by noting one more source of resistance to the idea of social injustice. To acknowledge rather than reject the charge that one is complicit in social injustice requires that one commit oneself to desist from the practice or reform it, if either of those is possible—and often that is more than a person can bring himself to do. One would lose esteem among friends, make less money, and no longer be in a position of privilege and power. That is too high a price. It is best to keep one's position of privilege, power, and pelf, fend off the charge in one way or another, and make generous contributions to charitable organizations. Not justice but charity: that is the way to go. Then nothing has to change. The reason social justice movements are almost always conflictual is that those who benefit from the status quo find the price of change too high.

Consider the great social justice movements of the past century and a half: the abolitionist movement was a social justice movement, the movement for the control of monopolies was a social justice movement, the campaign for the abolition of child labor was a social justice movement, the labor union movement was a social justice movement, the campaign for women's rights was a social justice movement, the passage of Social Security legislation was the result of a social justice movement, the civil rights movement was a social justice movement. The list goes on and on. How different our society would be if none of these movements for social justice had occurred. Though all justice is social, not all justice is social justice. Social justice is, however, an enormously important part of the whole.

6

Religious Intolerance and the Wounds of God

A Cry for Justice

They spoke of their ancestral lands being expropriated. They spoke of their ancient olive orchards being bulldozed. They spoke of their houses being dynamited after the family was given one hour to remove its belongings. They spoke of humiliating searches at airports and at checkpoints scattered around their country. They cried out for justice. And they asked why no one heard their cry.

This was my first contact with Palestinians. It happened at a conference on Palestinian rights on the west side of Chicago in May, 1978. About 150 Palestinians were in attendance. The reason these evils had befallen them was that they were not Jewish. Had they been Jewish, none of it would have happened.

A year or so later I went to the Middle East; I have gone several times since. I went to the West Bank—the "occupied territory," as the Palestinians call it—and saw for myself the expropriated land, usually on the crest of hills, the crest now covered with gleaming new residences exclusively for Jews, paid for in good measure by American funds. I saw where the olive orchards had once been. I saw two families standing next to the heaps of rubble that had been their homes until the middle of the night before.

I went to Israel and talked to Jews and Palestinians. I heard from the Palestinians about the many ways in which their not being Jewish resulted in their being treated as second-class citizens. I heard progressive Israelis confirm this charge. I listened to the "spiel" of the leader of the so-called Jerusalem Embassy, an American evangelical dispensationalist organization committed to supporting the Israeli cause. He seemed either unaware that there were Christians in the Middle East or utterly indifferent to what Israel's policies and America's support of those policies were doing to them. When a question was raised afterwards, it turned out that he was not unaware. These were not real Christians, he said. Nor was he indifferent. The Palestinians, Christian and Muslim alike, ought to leave. God gave this land to the Jews.

What strange turns religious intolerance takes. The patent anti-Semitism that surfaced in the famous Dreyfus case in France in the late 1800s, coming after one hundred years of European enlightenment, led Theodor Herzl to conclude that Jews would never be fully accepted in Europe. The solution he proposed was that Jews establish their own state somewhere—he had no strong preference as to where that should be. The Holocaust impelled many of the surviving Jews to leave their homelands after the Second World War and emigrate to the Middle East. Their arrival was instrumental in the founding of the state of Israel—from its beginning, a Jewish state. And now this same people, who had endured so much suffering over the centuries for no other reason than that they were Jewish, were seizing the ancestral lands of the Palestinian inhabitants, destroying their livelihood, dynamiting their homes. It should be added that whereas many if not most of the founders of the State of Israel understood Jewishness more in ethnic than religious terms, that is not true of the present-day population of Israel; it is even less true of the Jewish settlers in the West Bank.[1]

A story similar to the one I have just now told about the treatment by the Jewish State of Israel of those who are not Jews could be told about the treatment by Christians of those who are not Christian, by Muslims of those who are not Muslim, by Hindus of those who are not Hindu, and so forth. From all the stories that could be told, my only reason for selecting the one I did tell is that this is the one I happened to become directly acquainted with.

In this chapter I shall present a case for religious tolerance that draws on a near-forgotten theme in the Christian theological tradition: given the assumption that religious intolerance is unjust, to be intolerant of the other person's practice of her religion is to wrong God.

This theme, of injustice as the wronging of God, does not, all by itself, constitute a full case for religious tolerance; one has to add, for example, the assumption just mentioned, that religious intolerance is unjust. So before developing the theme, let me say a bit about the nature of tolerance, identify the

---

1. Mark Braverman, himself Jewish, argues in his courageous book *Fatal Embrace* that the root cause of Israel's discriminatory treatment of those who are not Jewish within the State of Israel and within the occupied territory is the conviction of Jewish exceptionalism that is lodged deep in the mentality of religious and non-religious Jews alike.

structure that a full case for religious tolerance would have, and pinpoint the contribution to that structure of the theme that we will be discussing.

The Nature of Tolerance and the Reasons for Practicing It

Tolerance is not indifference. It is incompatible with indifference; indifference makes tolerance impossible. If I believe that all religions are as good as my own in arriving at God, in putting us in touch with the Real, or whatever, I will not *tolerate* your practice of your religion; I will be *indifferent* as to which religion you practice. Tolerance is likewise incompatible with prizing your practice of some religion different from my own—"So interesting to have a Hindu in the neighborhood." Prizing of diversity makes tolerance impossible. When J. S. Mill urged that we prize disagreement on the ground that the clash of opinions makes the attainment of truth more likely, he was not urging tolerance of disagreement.

Some of what passes for religious tolerance in the Western world today is not tolerance but the prizing of diversity; even more of it is sheer indifference. It should be added, however, that few people are indifferent to all religions; even fewer prize all diversity. The liberal Christian who relishes having a progressive Hindu in the neighborhood is likely to be upset if a right-wing teetotaling evangelical Christian moves in. His being upset by having a right-wing evangelical Christian in the neighborhood, but not by a progressive Hindu, means that the presence of the evangelical Christian offers him an opportunity to practice tolerance whereas the presence of the progressive Hindu does not.

Tolerance and intolerance of someone's practice of their religion are alike in that both presuppose that one *disapproves* of that practice. One tolerates their practice of their religion if one disapproves of it but nonetheless puts up with it. Or more precisely: if one *voluntarily* puts up with it. If one puts up with the other person's practice of his religion only because the law compels one to do so, that is not tolerance.

Disapproval varies in intensity, as it does in what it is about the other person's practice of his or her religion that bears the brunt of one's disapproval. Perhaps what annoys me is the mere fact of a seemingly rational adult believing such silly nonsense, perhaps it is the fact that he makes me feel unsure and uneasy about my own religion, perhaps it is his unwillingness to participate in our nation's wars. Tolerance and intolerance likewise vary in intensity, and they too come in many forms. Though I may not advocate your being coerced into not practicing your religion and instead practicing some other, I may shun you, ridicule you, mock you, advocate that you not be treated equally with the rest of us by the state, advocate that you have fewer civil rights than the rest of us, and the like. In not advocating that you be coerced I am, so far forth, putting up with your practice of your religion; in nonetheless mocking your religion I am not putting up with your practice of it. My behavior is a mixture of tolerance and intolerance.

Given that I disapprove of your practice of your religion, tolerance becomes a live option for me only if I believe that my own religion and morality permit it. Herein lies the greatest obstacle to tolerance: many religious people, down through the ages and yet today, believe that their religion obligates them not to tolerate the other. God demands that heresy be stamped out. Allah demands the elimination of the infidel. What made possible the emergence of widespread religious tolerance in the West was a deep theological alteration in the mentality of Western Christians.

And what is it that motivates people to go beyond believing that tolerance is permissible to actually tolerating the practice of a religion of which they disapprove? Sometimes what motivates them is consequentialist considerations: vivid awareness of the great personal and social evils that flow from intolerance coupled, perhaps, with the attraction of the personal and social goods that they think tolerance is likely to yield. It was the appalling bloodiness of the wars of religion in the seventeenth century that led European Christians to conclude that whatever was to be said for religious intolerance, it came at too high a price.

A consequentialist case for tolerance is unstable, however. Circumstances may change, so that the personal and social costs of intolerance no longer seem unacceptable. The more fundamental case for religious tolerance is that intolerance is *unjust*; it wrongs the person who is treated with intolerance. It wrongs her because *qua* human person she has dignity, worth. To be intolerant toward her practice of her religion is to violate that dignity, to treat her as if she did not have that worth. And that is to wrong her.

Thus a full case for religious tolerance that employed the resources of Christian Scripture and the Christian theological tradition would argue, first, that Christian Scripture and theology permit religious tolerance; from there it would go on to argue that human persons, one and all, have dignity, and it would conclude by arguing that religious intolerance is a violation of that dignity. In this essay I will assume that these three claims can be defended on the basis of Christian Scripture and the Christian theological tradition. Rather than arguing for them here,[2] I will point to a theme in the Christian

---

2. I have done that in my essay, "Do Christians Have Good Reasons for Supporting Liberal Democracy," 229–48.

tradition concerning the import or significance of perpetrating on someone the injustice of religious intolerance—or of any other sort of injustice. To treat someone unjustly, to violate their worth or dignity, is not only to wrong them but is also to wrong *God*. To the best of my knowledge this theme was more prominent in the thought of John Calvin than in any other theologian from the tradition; for that reason, my development of the theme will take the form of an exposition of Calvin's theology of social injustice.

The Augustinian Background[3]

To fully understand the boldness of Calvin's thought on these matters we must be reminded of the pattern of thought on the place of suffering in human and divine life that was dominant in Calvin's predecessors. Obviously this is not the place to survey and summarize more than a thousand years of thought. So I shall confine myself to looking at Augustine, on the ground that his views on these matters both expressed a mentality that was already well entrenched in his day and that powerfully shaped the thought of his successors. The views of Augustine that I will summarize are those developed in the *Confessions* and in two other books that he wrote at approximately the same time, *Of True Religion* and *On Christian Doctrine*. Late in his life, when he wrote *The City of God*, his views had changed somewhat.[4]

In a passage from Book IV of the *Confessions*, Augustine exposes to full view the grief that overwhelmed him upon the death of a school friend from his home village of Tagaste in North Africa.

> My heart grew somber with grief, and wherever I looked I saw only death. My own country became a torment and my own home a grotesque abode of misery. All that we had done together was now a grim ordeal without him. My eyes searched everywhere for him, but he was not there to be seen. I hated all the places we had known together, because he was not in them and they could no longer whisper to me, "Here he comes!" as they would have done had he been alive but absent for a while. . . . My soul was a burden, bruised and bleeding. It was tired of the man who carried it, but I found no place to set it down to rest.[5]

The death of his friend occurred before Augustine's embrace of Christianity, the death of his mother, after. That embrace made his response to his

---

3. What follows in this essay is substantially the same as my "The Wounds of God: Calvin's Theology of Social Injustice," 14-22.

4. On the change, see chapter 8 of Wolterstorff, *Justice: Rights and Wrongs*.

5. Augustine, *Confessions*, IV.4.7.

mother's death profoundly different from that to his friend's death. "I closed her eyes," he says,

> and a great wave of sorrow surged into my heart. It would have overflowed in tears if I had not made a strong effort of will and stemmed the flow, so that the tears dried in my eyes. What a terrible struggle it was to hold them back! As she breathed her last, the boy Adeodatus [Augustine's son] began to wail aloud and only ceased his cries when we all checked him. I, too, felt that I wanted to cry like a child, but a more mature voice within me, the voice of my heart, bade me keep my sobs in check, and I remained silent.[6]

Augustine's struggle for self-control was not successful. He reports that after the burial, as he lay in bed thinking of his devoted mother, "the tears which I had been holding back streamed down, and I let them flow as freely as they would, making of them a pillow for my heart. On them it rested." So now, he says to God, "I make my confession.... Let any man read it who will. ... And if he finds that I sinned by weeping for my mother, even if only for a fraction of an hour, let him not mock at me ... but weep himself, if his charity is great. Let him weep for my sins to you." The sin for which Augustine wants the person of charity to weep is not so much the sin of weeping over the death of his mother as the sin of which that weeping was a sign. I was, he says, "guilty of too much worldly affection."[7]

How are we to understand the mentality coming to expression here? Along the following lines, I suggest. Augustine, with all the ancients, held that to be human is to be in search of happiness—*eudaimonia* in Greek, *beatitudo* in Latin. Furthermore, Augustine aligned himself with the Platonic tradition in his conviction that one's love is the fundamental determinant of one's happiness. Augustine never imagined that we human beings could root all love out of our lives.

It was as obvious to Augustine as it is to all of us that grief ensues when that which we love is destroyed or dies. In reflecting on his grief over the death of his friend, he says,

> I lived in misery like every man whose soul is tethered by the love of things that cannot last and then is agonized to lose them. ... The grief I felt for the loss of my friend had struck so easily into my inmost heart simply because I had poured out my soul

---

6. Augustine, *Confessions*, IX.12.
7. Augustine, *Confessions*, IX.12.

upon him, like water upon sand, loving a man who was mortal as though he were never to die.[8]

The cure is to detach one's love from such objects and attach it to something immutable and indestructible. For Augustine, the only candidate was God. "Blessed are those who love you, O God. . . . No one can lose you . . . unless he forsakes you."[9]

Augustine should not be interpreted as opposed to all enjoyment of earthly things: of food, of drink, of conversation, of visible beauty, of music. Suspicious and wary, yes; opposed, no. His point in the *Confessions* is only that we should root out all love for things whose death or destruction would cause us grief. To enjoy the taste of kiwi fruit is acceptable provided one's enjoyment is not such that, should kiwi fruit prove unavailable, one grieves. Though we must not love the world, we may enjoy it. Yet it must be admitted that Augustine says little or nothing by way of grounding the legitimacy of such enjoyment. In the famous passage in Book X of the *Confessions* where the things of creation speak, what they say is not "receive us with enjoyment as God's blessing" but "turn away from us to our maker." Further, Augustine was fond of saying that things of this world are to be used (*uti*) whereas God and God alone is to be enjoyed (*frui*).

Augustine held that the struggle to eliminate one's love for earthly things is never complete in this life; the newly oriented self never wholly wins out over the old. That introduces a new mode of grief into our lives— this a legitimate mode. We are to grieve over the repetitious reappearance of the old self—and correspondingly, to rejoice over the extent of its disappearance. And also—most extraordinary—we are to grieve over the sins of others and to rejoice over their repentance. Each of us is to be joined in a solidarity of rejoicing and grieving with all humanity—rejoicing and grieving over the *right* things, however, namely, over the religious condition of our souls.[10] I am to rejoice and grieve over the religious condition of my soul and, in the very same way, over the religious condition of your soul. This exception is important. Yet the general rule is that we are to struggle to eliminate grief from our lives by struggling to concentrate our love on God alone.

---

8. Augustine, *Confessions*, IV.6.8.
9. Augustine, *Confessions*, IV.9.
10. In *The City of God*, Augustine holds that it is also appropriate to grieve over the misfortunes that befall ourselves and our fellows, the implication being that we are not to aim to achieve, here in this present life, full and complete happiness. As we shall see, Calvin is basically in agreement with late Augustine on this point.

All this has been about us human beings. What Augustine says about God is the more or less obvious counterpart. God's life is through and through blissful. In God there is no emotional disturbance. Of sympathy, *Mitleiden* with those who are suffering, God feels nothing, as also God feels no pain over the shortfall of godliness in God's errant creatures. God's state is what the Greeks called *apatheia*. God dwells eternally in blissful non-suffering *apatheia*. Nothing that happens in the world alters God's unperturbed serenity. God is not oblivious to the world; there is in God a steady disposition of benevolence toward God's human creatures. But this disposition to act benevolently proceeds on its uninterrupted successful course whatever transpires in the world.

For this understanding of God, Augustine and the other ancients had fundamentally two reasons. First, they were persuaded that God's existence is perfect existence, and they could not imagine perfect existence as anything other than undisturbed bliss through and through. And since they thought that God was changeless, they did not think that God's perfect existence was something God had to await; that would itself have been a mark of imperfection.

Second, they held that if God were to suffer and grieve, something outside God would have to bring that about in God—humanity's evil-doing, for example. But God's changeless character and existence is not affected by anything outside Godself. God is the unconditioned condition of everything not identical with God. It was these two lines of thought, God's enjoying perfect existence and God's being the unconditioned condition, that led to the doctrine of the blissful apathy of God—or as it was traditionally called, God's impassibility.

Calvin on Injustice as Wronging God

Let us now turn to Calvin, beginning with a few statements by Calvin of his theology of social injustice, and then tracing the path that led Calvin to his bold claims. In the course of carrying out his project of commenting on the books of the Bible, Calvin, in his *Commentary on Genesis,* was confronted with the following passage:

> I will demand an account of every man's life from his fellow man. He who sheds man's blood shall have his blood shed by man, for in the image of God man was made. (Gen 9:5–6)

Calvin comments as follows:

> [M]en are indeed unworthy of God's care, if respect be had only to themselves; but since they bear the image of God engraven on them, he deems himself violated in their person. Thus, although they have nothing of their own by which they obtain the favor of God, he looks upon his own gifts in them, and is thereby excited to love and to care for them. This doctrine, however, is to be carefully observed, that no one can be injurious to his brother without wounding God himself. Were this doctrine deeply fixed in our minds, we should be much more reluctant than we are to inflict injuries.[11]

The thought is striking. God "deems himself violated in their person," "no one can be injurious to his brother without wounding God himself." As if to make clear that speaking thus was not some fancy rhetorical flourish on his part, not to be taken seriously, Calvin adds that this doctrine "is to be carefully observed." It is to be "deeply fixed in our minds." To inflict injury on a fellow human being is to wound God. Behind and beneath the social misery of our world is the suffering of God. To pursue justice is to relieve God's suffering. If we really believed that, we would be much more reluctant than we are to inflict injuries.

A second passage worth having in hand before we trace out the path that led Calvin to these striking and provocative conclusions occurs in his *Commentary on Habakkuk*. The text on which he is commenting is this:

> The arrogant man shall not abide. His greed is as wide as Sheol, like death he never has enough. He gathers for himself all nations, and collects as his own all peoples. Shall not all these take up their taunt against him, in scoffing derision of him, and say, Woe to him who heaps up what is not his own—for how long?—and loads himself with pledges! (Hab 2:5–6)

Commenting especially on the cry "how long?" Calvin says the following:

> [T]his also is a dictate of nature. . . . When any one disturbs the whole world by his ambition and avarice, or everywhere commits plunder, or oppresses miserable nations—when he distresses the innocent, all cry out How long? And this cry, proceeding as it does from the feeling of nature and the dictate of justice, is at length heard by the Lord. For how comes it that all, being touched with weariness, cry out How long? except that they know that this confusion of order and equity is not to be endured? And this feeling, is it not implanted in us by the Lord?

---

11. Calvin, *Commentary on Genesis*, 9:5–6.

> It is then the same as though God heard himself, when he hears the cries and groanings of those who cannot bear injustice.[12]

Again the thought is striking. The cries of the victims of injustice are the cry of God. The lament of the victims as they cry out "how long?" is God giving voice to God's own lament.

Calvin's Anti-Augustinian Position on Enjoyment and Grief

What was the line of thought that led Calvin to such an extraordinarily bold theology of social injustice? A good place to begin is with his opposition to the Augustinian position on the place of grief in human life, namely, that we are to pursue the elimination of all grief by struggling to love God and God alone, with the exception that one is to grieve over one's own failure and that of one's fellows to accomplish this project. "Among the Christians," says Calvin, "there are also new Stoics, who count it depraved not only to groan and weep but also to be sad and care ridden."[13] On this they are quite wrong.

> [Our goal] is not to be utterly stupefied and to be deprived of all feeling of pain. Our ideal is not that of what the Stoics of old foolishly described [as] "the great-souled man," one who, having cast off all human qualities, was affected equally by adversity and prosperity, by sad times and happy ones—nay, who like a stone was not affected at all.[14]

One reason for repudiating the Stoic ideal is that it paints "a likeness of forbearance that has never been found among men, and can never be realized".[15] In setting before us this impossible ideal it distracts us from the attitude toward suffering that we ought in fact to cultivate.

> Thus afflicted by disease, we shall both groan and be uneasy and pant after health, thus pressed by poverty, we shall be pricked by the arrows of care and sorrow, thus we shall be smitten by the pain of disgrace, contempt, injustice, thus at the funerals of our dear ones we shall weep the tears that are owed to our nature.[16]

Calvin had a second reason for rejecting the Stoic ideal.

---

12. Calvin, *John Calvin's Bible Commentaries on Habakkuk*, 2:5–6.
13. Calvin, *Institutes*, III.viii.9.
14. Calvin, *Institutes*, III.viii.9.
15. Calvin, *Institutes*, III.viii.9.
16. Calvin, *Institutes*, III.viii.10.

Our Lord and Master has condemned [it] not only by his word, but also by his example. For he groaned and wept both over his own and others' misfortunes. And he taught his disciples in the same way. "The world," he says, "will rejoice, but you will be sorrowful and will weep" (John 16:20). And that no one might turn it into a vice he openly proclaimed, "Blessed are those who mourn" (Matt. 5:4). No wonder! For if all weeping is condemned, what shall we judge concerning the Lord himself, from whose body tears of blood trickled down (Luke 22:44)? If all fear is branded as unbelief, how shall we account for that dread with which, we read, he was heavily stricken (Matt 26:37, Mark 14:33)? If all sadness displeases us how will it please us that he confesses his soul "sorrowful even to death" (Matt. 26:38)?[17]

The discipline that we are to undertake in the face of sickness, death, poverty, disgrace, indignity, and injustice is not the discipline of no longer grieving over these, of becoming indifferent. Following the example of Christ, we are to let our God-given nature take its course, paying to justice the honor of grieving upon being treated unjustly, paying to life the honor of grieving upon the death of those we love. We are to let our wounds bleed, our eyes tear. The discipline we are to undertake is the discipline of becoming patient in suffering. I shall have something to say shortly about the nature of Calvinist patience and why Calvin thinks it appropriate.

Calvin's opposition to Stoicism and Augustinianism, then, was grounded in his conviction that they set for us an impossible and inappropriate ideal, contrary to our created nature, thus distracting us from the achievable and appropriate ideal of patience in suffering. But it is easy to see that his attitude toward grief also fits in with, and is supported by, his attitude toward enjoyment of the things of this world.

In a remarkable passage in the *Institutes*,[18] Calvin argues that of grasses, trees, and fruits we should appreciate not only their utility as nourishment but their beauty of appearance and pleasantness of odor and taste, of clothes we should appreciate not only their utility for keeping us warm but their comeliness, and of wine and oil we should appreciate not only that they are useful but that wine gladdens the heart and oil makes one's face shine. As if with his eye on Augustine's use/enjoyment distinction, he asks rhetorically whether God did "not, in short, render many things attractive to us, apart from their necessary use?" He answers that God did. So let this "be our principle, that the use of God's gifts is not wrongly directed when

17. Calvin, *Institutes*, III.viii.9.
18. Calvin, *Institutes*, III.x.2.

it is referred to that end to which the Author himself created and destined them for us, since he created them for our good, not for our ruin."

Augustine saw the things of the world almost exclusively as the *works* of God; hence he urges us to look away from them to their maker. They are to be seen as benefit only so far as they are useful for our continued existence and for our devotion to God. Pervasive in Calvin, by contrast, is the insistence that we are to see the things of the world not only as God's works but also as God's *gifts* to us, gifts not only in their utility but also in their being enjoyable. "This life," says Calvin, "however crammed with infinite miseries it may be, is still rightly to be counted among those blessings of God which are not to be spurned. Therefore, if we recognize in it no divine benefit, we are already guilty of grave ingratitude toward God himself."[19]

One cannot overemphasize the pervasiveness of this theme in Calvin of the world as God's gift to us for use and enjoyment, and of the counterpart theme of the propriety of gratitude. Never, in this regard, was there a more sacramental theologian than Calvin, one more imbued with the sense that in world, history, and self, we meet God. "Away, then, with that inhuman philosophy which, while conceding only a necessary use of creatures, not only malignantly deprives us of the lawful fruit of God's beneficence but cannot be practiced unless it rob a man of all his senses and degrade him to a block."[20]

On Bearing the Image of God

I said that to understand Calvin's theology of social injustice and to appreciate its boldness we must discern his anti-Stoical and anti-Augustinian view as to the place of grief in human existence, and, correspondingly, his view as to the place of enjoyment. One does not say to the person suffering injustice that she should not care about justice so much that she grieves over its violation—that she should love only God. To the contrary, one encourages grief. But there is a second component as well in the path that led Calvin to his radical conclusions, namely, his thoughts on the image of God in human beings.

"'So man was created in the image of God,' in him the Creator himself willed that his own glory be seen as in a mirror."[21] What Calvin means, of course, and what he says in his Latin, is not that male human beings were created in God's image but that male and female human beings alike were

19. Calvin, *Institutes*, III.ix.3.
20. Calvin, *Institutes*, III.x.3.
21. Calvin, *Institutes*, II.xii.6.

created in the image of God. "God looks upon Himself, as one might say, and beholds himself in men as in a mirror."[22] "God's children are pleasing and lovable to him, since he sees in them the marks and features of his own countenance.... Whenever God contemplates his own face, he both rightly loves it and holds it in honor."[23]

God beholds what God has made. God observes that human beings are icons of Godself. God observes that they mirror God, that they image God, that they are likenesses of God. In this God delights. And this evokes God's love for them. God delights in all God's works. But human beings are singled out from other earthlings in that, in them, God finds God's perfections most clearly mirrored back to Godself.

A consequence of the fact that each human being mirrors God is that we as human beings exist in profound unity with each other: to see another human being is to see another creature who delights God by mirroring God. No more profound kinship among God's creatures can exist than this. Furthermore, each of us mirrors God in the same respects—though, as we shall see shortly, some do so more, some less. Thereby we also, in a derivative way, resemble each other. One could say that we mirror each other. In looking at you and me, God finds Godself mirrored. Accordingly, in my looking at you I too discern, once my eyes have been opened, that you mirror God—and that you mirror me. I discern myself as in a mirror. I discern a family likeness. As Calvin puts it, "we cannot but behold our own face as it were in a glass in the person that is poor and despised ... though he were the furthest stranger in the world. Let a Moor or a Barbarian come among us, and yet inasmuch as he is a man, he brings with him a looking glass wherein we may see that he is our brother and neighbor."[24] There were those who argued that the image of God in us can be, and in some cases has been, eliminated. Calvin disagreed.

> Should anyone object, that this divine image has been obliterated, the solution is easy; first, there yet exists some remnant of it, so that man is possessed of no small dignity; and secondly, the Celestial Creator himself, however corrupted man may be, still keeps in view the end of his original creation; and according to his example, we ought to consider for what end he created

---

22. John Calvin, "Sermon on Job 10:7," quoted in Torrance, *Calvin's Doctrine of Man*, 39.

23. Calvin, *Institutes*, III.xvii.5.

24. Calvin, "Sermon on Galatians 6:9–11," quoted in Wallace, *Calvin's Doctrine of the Christian Life*, 150.

men, and what excellence he has bestowed upon them above the rest of living things.[25]

There is nothing that can happen to a human being, and nothing a human being can do, to bring it about that the image of God in that person is obliterated. Though a human being's mirroring of God can be painfully distorted, blurred, and diminished, it cannot be eliminated.

Naturally we want to know wherein lies our iconicity. In what respects do we mirror God back to Godself and then to each other? Calvin offers two rules of thumb for answering this question. First, our iconicity is to be discerned in what differentiates us from other earthlings: "the likeness of God extends to the whole excellence by which man's nature towers over all the kinds of living creatures."[26] Second, keeping in mind that our likeness to God can be increased and diminished, we must employ the rule that the fundamental goal of our human existence is to become as like unto God as possible—or to use the language of the Eastern Orthodox Church, to become as "divinized" as possible. And what would a human being's full likeness to God be like? We apprehend the answer to that question in Jesus Christ, who was "the express image of the Father."

When we follow these two rules of thumb, looking at our uniqueness and looking at Jesus Christ, one thing we learn is that those of us who are capable of functioning as persons are like God in being capable of understanding; and the more our understanding expands—especially our understanding of God—the more we become like God. We also learn that those of us who are capable of functioning as persons are like God in being capable of governing our affections and thereby our actions; and the more upright our heart is, the more like God we are. For Calvin, these two are the principal resemblances. But there are others as well. Our (mandated) governance of creation is a mirroring of God's governance, and our formation of communities is a mirroring of that perfect community which is the Trinity. No doubt some of us today would wish to add other themes—for example, that our creativity is a mirroring of God's creativity.

Love, Justice, and the Image of God

Calvin grounds the claims of love and justice in this phenomenon of our mirroring God. The standard picture of Calvin is that obligation, duty, responsibility, and the call to obedience loom large in his thought; and indeed

---

25. Calvin, *Commentary on Genesis*, 9:6.
26. Calvin, *Institutes*, I.xv.4.

they do. Yet for Calvin there is something deeper than these. All of us in our daily lives are confronted with other human beings. We find ourselves in the presence of another who, by virtue of being an icon of God, makes claims on us. Moral reflection can begin either from the responsibility of the agent toward the other or from the moral claims of the other on the agent. The degree to which Calvin begins from the moral claims of the other is striking. The pattern is displayed with great insistence in this passage:

> The Lord commands all men without exception "to do good." Yet the great part of them are most unworthy if they be judged by their own merit. But here Scripture helps in the best way when it teaches that we are not to consider what men merit of themselves but to look upon the image of God in all men, to which we owe all honor and love. . . . Therefore whatever man you meet who needs your aid, you have no reason to refuse to help him. You say, "he is a stranger"; but the Lord has given him a mark that ought to be familiar to you, by virtue of the fact that he forbids you to despise your own flesh. You say, "he is contemptible and worthless"; but the Lord shows him to be one to whom he has deigned to give the beauty of his image. You say that you owe nothing for any service of his; but God, as it were, has put him in his own place in order that you may recognize toward him the many and great benefits with which God has bound you to him. You say that he does not deserve even your least effort for his sake; but the image of God, which recommends him to you, is worthy of your giving yourself and all your possessions. Now if he has not only deserved no good at your hand, but has also provoked you by unjust acts and curses, not even this is just reason why you should cease to embrace him in love and to perform the duties of love on his behalf. You say, "he has deserved something far different of me." Yet what has the Lord deserved? . . . It is that we remember not to consider men's evil intention but to look upon the image of God in them, which cancels and effaces their transgressions, and with its beauty and dignity allures us to love and embrace them.[27]

Several things is this passage are striking, in addition to the insistent grounding of the claims of love and justice in our ineradicable iconicity. One is Calvin's adamant insistence that, given that it is our iconicity that grounds these claims, the virtue of the other person or lack of virtue is irrelevant. Always the perpetrators of injustice want it otherwise. If the so-called blacks in South Africa just behaved, they would be given a voice in their

---

27. Calvin, *Institutes*, III.vii.6. Translation slightly altered.

governance. If the Palestinians just behaved, the ending of the occupation of their land could be considered.

But how exactly does the fact that each of us is an image of God ground our claim to love and justice from our fellows? One would expect Calvin to say that it is the great *dignity* that supervenes on being an image of God that grounds the claim of the other on me. This dignity calls for respect; and there is no other way of showing the appropriate respect than by love and justice. Calvin does speak this way now and then. But his emphasis falls elsewhere. It falls, for one thing, on the fact that the other has claims on my love and justice because she and I are kinfolk in the deepest possible way, namely, by virtue of jointly imaging God. This comes out vividly in a passage from his *Commentary on Isaiah*. The passage on which he is commenting is this:

> Is not this the fast that I choose, to loose the bonds of injustice, to undo the thongs of the yoke, to let the oppressed go free, and to break every yoke? Is it not to share your bread with the hungry and bring the homeless poor into your house, when you see the naked, to cover them, and not to hide yourself from your own flesh? (Isa 58:6-7)

Calvin's comment runs (in part) as follows:

> It is not enough to *abstain* from acts of injustice, if you refuse your assistance to the needy.... By commanding them to "break bread to the hungry," God intended to take away every excuse from covetous and greedy men, who allege that they have a right to keep possession of that which is their own.... And indeed, this is the dictate of common sense, that the hungry are deprived of their just right, if their hunger is not relieved.... At length he concludes—*and that you hide not yourself from your own flesh*. Here we ought to observe the term *flesh*, by which he means all men universally, not a single one of whom we can behold, without seeing, as in a mirror, "our own flesh." It is therefore a proof of the greatest inhumanity, to despise those in whom we are constrained to recognize our own likeness.[28]

In short, to fail to treat one's fellow human beings with love and justice is to fail in the duties of kinship, and thereby to act with "the greatest inhumanity."

---

28. Calvin, *Isaiah 49–66*, 233–34.

Injustice as Wronging God

There is a second way in which the iconicity of the other human being grounds her claim on me to love and justice, in addition to the fact that we are kin; it is this other way that our discussion has been moving towards. "God himself, looking on human beings as formed in his own image, regards them with such love and honor that he himself feels wounded and outraged in the persons of those who are the victims of human cruelty and wickedness"[29]

For Calvin, the demands of love and justice lie not first of all in the *will* of God, which is what much of the Christian tradition has held, nor in the *reason* of God, which is what most of the rest of the tradition has held. They lie in God's sorrow and in God's joy, in God's suffering and in God's delight. If I abuse something that you have made and that you love, then, at its deepest, what has gone wrong is not that I have violated your command not to abuse that object of your affection—though you may indeed have issued such a command, in which case I will have disobeyed it. It lies first of all in the fact that I cause you sorrow by riding roughshod over your affections. The demands of love and justice are rooted, so Calvin suggests, in what Abraham Heschel in his book on the Hebrew prophets called the *pathos* of God. To treat unjustly one of these human earthlings in whom God delights is to bring sorrow to God. To wound God's beloved is to wound God. The demands of justice are grounded in the fact that to commit injustice is to inflict suffering on God. They are grounded in the vulnerability of God's love for us, images of God. God is not *apathē*.

Though I do not propose developing it here, it is worth noting that this theme of the wounding of God is also given a specifically Christological and sacramental development in Calvin. At one point in his discussion of the Eucharist he says,

> We shall benefit very much from the sacrament if this thought is impressed and engraved upon our minds, that none of the brethren can be injured, despised, rejected, abused, or in any way offended by us, without at the same time injuring, despising, abusing Christ by the wrongs we do, . . . that we cannot love Christ without loving him in the brethren.[30]

---

29. Wallace, *Calvin's Doctrine of the Christian Life*, 149.
30. Calvin, *Institutes*, IV.xvii.38.

Calvinist Patience

Before concluding, we must return to Calvin's doctrine of patience. Recall that Augustine said that we should struggle to withdraw all love for things whose death or destruction would cause us grief. Calvin's position was profoundly different. We should not try to alter our created nature; we should honor it. To indignity, death, injustice, and a multitude of other evils in this life, grief is not only the normal but the appropriate response. The discipline to be undertaken is not that of withdrawing all our attachments but that of being patient in our suffering. Patient grief is to be our stance.

When confronted with the prospect of the occurrence of some event likely to cause one grief, one can pursue the Augustinian course of struggling to alter one's nature so that, when the event occurs, one feels no grief. But one can also pursue the opposite course of trying to avert the occurrence of the event. Did Calvin, in commending patience, mean to recommend that we also renounce this latter course? Did he mean to say that we should no more seek to change the world than to change ourselves—that we should allow the threatening episodes to flow over us? Should we simply put up with religious intolerance, for example? Is Calvinist patience passive acceptance?

The suggestion lacks even initial plausibility. What characterized the Calvinist movement as a whole was its dynamic restlessness, this to be traced in good measure to Calvin himself—to his words but also to his actions in Geneva. It is true that when it came to the political realm, Calvin insisted that those not in positions of political authority were not to revolt. But not revolting is very different from passively accepting—as we all know, and as the members of the Geneva city council experienced, to their dismay, in their conflicts with Calvin.

Calvin vigorously and unflinchingly denounced corruption in the church, tyranny in the polity, and inequity in the economy. And though it would not be inconsistent to denounce bishops, tyrant, and bosses while yet counseling passive acceptance of their orders and actions, Calvin regularly took the next steps of urging resistance to evil and struggle for reform, and of himself practicing what he preached. In a famous passage from his *Commentary on Daniel,* Calvin, while not recommending revolt even as a last resort, unmistakably recommends defiant disobedience.

> Earthly princes lay aside all their power when they rise against God and are unworthy of being reckoned in the number of mankind. We ought rather strictly to defy them than to obey them whenever they are so restive and wish to spoil God of his rights and, as it were, to seize upon his throne and draw him down from heaven (Daniel 6:22).

Given the situation depicted in the book of Daniel, one might wonder whether Calvin here has his eye exclusively on infringements on the free exercise of one's religion. When we are denied freedom of worship, we must disobey. But in his discussion of patience in the *Institutes* Calvin puts the struggle for justice and the struggle for free exercise of religion on the same footing. We are called to both, and both may yield suffering and the honor of the martyr.

> To suffer persecution for righteousness' sake is a singular comfort. For it ought to occur to us how much honor God bestows upon us in thus furnishing us with the special badge of his soldiery. I say that not only they who labor for the defense of the gospel but they who in any way maintain the cause of righteousness suffer persecution for righteousness.[31]

In short, Calvinist patience is not the patience of passive acceptance but the patience of one who suffers as she struggles against the world's evils. It is the paradoxical unstable combination of patiently grieving over the deprivation and injustice that befalls us while struggling to alleviate that deprivation and undo that injustice.

In Conclusion

In this essay I have taken for granted that intolerance toward a person's practice of his or her religion is an affront to that person's dignity and therefore unjust. Rather than employing the resources of Christian Scripture and the Christian theological tradition in support of that claim, I have called attention to a theme in the tradition concerning the significance of the injustice of religious intolerance—and of any other form of injustice. To perpetrate the injustice of religious intolerance on a fellow human being is to wrong God; the cries of those who are persecuted or demeaned on account of their religion are giving voice to God's suffering.

The theme we have explored, of injustice as the wronging of God, does not by any means exhaust the significance of injustice. My discussion has assumed that injustice also, for example, bears the significance of being a violation of the victim's human dignity; and along the way Calvin has suggested that it bears the significance of being abuse of one's kin. The theme we have explored is one that is not prominent in the Christian theological tradition as a whole; its lack of prominence was one of my reasons for presenting it. Though not prominent in the tradition as a whole, it was prominent in

---

31. Calvin, *Institutes*, III.viii.7.

the thought of John Calvin. It is for that reason that my presentation of the theme has taken the form of expounding Calvin.

No matter how much one may dislike the religion of the other person, she nonetheless bears the image of God and is on that account beloved of God. To treat her with intolerance is to wrong her. To wrong her is to wrong God. If we believed this, and believed it firmly, we would be much more reluctant than we are to treat someone with intolerance. And it makes no difference whether our intolerance is grounded in our religion or in something else.

7

Modern Protestant Developments in Human Rights

A new narrative of the origin of the idea of natural human rights has been emerging in recent years. Three books stand out. Brian Tierney, in his 1997 publication, *The Idea of Natural Rights: Studies on Natural Rights, Natural Law and Church Law: 1150–1625*,[1] shows that the idea of natural human rights was explicitly formulated and often employed by the canon lawyers of the 1100s. John Witte, in his 2007 publication, *The Reformation of Rights: Law, Religion, and Human Rights in Early Modern Calvinism*,[2] shows that the idea was employed almost incessantly by the early Calvinists. And the earlier 1979 publication by Richard Tuck, *Natural Rights Theories: Their Origin and Development*,[3] goes some way toward filling in the gap between the period that Tierney focused on and that on which Witte focuses.

The old and still popular narrative holds that the idea of natural human rights was created by the individualistic political philosophers of the Enlightenment, notably Hobbes and Locke. Those who espouse this narrative customarily add that the Enlightenment was a secular, anti-Christian movement. What the new counter-narrative shows beyond a doubt is that the idea was given birth some six centuries earlier by medieval Christian thinkers, and that it continued to be used through the centuries by Catholic writers and, once Protestantism arose, by Protestant writers as well. Hobbes and Locke inherited the idea from their Christian forebears.

Should a young scholar become acquainted with this new narrative and then later read around in Protestant writings of the twentieth century, he will be surprised to discover that the idea of natural human rights is seldom employed in these writings, and when it is, it is so usually in an

---

1. Tierney, *The Idea of Natural Rights*.
2. Witte, *The Reformation of Rights*.
3. Tuck, *Natural Rights Theories*.

off-hand manner. Opposition to the idea is far more common than systematic employment. The word "rights" does not occur in the index to Dietrich Bonhoeffer's *Ethics,* nor does it occur in the index to Reinhold Niebuhr's two-volume work, *The Nature and Destiny of Man*. In the index to the book on Christian ethics that Karl Barth wrote late in his career, *The Christian Life,* one does find the entry, "right of man." But when one looks up the two passages cited, one discovers that it was not human rights that Barth had in mind.

I mean to speak here only about Protestant *writing*, not about Protestant *writers*. It may well be that a good many of the twentieth-century writers who have systematically employed the idea of natural human rights and defended their doing so were in fact Protestants. I mean to speak about those writings that are clearly identifiable as located within the Protestant tradition of Christianity.

The story of what happened between early Calvinist Protestantism and the Protestantism of the twentieth-century, to account for this truly startling difference, remains to be told. Did the twentieth-century Protestant writers reject their Catholic and Protestant heritage knowing full well what they were rejecting? Or had historical amnesia set in? Clearly the latter. The twentieth-century Protestant writers betray no knowledge of the history that Tierney, Tuck, Witte, et al. have unearthed. When they refer or allude to a narrative of origins, that narrative is always the common secular-origins narrative. There is irony in this. Protestant writings of the twentieth century are full of attacks on secularism; ironic, then, that those same writings should buy into a central plank in the platform of modern secularism, namely, the secularist's telling of the story of the origins of the idea of natural human rights. Of course, typically there is a difference in how the story is told. When Protestant writers explicitly refer to the narrative, they almost always frame it as a story of decline; secular writers usually, though by no means always, frame it as a story of progress.

I am not sufficiently learned to be able to offer a survey of twentieth-century Protestant writings so as to determine when they had something significant to say about human rights, and when they did, what that was; but neither do I think that a survey would be of much use. Instead, I propose offering a typology of how the idea is treated by those who do mention it. Useful though typologies often are, they have the defect of ignoring individual nuances and of concealing from view how particular thinkers found themselves led to one and another of the typologized positions. The person who constructed the typology will have been aware of these particularities, but the typology itself abstracts from them. To compensate for this defect, I will in each case present the thought of a paradigmatic representative of the position. Of course, this in turn courts the distinct danger of annoying all those who have articulated one of the positions in my typology but whom I do not select as my example; to them, my apologies.

The Agapist Rejection of Human Rights

In a good deal of twentieth-century Protestant writing one finds a flat-out rejection of the idea of natural human rights. Sometimes this rejection takes the form of rejecting the idea of natural rights while affirming the importance of justice; in other cases it takes the more radical form of insisting that Christians should discard from their moral culture all considerations of justice and injustice. Let me begin with this latter, more radical, position.

This rejectionist position was most vividly presented, and most rigorously developed, by the Swedish Lutheran bishop Anders Nygren in his now-classic *Agape and Eros,* published in installments in the early 1930s. Whereas the Old Testament, said Nygren, is all about justice, agapic love has displaced justice in the life and teaching of Jesus. Jesus "enters into fellowship with those who are not worthy of it." His doing so is directed "against every attempt to regulate fellowship with God by the principle of justice."[4] "That Jesus should take lost sinners to Himself was bound to appear, not only to the Pharisees, but to anyone brought up and rooted in Jewish legal righteousness, as a violation of the order established by God Himself and guaranteed by His justice."[5] For them it was "a violation not merely of the human, but above all of the Divine, order of justice, and therefore of God's majesty."[6]

The point is unmistakable: the agapic love displayed and enjoined by Jesus does not supplement justice but supersedes it. "'Motivated' justice must give place . . . to 'unmotivated' love."[7] We are not to love the neighbor agapically *in addition to* treating her as justice requires; we are to love her *instead of* treating her as justice requires.

Part of what led Nygren to this conclusion was his conviction that in the second love command, "love your neighbor as yourself," Jesus was not just enjoining us to love everyone who is one's neighbor but to love the neighbor with that special form of love that came to be called *neighbor love* by the members of the twentieth-century agapist movement that Nygren was instrumental in inspiring. Nygren's great forebear on this point, that

---

4. Nygren, *Agape and Eros,* 86.
5. Nygren, *Agape and Eros,* 83.
6. Nygren, *Agape and Eros,* 70.
7. Nygren, *Agape and Eros,* 74.

Jesus was enjoining us to love the neighbor with a special kind of love, was Søren Kierkegaard in *Works of Love*.

What is that special form of love that Jesus enjoined us to have for every neighbor? It is love that takes God's loving forgiveness of the sinner as its model. Justice does not require forgiveness; one is not treating the person who wronged one unjustly if one finds it impossible to forgive him, or if one refuses to do so. Forgiveness is an act of gratuitous love. Agapic love in general is like forgiveness in this regard. Nygren often speaks of agapic love as *spontaneous*; the contrast he wants us to hear is, spontaneous rather than *required*. Agapic love is pure generosity, pure benevolence. Here is how Emil Brunner puts the point in *Justice and the Social Order*: love "does not render to the other what is his due, what belongs to him 'by right,' but gives of its own, gives precisely that to which the other has no right."[8] Agapic love is justice-blind.

Many members of the twentieth-century agapist movement took for granted that agapic love, though blind to what justice requires, would nonetheless not perpetrate injustice; Brunner, in *Justice and the Social Order*, is an example. Not so Nygren; he interpreted the landowner, in Jesus' parable of the laborers in the vineyard (Matt 20:1–16) as conceding the charge by those who had worked all day that he was treating them unjustly by paying them no more than the late-comers. "No matter," says the landowner on Nygren's interpretation, "am I not allowed to distribute my generosity as I wish?"

Very few Protestants, whether scholars or non-academics, have shared Nygren's clarity and rigor and been willing to follow him all the way to this conclusion. But the sense that Jesus enjoined us to love the neighbor with a form of love that pays no attention to justice—the sense that in the life and teaching of Jesus, love superseded justice—is common among twentieth-century Protestants. Nygren both articulated and reinforced this intuition. But if justice is superseded, then perforce natural human rights are superseded.

The Rejection of Natural Human Rights as a Lamentable Modern Invention

A less radical position than the one just considered affirms the importance of justice but rejects the idea of natural human rights. Justice has nothing to do with natural rights. The idea of natural rights is a lamentable invention of

---

8. Brunner, *Justice and the Social Order*, 17.

the individualist political philosophers of the Enlightenment—or perhaps of the late medieval nominalist, William of Ockham.

Those who espouse this position commonly credit the 1953 book of Leo Strauss, *Natural Right and History*, with introducing the crucial idea. Strauss distinguished between *natural law or right* and *natural rights*—in the plural. A right is something that someone *has*, something that he or she *possesses*. Strauss contrasts rights with *the obligatory* or *the right*—as in the phrase, "doing the right thing."

Having drawn this distinction, Strauss' central thesis was that whereas for most of Western history, thinkers have thought in terms of the right or the obligatory, in the Enlightenment the idea of the right was transmuted into the idea of rights, with Thomas Hobbes being the principal proponent. Whereas thinkers had once believed that there was a natural right order, or, if one prefers, a natural order of the right, this order determining the right or obligatory thing for a person of a certain sort to do in a certain situation, now they thought in terms of members of the social order bearing natural rights. "The fundamental change [was] from an orientation by natural duties to an orientation by natural rights," says Strauss.[9] Whereas it was once thought that a society is just insofar as it measures up to the natural order of the right, now it was thought that a society is just insofar as the natural and other rights of its members are honored.

Strauss saw this change as an important mark of the transition to modernity. And he left no doubt as to his judgment on the change. The idea of natural rights is an inextricable component in the atomistic and agonistic political philosophies that emerged in the Enlightenment; it cannot be extracted from such a context. The idea of natural rights carries possessive individualism in its DNA. The language of rights is for each of us asserting his claims, his entitlements, his rights, each against the other.

A decade or so after Strauss' 1953 publication, the French legal historian, Michel Villey, in a long series of publications, located the shift in conceptuality that Strauss had ascribed to the Enlightenment several centuries earlier, in fourteenth-century nominalism, with William of Ockham rather than Hobbes now being the principal culprit. Villey identified himself as part of the nineteenth- and twentieth-century neo-Thomist movement which sees Western philosophy as having reached its apogee in Thomas Aquinas and as having been in decline ever since.

In my presentation of this movement, I have said nothing thus far about Protestantism. The narrative and the moral drawn from it were neither originated by Protestants nor has their subsequent espousal been

---

9. Strauss, *Natural Rights and History*, 182.

monopolized by Protestants. Both the narrative and the moral have, however, been taken up by Protestant thinkers, so much so that I judge that this line of rejection of natural rights is now at least as common among Protestant scholars as the previous. Let me cite some passages from Joan Lockwood O'Donovan, who is, in my judgment, along with Oliver O'Donovan among the best Protestant proponents of the position.[10] "The modern liberal concept of rights belongs," she says, "to the socially atomistic and disintegrative philosophy of 'possessive individualism.'"[11]

> A close analysis of the history of the concept of subjective rights in the light of earlier theological-political conceptualization reveals a progressive antagonism between the older Christian tradition of political right and the newer voluntarist, individualist, and subjectivist orientation. The contrasting logic of the two orientations may be conveyed quite simply: where in the older patristic and medieval tradition, God's right established a matrix of divine, natural, and human laws or objective obligations that constituted the ordering justice of political community, in the newer tradition God's right established discrete rights, possessed by individuals originally and by communities derivatively, that determined civil order and justice.[12]

She then describes what she calls "the older traditions":

> In the older traditions, the central moral-political act on the part of ruler and ruled alike was to consent to the demands of justice, to the obligations inhering in communal life according to divine intention and rationally conceived as laws. The ruler commanded, legislated, and issued binding judgments, but these acts were to embody his consent to an order of right and obligations binding his own will. The subject was obligated to obey the ruler's commands, statutes, and judgments, not only because of his rightful authority, but also because these acts conformed to the requirements of justice.[13]

Given what she sees as the patent incompatibility between the idea of natural human rights and sound Christian theology, an obvious question for O'Donovan is "why Christian thinkers have been and are willing" to buy

---

10. Oliver O'Donovan's statements of the position tend to be scattered about, occurring in the context of his treatment of other topics. His most sustained statement of the position is: O'Donovan, "The Language of Rights and Conceptual History," 193–207.

11. O'Donovan "Natural Law and Perfect Community," 20.

12. O'Donovan, "The Concept of Rights in Christian Moral Discourse," 145.

13. O'Donovan, "The Concept of Rights in Christian Moral Discourse," 145.

into the idea. Why have they been "willing to adopt a child of such questionable parentage as the concept of human rights?" It is, she adds, a "question that has yet to be satisfactorily answered."[14]

It is important to add an explanatory qualification. The right-order theorists are not opposed to all rights talk. They are opposed to all talk of *natural* rights; they hold that there are no such rights. But as for talk about so-called *positive* rights, they are wary but not dismissive. Oliver O'Donovan puts the point well:

> The language of subjective rights (i.e., rights which adhere to a particular subject) has, of course, a perfectly appropriate and necessary place within a discourse founded on law. One's "right" is the claim on which the law entitles one to demand performance.... What is distinctive about the modern conception of rights, however, is that subjective rights are taken to be original, not derived.... The right is a primitive endowment of power with which the subject first engages in society, not an enhancement which accrues to the subject from an ordered and politically formed society.[15]

Rights-Talk Useful but Dispensable

A third position that one finds in Protestant writings of the twentieth century is that talk of natural human rights is sometimes useful, but always dispensable; one could make the same point with other concepts. Let me take the book of Emil Brunner already referred to, *Justice and the Social Order*, as an example of the position. Brunner was second only to Barth in his prominence as a German theologian of the first six or so decades of the twentieth century.

"From time immemorial," says Brunner, "the principle of justice has been defined as the *suum cuique*—the rendering to each man of his due. ... Who or whatever renders to every man his due, that person or thing is just."[16] Brunner takes for granted that what can be said with the term "due" can also be said with the term "a right." "The sphere of justice embraces all that 'belongs,' all that is a man's due, all that he has a 'right to.'"[17]

---

14. O'Donovan, "The Concept of Rights in Christian Moral Discourse," 155.
15. O'Donovan, *The Desire of the Nations*, 262.
16. Brunner, *Justice and Social Order*, 17.
17. Brunner, *Justice and Social Order*, 17.

Immediately after connecting justice with what is due a person, Brunner adds that what is due a person is not exhaustively determined by "the positive law of the state, firstly because it is precisely the idea of justice which enables us to distinguish between a just and an unjust law, secondly because we also speak of justice in cases where there could be no recourse to a legal settlement by the state."[18] Justice is grounded in "an underived, primal order of things established by no human lawgiver."[19] "An action or an attitude of mind, a law or an institution, can only claim to be called 'just' if it corresponds to that primal order."[20] As one would expect, Brunner relates this primal transcendent order to God. We shall see later what he takes the relationship to be.

Justice, what is due a person, is intimately related to equality. There is, for one thing, the formal relationship to equality of our all being equally subject to the primal order of justice. As to the substantive relationship, Brunner thinks that Aristotle got it right when he said that to distribute goods justly is to distribute them equally:

> Aristotle was the first to enquire into the nature of justice and to recognize both the close connection of justice with equality and the dual nature of justice. The first, simple justice, which gives the same to each, he called arithmetical or contractual, the second, which gives the same to each according to a scale of actual inequality, he calls proportional, geometrical, or distributive. In this way he established a fundamental rule for all time, and we can understand why the theory of justice has at all times taken its stand on these Aristotelian definitions. We can even say that the theory of justice has never gone beyond Aristotle, but has always harked back to him.[21]

What neither Aristotle nor anyone else in pagan antiquity discerned, however, is the presence of a fundamental and ineradicable equality among human beings. "That conception of justice by which all human beings, old or young, man or woman, bond or free, have equal rights in the sense that they *ought* to be treated alike, is in essence derived from the revelation of Scripture, according to which God created man 'in his image.'"[22] "The

---

18. Brunner, *Justice and Social Order*, 17.
19. Brunner, *Justice and Social Order*, 17.
20. Brunner, *Justice and Social Order*, 18–19.
21. Brunner, *Justice and Social Order*, 27–28.
22. Brunner, *Justice and Social Order*, 34.

doctrine of the *imago Dei* . . . is the fundamental principle of the Protestant doctrine of justice."[23]

Christianity does not only affirm the dignity that we share equally as image bearers of God. It adds that God "calls [each] person into being and thereby endows him with responsibility, . . . every human being has his own personal dignity which resides in his predestination to personal being and is identical with the dignity of every other human being."[24] We are alike in being responsible to God.

To this we must add that "it is the will of the Creator that the individual human being should not be self-sufficient. . . . It is His will that human beings should be dependent on each other. . . . Creation has so disposed human beings that they must seek and have each other. . . . The uniqueness of each individual human being is the limitation of that individual, and from that limitation there arises mutual dependence."[25]

Let's pull these last two points together. "The cardinal factor is the direct responsibility of the individual to God implied in God's call, and the dignity and equality which result from it. The secondary . . . factor is the mutual dependence resulting from man's predestination to fellowship and its substratum in nature, individual limitation and idiosyncrasy. Hence, in the Christian idea of justice, equality and the equal right of all are primary, while the difference of what is due to each in the fellowship is, though not inessential, secondary."[26]

The fact that we are equal in the dignity we have on account of bearing the image of God, and likewise equal in the dignity we have on account of being called by God to responsible service, implies that, in fundamental ways, we are to be treated alike; justice requires equal treatment. The additional fact that we are created by God as unique persons each with a unique contour of social responsibilities implies that, once the requirements of equal treatment have been satisfied, we are to treat each person in a way that is due that unique person with her unique contour of responsibilities. One would like Brunner to develop this last point; but he does not. He remarks that "the child has a sacred right to be treated as a child and not as an adult. Its specific nature as a child implies *ipso facto* the right to be *treated* as a child."[27] In another passage he says that "what is due to the man is not the same as what is due

---

23. Brunner, *Justice and Social Order*, 36.
24. Brunner, *Justice and Social Order*, 40.
25. Brunner, *Justice and Social Order*, 43.
26. Brunner, *Justice and Social Order*, 43.
27 Brunner, *Justice and Social Order*, 51.

to the woman, although what is due to both as human beings is equal."[28] He contents himself with these quick examples.

We can now take up the topic of the relation of God to the primal order of justice. "The law of justice is also the law of a divine will," stated Brunner. "Underlying the *suum cuique* there is the order of creation, the will of the Creator which determines which is each man's due."[29] But just how is the will of the Creator related to what is each person's due? Does God create human beings as equal in the dignity of each bearing the image of God but unique in the way that he or she is human and related to others? Does God then call each to serve in accord with her particularity so that all alike have the dignity of being called by God while at the same time each has a unique contour of responsibility? And does God then *in addition* to these acts of creation and call *determine* what is each person's due? Or do the equalities and inequalities of creation and call already determine what is due each person, so that no additional declaration of what is due people is required? Suppose those equalities and inequalities do already determine what is due each person. Does God then *in addition command* us to treat each other in accord with what is due us? Is it that additional command which is the primal order of justice of which Brunner speaks? Or was no such additional command required for there to be a primal order of justice? Is the primal order of justice simply that whole complex of equalities and inequalities which make things due us? If Brunner's view was the first of these three possibilities, there would be no significant difference between his view on this point and that of Joan and Oliver O'Donovan.

Though Brunner is less clear on the point than one would wish, I think the evidence points toward the last of the three possibilities mentioned. That seems to me clearly the most plausible interpretation of the following passage:

> To every creature, there is given at its creation, with the mode of being manifested in it, its law of life. Its right is given, its scope delimited, what is due and what is not due to it is determined. . . . The fact that every human being, without prejudice to his specific mode of being, is, like every other, a creature who must give an account of himself, . . . therein every human being has his dignity as a human being, which is identical with that of every other human being. . . . That is the equality of men founded in creation, the source of the eternal inalienable rights of man. . . . At the same time, however, every human being is endowed by

---

28. Brunner, *Justice and Social Order*, 50.
29. Brunner, *Justice and Social Order*, 48.

the Creator with a specific mode of being.... Both their equality of dignity as human beings, as persons, and their inequality in kind and function are established by creation. Both must, as it were, be acknowledged, both are due and must be taken into account in the allocation of rights and duties.[30]

The picture here is clearly not that of God first creating and calling and then, in addition, doing something else to establish the primal order of justice. The creating and calling establish the order.

In presenting Brunner's view, I have several times spoken of the *dignity* we share equally on account of all bearing the image of God and on account of all being called by God to responsible service. Rather often Brunner speaks of dignity in this connection. But dignity is not what is most fundamental in his theory. What is most fundamental is the idea of something being due a person, plus the Aristotelian thesis that what is due a person is equal treatment of the relevant sort. What is important about the *imago Dei* is not that every human being possesses a certain dignity on account of bearing the *imago*—though every human being does possess that dignity; what is important is that human beings are all *alike* in bearing the *imago Dei*. Likewise, what is important about being called by God to responsible service is not that every human being possesses a certain dignity on account of being called—though every human being does possess that dignity; what is important is that human beings are all *alike* in being called by God. Brunner's theory of justice is an Aristotelian equality-based theory, not a dignity-based theory.

Aristotle did not speak of rights. He *could* have spoken of rights; he could have said that we all have a right to equal treatment. But he did not. He defines justice as equal treatment, assumes that we should treat people justly, and lets it go at that. So too for what Brunner appropriates from the Roman jurists, namely, the idea of something being due a person. One could speak of a right at this point.[31] One could say that if something is due a person, then that person has a right to it. Now and then Brunner does say this. But it is entirely incidental. He can say everything he wants to say without ever using the concept of *a right*, using only the concept of something being *due* a person.

Brunner never stands back to reflect on the role of the concept of *a right* in his thought; he never says that the concept is useful but dispensable. But that is how the concept does in fact function in his thought.

---

30. Brunner, *Justice and Social Order*, 49–51.
31. Donahue, "*Ius* in Roman Law."

Human Rights as Indispensable but Not Fundamental

Another position that one finds in Protestant writings of the twentieth century is that talk of natural rights is indispensable, but that natural rights themselves are not fundamental in the moral order. More fundamental are duties; rights are grounded in duties. If you are obligated to do something, then you have a right to do that, along with a right to do whatever else is necessary as a means. And if your obligation to do the thing in question is a natural obligation, an obligation not generated by any act on the part of human beings, then the correlative rights must also be natural.

Those Christians who sense that talk about human rights is getting at something of deep importance but who, at the same time, feel uneasy with giving natural rights a fundamental place in the moral order, are often inclined toward this view. Thus it is that one finds this account of human rights being employed every now and then in official ecclesiastical declarations. Here is an example taken from "The United Church Pronouncement on Human Rights":

> [B]ecause of God's claim upon all God's creatures human rights have to do with the basic answerability or responsibility of being a human creature.... The fundamental human right is the right to be responsible to God. Human rights and human duties are two sides of the same coin.... In view of God's claim upon God's human creatures, rights are given by God as the means for all human beings to fulfill their duties before God's righteousness. Thus human rights are what people need in order to fulfill their fundamental task of becoming a human person, that is, fulfilling their calling as the image of God.[32]

Paul Ramsey, who taught Christian ethics for many years at Princeton University, is as articulate a defender of this position as any. Here is what he says in his essay, "The Created Destination of Property Rights":[33]

> [I]f human rights are the rights of fellow humanity, "inalienably" connected with this human nature in us and with our life with fellow-man and with our duties to other men, then rights must be whatever it is necessary for me to have in order to be with and for fellow man. If I have an inalienable natural right to

---

32. The full text of the Pronouncement is to be found in Appendix IV of Stackhouse, *Creeds, Society, and Human Rights*, 298.

33. The essay is the first chapter in Ramsey, *Christian Ethics and the Sit-In*.

life simply by my being a man, this is because life is the single most basic precondition to human existence in covenant.[34]

It is of natural human rights that Ramsey is explicitly speaking in this passage. But that he means his thesis concerning the connection between rights and duties to be understood more generally is clear from an earlier passage in the essay:

> [T]he state and its law as an ordinance of creation, natural justice, human and legal rights and social institutions generally, so far as these have a positive purpose under the creative, governing, and preserving purposes of God—all are the external basis making possible the actualization of the promise of covenant; while covenant or fellow humanity is the internal basis and meaning of every right, true justice, or law.[35]

Ramsey's use in this passage of the distinction between "external basis" and "internal basis" is an allusion to Karl Barth's apothegm that covenant is the internal basis of creation and creation, the external basis of covenant. God's covenant dealings with humankind is the purpose of creation; God's creation of humankind makes those covenant dealings possible.

God's covenant dealings with humankind have the overarching character, according to Ramsey, of God's being *for* humankind; and as a component of God's being *for* humankind, God asks of us that we be *for* our fellow human beings. God's being for humankind is God's mercy, God's "steadfast covenant-love"; our being for each other is correspondingly our mercy, our charity, our neighbor-love.[36] It follows that "the requirements of charity, or of steadfast covenant-love, and the requirements of justice, or of natural right, are ultimately inseparable."[37] "In being *for* fellow man is revealed the internal basis of any sort of justice, or the meaning and intentionality there were present all along in that life of man *with* man which God directs in creating, preserving, and governing the world by means of the social order. His rights are a man's capability to covenant."[38]

Ramsey observes that if one looks at love through the lens of justice, rather than looking at justice through the lens of love, then one has to acknowledge that "justice bears only the external marks of man's destiny for steadfast covenant-love. It provides only the external possibility of covenant,

---

34. Ramsey, *Christian Ethics and the Sit-In*, 37.
35. Ramsey, *Christian Ethics and the Sit-In*, 25–26.
36. Ramsey, *Christian Ethics and the Sit-In*, 26.
37. Ramsey, *Christian Ethics and the Sit-In*, 26.
38. Ramsey, *Christian Ethics and the Sit-In*, 30.

or a minimum sign and promise of this." Accordingly, "the fellow humanity of man that shows forth in the order of justice" can perhaps best be described "as the life of man *with* fellow man (not *for* him)."[39] Nonetheless,

> to be *for* fellow man (charity) and to be *with* fellow man (justice) indicates the permeability of justice to charity. Charity (*for* fellow man) is the internal basis and meaning of natural justice (*with* fellow man), as justice in turn is the promise and possibility of close meeting and steadfast covenant. This has to be said of every human right.... Human rights all bear the marks of the primal justice of man's creation for fellow humanity.[40]

Why the Preceding Views Are Untenable

The last position in our typology is that the discourse of natural human rights is indispensable, and that natural rights themselves are as fundamental in the moral order as duties. Since this is the position that I have myself developed in *Justice: Rights and Wrongs*, and that I develop somewhat further in *Justice in Love*, let me take my own account as our example of this position. Before I present my account, however, I must briefly indicate why I find each of the preceding views unsatisfactory. Everything I say here by way of critique is developed more fully in *Justice: Rights and Wrongs*.

To the best of my knowledge, all those twentieth-century writers who shared Nygren's conviction that Jesus, in the second love command, enjoined a special kind of love for all those who are one's neighbors, also shared his conviction that such love pays no attention to what justice requires. Neighbor-love is purely gratuitous benevolence. Nygren was one of the relatively few in the movement who seriously addressed the question whether such love might sometimes do what justice forbids. (Reinhold Niebuhr was another.) He answered the question as I think it must be answered. Such love *does* sometimes do what justice forbids. Nygren's view was that, in such a case, Christianity calls us to remain faithful to love and say farewell to justice. That position seems to me incoherent.

Take the parable of Jesus that Nygren himself used as an example, that of the laborers in the vineyard. Nygren interprets the landowner as conceding that he had treated the early workers unjustly but insisting that he was permitted to dispense his generosity as he wished. But if the landowner did indeed wrong the early workers by treating them as he did, then they had a

---

39. Ramsey, *Christian Ethics and the Sit-In*, 26.
40. Ramsey, *Christian Ethics and the Sit-In*, 26-27.

right with respect to him that he not treat them that way. And if they had a right with respect to him that he not treat them that way, then he, conversely, had an obligation toward them not to treat them thus. But if he had an obligation not to treat them thus, then it cannot be the case that he was permitted to do that. If one is obligated not to do something, then one is not morally permitted to do it. The standard agapist understanding of neighbor-love cannot be correct; love must be understood in such a way as to incorporate seeing to it that one does what justice requires.[41]

My difficulties with the second position in our typology will already have been evident to the reader. An essential part of this position is the embrace of one or another version of the narrative which claims that the idea of natural rights had its origins in atomistic and agonistic political philosophies; those who espouse the position then add that these origins cannot be shucked off. There are two ways of responding to these claims: one can develop a theory of natural rights that is clearly not agonistic and atomistic, or one can challenge the historical claims. Let me here confine myself to the latter. We know now that the canon lawyers of the twelfth century employed the idea of natural human rights; they were not possessive individualists. We also know now that the idea was employed by the early Calvinists; they too were not possessive individualists. My own view, which I do not have the space here to defend, is that the existence of natural rights, both ours and God's, was assumed though not conceptualized by the writers of the Old and New Testaments.

Brunner is correct in observing that Aristotle's equality-account of justice has been taken as "gospel truth" for millennia. To me it seems, however, not only not to be gospel truth but to be clearly false. Is it at all plausible to say that what is wrong with rape is that the rapist is not distributing benefits and burdens equally? Or suppose that a teacher sets up an extremely onerous system of grading, so onerous that there is no chance of anyone getting an A no matter how gifted and informed he may be. The teacher, in applying the system, may be equitable to a fault; everybody is graded in proportion to how well he or she did. But most of the students have been wronged, treated unjustly.

Lastly, the Ramsey position. Ramsey holds that if one ought to do something, then one has a right to do it; and conversely, if one has a right to do something, then one has an obligation to do it. Distinguish between permission-rights and claim-rights. If one ought to do something, then one is morally permitted to do it; one has a permission-right to do it. But natural human rights are claim-rights, not permission-rights. The relevant

---

41. In *Justice in Love*, I develop such an alternative account of love.

claim-right here would be the claim-right to be *free* to do what one ought to do. It is less obviously true that if one is obligated to do something, then one has the claim-right to be free to do it, than it is that one has the permission-right to do it. But rather than pondering the truth or falsehood of that thesis, let us consider the other side of Ramsey's thesis, that all rights are implications of duties. The Alzheimer's patient has no duties; yet she has rights. And the person who pruriently spies on me but does nothing with what he learns, other than enjoy it privately, in no way impairs my ability to carry out my responsibilities; nonetheless he has deprived me of my right to privacy.

Indispensable and Fundamental

My account of rights is a dignity-based account. A right is a legitimate claim to the good of being treated a certain way by one's fellows—or in the limiting case, by oneself. But there are many ways of being treated by one's fellows to which one does not have a right even though it would be a good in one's life to be so treated. The goods to which we have rights are a subdivision of goods in general. One of the most daunting challenges facing anyone who wishes to give an account of rights is to explain what it is that accounts for the fact that one has a right to some of the ways of being treated that would be a good in one's life but not to others.

My view is that one has a right to being treated a certain way by another just in case, were the other not to treat one that way, the other would be treating one with under-respect. He would not be treating one in a way that befits one's worth; he would be treating one in a way that would only befit someone or something of less worth. Rights are what respect for worth requires. We each have worth on account of one or another feature, accomplishment, or relationship in which we stand. And many of our actions have what one might call respect/disrespect import. One is wronged, deprived of what one has a right to, when the respect/disrespect import of how one is treated does not befit one's worth, when it would only befit someone of less worth.

The other comes into my midst bearing worth. By virtue of bearing that worth she has rights with respect to me; she is susceptible of being wronged by me. But I also have worth; thereby I have rights with respect to her and am susceptible of being wronged by her. The situation is entirely symmetrical. The language of rights and of being wronged is for bringing these realities to speech. The language is often abused; the possessive individualist insistently calls attention to his own rights while brushing aside those of the other. That is what those who want to get rid of rights-talk, on the ground that it expresses and abets possessive individualism, call attention to. But it is not the rights-talk that is at fault; it is the possessive individualism. Every component of our moral vocabulary suffers from abuse; if abuse of some component was a good ground for discarding it, we would have no moral vocabulary left.

Ramsey was right to contend that there is an intimate connection between rights and duties. The connection is not that which he suggested, however, but that which is expressed in the following principle of correlatives: if R is the sort of being that can have rights, then R has a right against S to S's doing X if and only if S has an obligation toward R to do X. Mary has a right against John to John's not insulting her if and only if John has an obligation toward Mary not to insult her.

It is tempting to conclude from the principle of correlatives that rights-talk is, after all, dispensable in favor of duty-talk—though if that were true, it would be equally true that duty-talk is dispensable in favor of rights-talk. Neither inference is correct. The principle of correlatives is what philosophers call a *synthetic necessary* truth; though necessarily true, it is not true by virtue of the meanings of the words plus the law of non-contradiction. When one says that Mary has a right with respect to John to John's not insulting her, one is not saying the same thing in different words as when one says that John has an obligation toward Mary not to insult her.

The language of duty brings to speech (one aspect of) the moral significance of *what we do*; the language of rights brings to speech the moral significance of *how we are done unto*. If John insults Mary, then the moral significance for himself of what he has done is that he is guilty; the moral significance for Mary of what he has done is that she has been wronged. The moral order has two fundamental dimensions, interlocking but distinct, the agent-dimension and the recipient- or patient-dimension. The language of duty, responsibility, and the like is for bringing to speech the agent-dimension; the language of rights is for bringing to speech the recipient-dimension.

And what, lastly, about natural human rights? These are rights that one has by virtue of the worth one has just *qua* human being. What accounts for such worth? Far and away the most common view among Christian writers has been that it is bearing the *imago Dei* that gives each of us the worth that grounds human rights; we saw that to be Brunner's view. I think the claim has been made far too quickly; too little attention has been paid to those who are severely impaired—Alzheimer's patients, those who are cognitively impaired from birth, and so forth. Brunner connects the *imago Dei* to being a creature called by God to responsible service;

the Alzheimer's patient cannot engage in responsible service. We need an understanding of the *imago Dei* such that those who are severely impaired nonetheless bear the *imago Dei*. But then it becomes a question whether bearing the *imago Dei* gives a creature sufficient worth to ground human rights. My own view is that we have to bring into the picture a worth-bestowing relation to God that even the most impaired human beings possess. God loves redemptively all who bear the *imago Dei*—loves them equally and loves them perpetually. It is the worth we have on account of being so honored by God that grounds natural human rights.

Art

8

Human Flourishing and Art That Enhances the Ordinary

Most people, when reflecting on the contribution of art to human flourishing, have in mind absorbed attention to some work of the arts: attentive viewing, attentive listening, attentive reading. The question they address is how that activity promotes the flourishing of those who engage in it.

Absorbed attention to some work of the arts is a distinct and complex activity. It requires leisure, respite from one's ordinary activities. To do it well requires training, both informal and formal. A great deal has been written about what goes into doing it well and about the rewards of doing it well.

In this essay I want to explore a very different way in which art contributes to human flourishing. Instead of taking us away from our ordinary activities, art often enhances those activities. I am well aware of the fact that many lovers of art are disdainful of such art; they dismiss it as "functional art," art in the service of interests outside itself. In this essay, I will not challenge that put-down.[1] My goal will be achieved if, by the end of the essay, the reader has some glimpse of how impoverished our flourishing would be if our lives were devoid of art that enhances our ordinary activities.

A general analysis of the ways in which art enhances our ordinary activities would necessarily operate at a high level of abstraction. I think it better to analyze in more detail and with greater specificity just one art. For no particular reason, I have chosen music. Even within music I will not attempt a general analysis of how music enhances our ordinary activities. Instead, I will first analyze how, in work songs, music enhances

---

1. I have addressed it at length in, Wolterstorff, *Art Rethought: The Social Practices of Art.*

manual labor; I will then take and expand what we have learned for an analysis of liturgical singing.[2]

There are, of course, many different understandings of human flourishing, the differences due, in good measure, to different worldviews; naturalists understand flourishing very differently from how humanists understand it. So before I set out, let me briefly explain how I understand flourishing.

My understanding is a Christian understanding. Even among Christians, however, there are different understandings of flourishing; so let me be more specific. I understand flourishing to be what the writers of the Hebrew Bible/Old Testament called *shalom*. An entire essay could be devoted to analyzing the concept of shalom in the Hebrew Bible/Old Testament. Here let me just say that shalom consists of being rightly related to God, to one's fellow human beings, to oneself, to the natural world, and to society and culture, and of finding joy in being so related.

In English translations of the Hebrew Bible/Old Testament, "shalom" has traditionally been translated as "peace." If shalom is what I have just now said it is, "peace" is obviously a very poor translation. In some recent translations it is translated as "welfare." That is better, but still inadequate. "Welfare" has economistic connotations; we speak of "the welfare state." I think "flourishing" is the best translation. Shalom is flourishing, flourishing in all one's relationships: to God, to one's fellows, to oneself, to the natural world, to society and culture. It has both a normative component, being *rightly* related, and an affective component, finding *joy* in being so related.

Sung Work

Songs *about* work are sometimes called "work songs." By the term "work songs" I will not mean songs *about* work but songs sung as an *accompaniment* to work, specifically, manual work.[3]

The labor that work songs accompany can be performed without the songs: spinners can spin and rowers can row without singing. Sometimes the singing establishes a rhythm that is essential for coordinated activity by the laborers; but there are other ways to establish a rhythm for the work than by singing. From the standpoint of getting the work done, the singing is

---

2. In this essay, by the term "ordinary activities" I mean, activities not focused on some work of the arts. In that sense of the term, praising God is an ordinary activity. In other ways it is, of course, not at all ordinary.

3. Some of what follows is taken from my discussion of work songs in Wolterstorff, *Art Rethought*, chapter 16.

unnecessary. It is an addition, an excess. Except for those atypical cases in which some overseer orders the workers to sing, it is a gratuitous excess.

Just as the work can be done without the singing, so too the singing can be done without the work; that is what happens when work songs are performed in concert. With respect to the work, the singing is an excess; with respect to the singing, the work is an excess.

The situation is not entirely symmetrical, however. Usually the work is already there; the singing is not. Though the singing and the working are each an excess with respect to the other, usually the workers feel that the singing accompanies the work, not that the work accompanies the singing. In the term "work songs," the word "work" is the modifier and the word "songs" is the substantive. Our terminology would better reflect the typical reality of things if, instead of speaking of work songs, we spoke of *sung work*.

I spoke above of the singing as *accompanying* the work; I might also have spoken of the work as accompanying the singing. We can describe what takes place either as singing while working or as working while singing. Either way, however, the word "accompany" is misleading. It suggests mere simultaneity. The singing and the working do, of course, occur simultaneously; but their relation goes beyond that. It is integral. Music piped into a factory as background music would be a mere accompaniment to the work.

When workers sing while working, they create an entity of a new genre. There is now neither ordinary work accompanied by singing nor singing accompanied by ordinary work. There is now *sung work*, an entity of a different genre, a hybrid, a blend of singing and working in which the singing and the working "coinhere"—to borrow a term from theology of the Trinity. Ted Gioia, in his fine book *Work Songs*, remarks, "the work of the poorest laborer is still a process of creating and of making something where before there was nothing."[4] Singing while working is a manifestation of human creativity; the gratuitous excess represented by sung work is a *creative* excess.

In situations of labor under duress, this creative excess is the manifestation of a spirit that refuses to be reduced to mere utility—refuses to be reduced to a mere hoer of cotton or a mere splitter of rocks. By singing while laboring under duress, the workers manifest an indomitable sense of their ineradicable dignity. Speaking of some work songs from the country of Georgia, Gioia remarks that their spirit "was not all that different from work songs [from] the American state of Georgia. Both groups of workers managed to capture the strange, paradoxical combination of a wail of misery and an uplifting statement of human dignity as expressed in labor. Such music simultaneously

---

4. Gioia, *Work Songs*, 257.

complains and exults, denies and accepts, pushes forward and holds back."[5] One can understand why overseers in prisons sometimes refused to allow the prisoners to sing.[6] They wanted to crush their spirit. The singing was an indication that they had not yet succeeded. It was an act of resistance on the part of the workers to the attempt to crush their spirit. So the overseers forbade singing. They preferred sullen silent acquiescence.

Prison Songs is a recording made by Alan Lomax in 1947–48 of songs sung by prisoners in the Parchman Farm prison in Mississippi.[7] In 1996 a researcher played this recording for a group of ex-prisoners living in the South Bronx and asked them what they thought about it. One said, "They sing for inspiration, survival. They were uplifting themselves." Another said, "You're trying to save your sanity. . . . You'd lose your spirit if you didn't sing." A third said that the songs were a manifestation of the

> will of the human spirit. That will is something within me. It says that I have something that I can do to get myself out of this, too, or get through this day, or cope with tomorrow, and not just lay back and hope that someone else will come to my rescue. So I think these songs have a great value, a great lesson: the will of the human spirit—the will to survive and go on, no matter what, and in spite of everything.[8]

The Singing Fits the Work

If the singing and the labor are to coinhere, the singing has to fit the work.[9] Thus it is that

> the work song follows musical rules of its own, far distant from the cultural and formal considerations that hold sway in virtually all other types of performance art. Indeed, in almost every regard the work song defies our conception of an "artistic performance." Its pace can be repetitive and predictable; often it strives to achieve effects that, in other settings, would be dismissed as merely monotonous. The time and setting of the performance, the number of singers—these factors and others are usually determined by external forces. No artists have less

---

5. Gioia, *Work Songs*, 257–58.
6. Gioia, *Work Songs*, 207.
7. Lomax, *Prison Songs*.
8. These comments are to be found in the booklet accompanying the CD.
9. In Wolterstorff, *Art in Action*, 96–121, I develop a theory of fittingness.

control over their "medium" than do the singers of these songs. The rhythms are typically slower than most other types of traditional songs, sometimes positively sluggish.[10]

Gioia quotes what Richard Henry Dana wrote in his 1841 memoir, *Two Years before the Mast*, about the difficulty sailors sometimes experienced in finding the right shanty for certain shipboard tasks. "Two or three songs would be tried, one after the other, with no effect—not an inch could be got on the tackles—when a new song struck up, seemed to hit the humor of the moment, and drove the tackles 'two blocks' at once."[11] For simpler tasks

> the crew might be forgiving of a less-than-ideal shanty: "Tom's Gone to Hilo" (or "John's Gone to Hilo") was simply too slow to serve as a proper tops'l halyard song—it invariably took ages to hoist a yard given its languorous tempo; but nonetheless it was popular with sailors, who liked its melody and often put it to use despite this functional limitation. Other songs only found their true calling over time, such as "Santa Anna," . . . which started life as a pumping shanty and gradually made its way to the capstan where it served yeoman's duty.[12]

Not only must the tempo of the song fit the tempo of the work. The rhythm of the song must likewise fit the rhythm of the work. Or in case the work does not have an inherent rhythm, the rhythm of the song has to be a rhythm that can be imposed on the work. For some types of work it was important, or even indispensable, that the actions of the individual workers be synchronized; in those cases, the singing had to have a rhythm that could serve that function. Track 2 on *Prison Songs*, "No More, My Lord," and track 13, "Early in the Mornin'," are fascinating examples of the point. Both are songs sung to the action of chopping wood; and in both cases, not only does the rhythm of the singing establish a rhythm for the swinging of the axes, but the ringing percussive sound of the axe-blows is an integral part of the music.

If the song is to fit the work, another requirement is that the expressive character of the song fit the nature of the work and the mood typical of those who perform the work. Gioia remarks that "no listener can hear the music of . . . traditional hunting cultures without sensing . . . joy and exultation, [the] expression of intense connection with the surrounding environment. The songs of herders and farmers are, by comparison, pensive and

---

10. Gioia, *Work Songs*, 60–61.
11. This is a quotation from Dana by Gioia, *Work Songs*, 121.
12. Gioia, *Work Songs*, 122.

sober, only rarely achieving the vivacity that is a constitutive element of the hunter's daily music."[13] In pastoral music, he says, "we can sense a plaintive, melancholy tone—perhaps inculcated by the long lonely hours spent by the herder with only the company of sounds."[14] Lumberjack songs, like hunter songs, are joyful; their "general tone of gaiety puts lumber camp songs almost in a class by themselves in the area of work-related music."[15] Writing about the music of African tribes, the ethnomusicologist Rose Brandel observed that these peoples do "not deliberately project the 'work music' upon the scene in the manner of modern factory psychologists. Rather, the music seems to be an expressive outgrowth of the labor itself."[16]

Singing While Working Makes the Work Go Better

Those who sang while working obviously found this new creation, sung work, to be more gratifying than the same work done without singing; that is why they sang. What was it about this new entity that they found more gratifying? The name of one of the inmates in the Parchman Farm Prison whom Alan Lomax interviewed was "Bama." When Lomax asked Bama why he and his fellow inmates sang, Bama said, singing makes the work "go so better."[17] Singing changes the work, modifies it, modifies it for the better; singing enhances the work, elevates it. Gioia sometimes describes the singing as "transforming" the work.[18]

The counterpart thing can be said about the effect of the work on the singing. The work modifies the singing, modifies it for the better, enhances it. About the seaman's shanty, Gioia says, "cut off from the activities that gave it meaning, the shanty has become just another song. This transition can only be lamented, for the work-a-day circumstances that gave birth to the shanty also imparted the rough-and-ready beauty that made them so inspirational and this charm all but disappears when the music is brought inside the concert hall or recording studio."[19]

Let us set off to the side the enhancement of the singing effected by its combination with the work and reflect on the enhancement of the work

13. Gioia, *Work Songs*, 26.
14. Gioia, *Work Songs*, 66.
15. Gioia, *Work Songs*, 141.
16. Quoted in Gioia, *Work Songs*, 56.
17. Lomax, *Prison Songs*, Track 12.
18. Gioia, *Work Songs*, xi; 4.
19. Gioia, *Work Songs*, 136.

effected by its combination with the singing. What is it about sung work that makes it more gratifying for the workers than work of the same sort performed without singing? In what way does the work "go so better?"

We have already taken note of one of the ways in which the singing makes the work go better: the rhythm of the singing coordinates the activity of the individual laborers. In addition, singing often energizes the workers. In Gioia's words, the songs "impart vitality and energy to an undertaking."[20] When accompanied by singing, tasks "have a stronger and more insistent force of momentum behind them."[21]

Singing enhances not only the work itself but the workers' experience of the work. The creative excess of the singing blurs the distinction between work and play by introducing a dimension of play into the work; this enhances their experience of the work. And when the singing is not solitary, as, for example, the singing of herdsmen often was, but is done together with others, the singing together heightens the workers' sense of solidarity.

Working together rather than individually—rowing a boat together, setting sails together—requires that each adjust what he or she is doing to what the others are doing; it requires mutual responsiveness. A sense of solidarity emerges. Singing together while working together adds a new level of responsiveness; now each participant must not only adjust his or her work to the work of the others but his or her singing to the singing of the others. From this new level of responsiveness an even stronger sense of solidarity emerges. Add to this that in singing the same words they are voicing the same sentiments. Is it fanciful to see in this heightened sense of solidarity a sign of shalom, using "sign" in the sense in which the word is used in the Gospel of John? The signs that Jesus performed were samples of shalom that pointed to a shalom beyond themselves.

In these ways, and no doubt others, singing enhanced the experience of the work, whether or not the work was pleasant. It was especially when the work was unpleasant, however, that singing was important. Much of the work that human beings have performed while singing is tedious or laborious. The singing alleviates the unpleasantness; it makes the time go faster. It does this not by distracting the workers from the work, in the way that reading a gripping novel distracts one for a while from the pain in one's foot; the workers still attend to the work. But their attention is now divided between the work and the singing. I quoted three words from what Bama said to Lomax when Lomax asked him why he and his fellows sang while working. Here is more of what Bama said in answer to Lomax's question:

20. Gioia, *Work Songs*, 178.
21. Gioia, *Work Songs*, 178.

> When you singin', you forgit, you see, and the time just pass on "way" but if you just get your mind devoted on one something, it look like it will be hard for you to make it, see, make a day. The day be longer, look like. So to keep his mind from being devoted on just one thing, why he'll practically take up singin', see.

In short, singing while working leads the workers no longer to focus exclusively on the tedium and laboriousness of the work.

Singing While Working Is an Intrinsic Good

I posed the question, what was it about sung work that made it more gratifying than the same work done without singing. The answer I have offered thus far took its cue from a comment made to Alan Lomax by Bama: singing makes the work "go so better." Singing has the effect of modifying the work, modifying it for the better, enhancing it; and singing has the effect of modifying the workers' experience of the work so that it feels less tedious and laborious. Singing coordinates the activity of the workers, energizes them, and makes them no longer preoccupied exclusively with their work.

These are functional considerations, beneficial effects of the singing on the work and on the workers' experience of the work. Gioia doubts that such functional considerations exhaust the matter; I think he is right about that.[22] His guess and mine is that the workers often found this expression of creativity on their part, this *gratuitous excess* as I have called it, intrinsically good. Yes, singing together while working does have the effects mentioned. But the workers also sang for the sheer joy of creating sung work; sung work was *an end in itself* in the structure of their activities. The labor as such was not an end in itself for them—not usually, anyway; it was the sung work that was an end in itself. Gioia quotes from Charles de Rochefort's 1666 publication, *The History of the Caribby-Islands*, "they do also by singing alleviate the hard labour they are addicted unto and yet what they do, seems to be done rather out of divertisement, and to avoid idleness, than out of any considerations of advantage that they make thereof."[23] Like artists in general, the workers found joy in their act of creation. Is it fanciful to see in that joy a sign of shalom?

---

22. Gioia, *Work Songs*, 56–59.
23. Gioia, *Work Songs*, 59.

An Excursus on Joy

How can prisoners experience joy in creating sung work when their overall condition is miserable, something they would never choose? To understand this apparently paradoxical situation, we need a brief excursus on joy.

Joy is an emotion. I judge that the best philosophical account of emotion currently available is that by Robert C. Roberts in his 2003 treatise, *Emotions: An Essay in Aid of Moral Psychology*. Let me present the core of Roberts' theory without, on this occasion, defending it.

Emotions always have an object: if one fears, there is something that one fears; if one envies, there is someone that one envies; if one grieves, there is something over which one grieves; and so forth. Emotions are in this way different from sensations: a tingling sensation in one's finger has no object, nor does a burning sensation on one's tongue. Sensations are, as it were, non-referential.

Roberts' central claim is that emotions are *concern-imbued construals*.[24] Here is the idea. An emotion incorporates a certain construal or interpretation of some segment of reality; if I construed that segment of reality differently, or not at all, I would not have the emotion in question. When I fear, I construe something as threatening my life or well-being; when I envy, I construe someone as superior to me in some way.

Construals are not sufficient for emotions, however; what is also required is concern. What one construes as so-and-so must concern one. My construal of something as threatening my life must concern me or I will not feel fear; my construal of Michael as superior to me in a certain way must concern me or I will not feel envy.

Concerns vary in how important they are to the person—to put the same point in other words, they differ with respect to their depth of ingression into one's personality. Some are so important to one that one cannot imagine oneself not having that concern; they are constitutive of one's identity. Relative importance is determined by which member of some pair one would choose to give up, if one could choose and had to choose.

Concerns also typically vary with respect to intensity, with the result that emotions typically vary with respect to intensity. Depending on the intensity of my concern over Michael's perceived superiority to me, I may feel intensely envious of him or only mildly envious.

Where, within the panoply of concern-imbued construals of reality, is joy located? Joy, I would say, occurs when it is important to one that things

---

24. The term that Roberts most often uses is "concern-*based* construals." His thought is not, however, that the construal is somehow *based on* the concern but that it is *imbued* or *infused with* the concern. He himself sometimes uses the term "imbued."

be a certain way and one construes them as being that way. Roberts gives a nice example of joy; let me quote what he says.

> I am surrounded by my children, who are playing happily, . . . showing signs of flourishing, of growing well in body, mind, and spirit. As I contemplate this goodly scene, I am filled with joy. On my analysis of emotion, my joy amounts to a concern-based construal of my children: I "see" them in terms of their well-being, and this term impinges satisfyingly on my concern for their well-being. If I do not see them in terms of this or some similar aspect of the scene (let us say I merely perceive the noise and motion as an impediment to my reading), then I will not feel joy; or if I perceive them in terms of their flourishing but without this perception impinging on my concern (I am assessing them clinically, with perfect detachment, and give them a high grade), then likewise I do not feel joy.[25]

The linguistic connection between the English terms "joy" and "enjoyment" leads one to think that these are basically the same phenomenon. If Roberts and I are right in holding that joy is an emotion, then clearly they are not the same. Enjoying something—enjoying the taste of the ice cream, enjoying the display of aurora borealis—is not having an emotion. One "feels" joy, grief, pride, guilt, and so forth; one does not "feel" enjoyment. So, too, one does not "feel" happiness. One can, of course, feel happy. But happiness is unlike joy in that often it has no object. One just feels happy. Feeling happy has causes but not an object. Feeling miserable is like happiness in that regard.

The fact that joy always has an object, whereas feeling miserable does not, explains how one can be miserable and yet experience joy. A passage in Paul's Second Letter to the Corinthians offers a vivid example of the point:

> As servants of God we have commended ourselves in every way: through great endurance, in afflictions, hardships, calamities, beatings, imprisonments, riots, labors, sleepless nights, hunger, by purity, knowledge, patience, kindness, holiness of spirit, genuine love, truthful speech, and the power of God, with the weapons of righteousness for the right hand and for the left; in honor and dishonor, in ill repute and good repute. We are treated as imposters, and yet are true; as unknown, and yet are well

---

25. Roberts, *Emotions*, 279. The passage continues: "Let us say, then, that joy is a construal of something in terms that satisfy one or more of one's concerns." Thus joy, as Roberts understands it, does not require that the concern in question be important to one. I doubt that one would naturally call it "joy" if the concern in question was unimportant to one; calling it "joy" would seem excessive.

known; as dying, and see—we are alive; as punished, and yet not killed; as sorrowful, yet always rejoicing. (2 Cor 6:4–10; NRSV)

Often miserable—hungry, beaten, deprived of sleep, imprisoned, maligned—*yet always rejoicing*. To rejoice is to express one's joy. No matter how miserable he often was, joy was a constant in Paul's life. In the passage quoted he does not say what it was that gave him joy no matter what his condition. We know from other passages what it was; he found joy in knowledge of the salvation that had come to humanity and to himself in the crucifixion and resurrection of Jesus Christ.

Liturgical Singing

Work songs have virtually disappeared from modernized societies; for most of us, they are a thing of the past. Elsewhere I have explored why that is.[26] Liturgical singing has by no means disappeared. Almost all enactments of Christian liturgies include singing. From Paul's letters we learn that that was true already in his day; he speaks of "psalms, hymns, and spiritual songs" (Col 3:6).[27] From its earliest days, the church has broken out into song.

Liturgical singing takes a number of different forms: the form of chanting a penitential psalm, the form of singing a prayer of confession, the form of singing the Creed, the form of singing a hymn of praise or thanksgiving. It is important to recognize the variety. Nonetheless, I think there will be no harm if, on this occasion, we simplify our discussion by focusing on hymns of praise and thanksgiving. Almost everything I have to say about such hymns applies to the other forms of liturgical singing as well.

What we have learned from our analysis of sung manual labor applies, *mutatis mutandis*, to hymns of praise and thanksgiving. Hymns are sung work, the "work" in this case being praise and thanksgiving addressed to God.

Just as workers can perform manual labor without singing, so too we can praise God without singing. We can praise God in spoken prose; often we do. With respect to the action of praising God, singing is an excess, a *gratuitous* excess; it is not necessary.

The musical excess is not just tacked on, however; it does not merely coexist with the praise. The singing and the praising are fused; they coinhere to create an entity of a new genre, namely, *sung praise*. In this fusion,

---

26. Wolterstorff, *Art Rethought*, 269.

27. "Spiritual songs" may well have meant *inspired songs*, that is, songs inspired by the Spirit.

the praise is altered, changed, transformed. Compared to prose praise, sung praise is an enhancement of praise in much the same way that sung work is an enhancement of manual labor. Singing elevates our praise, ennobles it, makes it more fitting to the one to whom it is addressed, namely God. Singing makes our praise "go so better."

Just now I contrasted prose praise with the sung praise of a hymn. To describe the situation that way, while not inaccurate, nonetheless ignores an important complexity. The text of a hymn is typically not prose but poetry, often not poetry of a sort and quality that would qualify it for inclusion in an anthology of poetry, but poetry nonetheless.[28] (The same is true of the text of most work songs.) It is a work of one of the arts, a poem.

The full structure of the situation is thus as follows. With respect to the action of praising God, the poetry is a gratuitous excess; it is not necessary. The poetry is not just tacked on to the praise, however; it does not merely coexist with it. The poetry and the praise are fused; they coinhere to create an entity of a new genre, poetized praise. In this fusion, the praise is altered, transformed. Compared to prose praise, poetized praise is an enhancement of praise. Poetry elevates our praise, makes it more fitting for addressing God. The poetry makes the praise "go so better."

The music is then, in turn, a gratuitous excess with respect to spoken poetized praise. But it is not just tacked on to the poetized praise; it is fused with it. The music and the poetized praise coinhere to create an entity of yet another genre, namely, sung poetized-praise. When a hymn is sung in praise of God, the praise, the poetry, and the music, all coinhere; there is a trinity of coinherence. And in this trinity of coinherence, the poetry elevates the praise and the music elevates the poetized-praise, ennobles it, makes it more fitting for addressing God. In the presence of God, the angels sing poetry; they don't speak in prose.

There is no such thing as generic praise of God. Whether the praise be in prose or poetry, the praise is concrete, specific. And it can always be interpreted in somewhat different ways. Thus it is that every musical setting of a text is an interpretation of the text. In his *Aesthetics*, Monroe Beardsley gives an interesting example of the point. He cites the musical phrase to which Palestrina, in his *Pope Marcellus Mass,* set the words of the Credo, "*descendit de caelis*," and the musical phrase to which Beethoven set the word "*descendit*" in the Credo of his *Missa Solemnis*. The phrase in Palestrina descends gradually over an expanse of nine notes from F above middle C to A below. The phrase in Beethoven plunges abruptly over the expanse of three notes

---

28. Some of the sung hymns in the Orthodox liturgy have prose texts. And the Creed is, of course, not poetry.

from B above high C to F above middle C. Beardsley remarks: "these are two descents, so to speak, but what different descents they are! In Palestrina the coming of Christ is a serene passage into the world from a realm not utterly remote; in Beethoven it is a dramatic plunge."[29]

The fusion of the music with a text alters our *experience* of the text, partly, but by no means only, because of how the music interprets the text. To sing a poem or to hear it sung is to experience it very differently from reading or reciting it, and also very differently from hearing it read aloud by someone else. Vivien Schweitzer is one of the regular music reviewers of *The New York Times*. In *The Times* of March 7, 2014, she reviewed a performance of Franz Schubert's *Die Schöne Müllerin* by Matthias Goerne and Christoph Eschenbach. Schubert's work is a setting of a cycle of poems by Wilhelm Müller. In the course of her review, Schweitzer quotes something that Müller wrote in his diary in 1815, before Schubert had set the poems: "I can neither play nor sing, and my verses lead but half a life until music breathes life into them. But courage! A kindred soul may yet be found who will hear the tunes behind the words and reflect them back to me." Müller was convinced that his own experience of his poems, not to mention that of the public, would not reach its full potential until they had been appropriately set to music. I do not know whether Müller ever heard Schubert's settings; but I think anyone would agree that Schubert's settings alter and enormously enhance our experience of the poetry.

My thesis has been that poetized praise is an enhancement of praise in prose, and that, in turn, sung poetized-praise is an enhancement of spoken poetized praise. Not always, of course; sometimes poetry deadens the praise, sometimes music deadens the poem. But it is the experience of all of us that, very often, the enhancement happens. So we continue to break out in song.

What is it about singing our praise, whether poetized or not, that enhances and elevates the praise? What is it about singing that makes the praise "go so better"? What is it about singing, "Oh Come All Ye Faithful, Joyful and Triumphant" that makes our praise so much better than just saying the words together? What is it about singing "A Mighty Fortress Is Our God" that makes our praise so much better than just saying the words together?

I *apprehend* what it is about singing our praise that makes it intrinsically better than speaking our praise; but I find myself incapable of describing it. Singing gives to our praise a certain lift; but I am incapable of *describing* that lift. And in any case, to say that it gives to our praise a certain lift is not to say anything different from saying that it elevates our praise. There have been studies by cognitive psychologists of the changes that occur

---

29. Beardsley, *Aesthetics*, 347.

in the brain when people sing together.[30] But knowledge of those changes in the brain is of no help in describing the enhancement of our praise that we *experience* when we sing a hymn together.

What I can do is put into words some of what makes praising God *together* better than praising God alone, especially when we praise God together in song. When discussing work songs, I noted that, in order to work together, each worker must adjust what he or she is doing to what the others are doing, and that singing together while working requires an additional level of mutual responsiveness. This additional mutual responsiveness both expresses and intensifies the workers' solidarity; they are in this together.

The same points apply, *mutatis mutandis*, to singing together hymns of praise and thanksgiving: mutual adjustment and responsiveness is required. This is especially true when the singing is in harmony. In Stacy Horn's book, *Imperfect Harmony: Finding Happiness Singing with Others*, there is a fascinating discussion of the mutual adjustment required for choral singing. Here is one passage in which she describes her experience of singing in a choir.

> You make a contribution of sound waves and airwaves, and something more complex, something you couldn't possibly produce on your own, comes back to you. You constantly adjust your contribution. . . . It requires more concentration than if you were producing sound or singing on your own, say, in the shower, and thus you really do get lost—in the sense that you can't worry about anything else in your life at that moment. . . . I've loved being able to listen to individual voices singing right next to me on parts other than my own. It's both energizing and stabilizing to be surrounded by all four parts. . . . After all, there aren't too many chances in ordinary life to be in perfect cooperation with other people. Singing fulfills that need.[31]

Good congregational singing requires the same sort of mutual responsiveness that Horn experienced in singing in a choir. The theologian David Ford makes the point well in a chapter that he calls "Communicating God's Abundance: A Singing Self": "the specific contribution of music to [the] building up of community in worship includes its encouragement of alertness to others, immediate responsiveness to changes in tone, tune and rhythm, and sharing in the confidence that can come from joint singing. Singing together embodies joint responsibility in which each singer waits on the others, is attentive with the intention of serving the common

---

30. See the discussion and references in Horn, *Imperfect Harmony*.
31. Horn, *Imperfect Harmony*, 120–21.

harmony."[32] The mutual responsiveness required by *together* praising God in song both expresses and intensifies the participants' solidarity, what Ford calls "community." Liturgical singing is a sign of shalom: it is a sample of shalom that points to a shalom beyond itself.

Singing hymns together not only enhances solidarity by virtue of the mutual responsiveness required for singing together. It also enhances solidarity by unifying the participants around what they are saying in their singing, sometimes leading them to say what they would not previously have said. I think here of a paragraph in the book by the African American theologian James Cone, *The Spirituals and the Blues*:

> Black music is unity music. It unites the joy and the sorrow, the love and the hate, the hope and the despair, of black people; and it moves the people toward the direction of total liberation. It shapes and defines black existence and creates culture structures for black expression. Black music is unifying because it confronts the individual with the truth of black existence and affirms that black being is possible only in a communal context.[33]

For many members of the African-American community, singing spirituals in church and elsewhere not only expressed and intensified their solidarity but was an act of defiance on their part. It was a declaration that their spirit had not been crushed, just as the singing of work songs by prisoners was a declaration that their spirit had not been crushed. The singing of their spirituals by African-Americans was, in this way too, a sign of shalom.

Joy in Liturgical Singing

Let me conclude with a few comments about joy in liturgical singing. When discussing work songs, I took note of the fact that workers sang not only for the beneficial effects on the work and their experience of the work but also, sometimes at least, for the sheer joy of singing while working: the joy of creating this new entity, sung work. Singing while working was an end in itself for them. The same is true for liturgical singing. We sing hymns for the sheer joy of creating together with our fellow congregants this new entity, sung poetized-praise. But I suggest that there are, in praising God in song, two other sources of joy as well.

Praising God is "work" that most liturgical participants find joy in doing. When discussing work songs, I noted that the manual labor that work

---

32. Ford, *Self and Salvation*, 122.
33. Cone, *The Spirituals and the Blues*, 5.

songs accompany is often tedious and onerous, not something that the workers would do if given a choice. Not always, of course. No doubt sailors sometimes found joy and satisfaction in setting sails; they would do it even if they did not have to. No doubt weavers sometimes found joy and satisfaction in weaving. But typically the work was tedious on account of its repetitiveness, and onerous. By contrast, believers find joy in praising God—not only joy in praising God in song, but joy in the very act of praising God. It is not tedious or onerous. It is something they *want* to do.

For the third source of joy in praising God in song, think back to the passage from St. Paul that I quoted earlier, in which he writes that, no matter how miserable and unhappy he often was, joy was nonetheless a constant in his life. No matter what afflictions and hardships he was undergoing, he found joy in the salvation that had come to humanity and to himself in the crucifixion and resurrection of Jesus Christ. When Christians sing hymns of praise and thanksgiving to God, they are singing of that which gives them deep joy. It is for this reason, especially, that they find themselves capable of singing hymns to God in times of adversity—or better, it is for this reason that they find themselves *impelled* to sing hymns to God in times of adversity. In this way, too, liturgical singing is a sign of shalom—a foretaste.

The Larger Point

In this essay I have analyzed the contribution that work songs and liturgical singing make to the flourishing of the participants. The overarching concept that I have employed is *enhancement*: singing while working enhances the work; singing our praise and thanksgiving enhances our praise and thanksgiving. It is primarily by this enhancement that the singing contributes to the shalom of the participants. The fact that the enhancement is a creative gratuitous excess means that there is more to the worth of those who sing than their utility: they are creators.

In my introductory remarks I indicated that I intended my analyses to call attention to, and illuminate, a larger point. That larger point is this: art in general contributes to our flourishing by enhancing our ordinary activities. To cite just one example in addition to music: architecture enhances the activities that we perform within our architectural enclosures. To this should be added the related point that art contributes to our flourishing by enhancing not only our ordinary activities but also the objects that we use in our ordinary activities: visual decoration enhances our books, our buildings, and so forth; ceramic art enhances our vessels. There can be no doubt that art that rewards absorbed attention contributes to human flourishing. I am inclined to think that, all in all, art that enhances the ordinary makes an even greater contribution. Might it be that, in general, human flourishing is best advanced by enhancing the ordinary rather than by trying to deny it or in some way to transcend it?[34]

---

34. I thank Matthew Croasmun and Ryan McAnnally-Linz for their helpful comments on an earlier draft of this essay.

9

What Sort of Worth Do Works of Art Have?[1]

In the spring of 2007, the distinguished American poet Donald Hall paid a visit to the University of Virginia. He read some of his own poetry to a large audience in Old Cabel Hall, taking some questions afterward. The next day he led a small seminar sponsored by the Institute for Advanced Studies in Culture. The seminar was about writing poetry. Hall frequently illustrated what he had to say by referring to changes he had made in some of his own poems between early drafts and final version. I remember one of those changes. In an earlier draft of one of his poems, he had spoken of a dog wagging its tail; he changed that to the dog swinging its tail. A student asked why he made that change. He answered, "because it made it a better poem." Those were his exact words.

If you were not present at the seminar and all you know about this episode is what I just told you, it would not be implausible to interpret Hall's response as a brush-off. But the remark came near the end of an hour in which Hall had been talking and fielding questions; and given what I had discerned of his character in this hour, it never crossed my mind that he had given the student a brush-off. He meant no more and no less than what he said: he changed the line because it made it a better poem. I wanted him to go on and explain why the change made the poem better. But maybe he felt he couldn't put into words why it made the poem better. Or—more likely, I think—his remark had an implicit question attached: "Because it made it a better poem. Don't you agree?"

Hall's simple remark initiated in me a long chain of reflections about the sort of worth that works of art have. Those reflections have been relatively brief, and episodic rather than sustained; they remain unfinished

---

[1]. This is the text of a talk given to the philosophy department of the University of Virginia in the October, 2011.

and incomplete. Nonetheless, I decided to stick my neck out today, present to you the conclusions to which I have thus far been led, and invite your response.

Upon returning home from Hall's seminar, I looked up a passage written in 1785 by the German author Karl Philipp Moritz. I knew the passage from its quotation by M. H. Abrams in his essay, "Art-as-Such: The Sociology of Modern Aesthetics."[2] My previous response to the passage had been a blend of fascination, bafflement, and rejection. The passage goes like this:

> In the contemplation of the beautiful object . . . I contemplate . . . something which is *completed*, not in me, but *in its own self*, which therefore constitutes a whole in itself, and affords me pleasure *for its own sake*.[3]

> While the beautiful draws our attention exclusively to itself . . . we seem to lose ourselves in the beautiful object; and precisely this loss, this forgetfulness of self, is the highest degree of pure and disinterested pleasure that beauty grants us. In that moment we sacrifice our individual being to a kind of higher being. . . . Beauty in a work of art is not pure . . . until I contemplate it as something that has been brought forth entirely for its own sake, in order that it should be something complete in itself.[4]

What I found annoying in this passage was the suggestion that works of art belong to a higher kind of being than human beings; I do not accept that. What I found baffling was Moritz's apparent obliviousness to the fact that while he was declaiming that a work of art is brought forth entirely for its own sake, he was assuming that works of art exist for the pleasure to be got in contemplating them. And as to why I found it fascinating—well, it is fascinating, don't you agree?

Hall's comment made the passage look quite different from how it had looked before. I was still annoyed with the suggestion that works of art are of greater worth than human beings. But was I perhaps wrong in thinking that Moritz was assuming that works of art are instrumental to the pleasure to be got in contemplating them? Was he perhaps saying that works of art have *intrinsic* worth? Notice that Donald Hall's answer to the student's question was not that he had changed the line because he thought his audience would getter pleasure from reading the revision. He changed it because it made a better poem.

2. Included in, Abrams, *Doing Things with Texts*.
3. Abrams, *Doing Things with Texts*, 156.
4. Abrams, *Doing Things with Texts*, 156.

The reason I found Hall's remark so striking is that it awoke me from a dogmatic slumber, a slumber that had lasted ever since I first began to study aesthetics. Probably I was the only person in the room to be sufficiently struck by Hall's remark to remember it; the others were either not in the dogmatic slumber that I was in, or they were, but were not jolted out of it by his comment. Before I explore with you the line of thought initiated in me by Hall's remark, and by the reflections sparked in me by the passage from Moritz, I want to set before you the nature of my dogmatic slumber. That will highlight the significance of the line of thought that I want to set before you today.

Every articulate theory of the modern or contemporary period concerning the worth of works of art that I am acquainted with is an *instrumentalist* theory. There are brief passages, such as that from Moritz, that point in another direction. But every developed, articulated theory that I know of is an instrumentalist theory. Works of art do not have intrinsic worth. Their worth lies in their serving to bring about something else that is of intrinsic worth. The "something else" that is of intrinsic worth is an experience of a certain kind, coupled, perhaps, with certain effects of that experience. The deepest disagreements among modern theories of artistic worth are disagreements over the nature of that experience.

The *emotivist* tradition, represented preeminently by Tolstoy and Collingwood, insists that the intrinsically valuable experience that imparts worth to works of art is an emotion of a certain sort, or perhaps a certain range of emotions. The *alethic* tradition (from the Greek for "truth," "*aletheia*"), of which Hegel, Heidegger, Adorno, and Marcusse are prominent representatives, insists that the fundamental worth of works of art is to be located in their giving us knowledge of certain sorts. And the *aestheticist* tradition, represented by many writers, Kant and Monroe Beardsley prominent among them, holds that the worth-imparting experience is what has come to be called the *aesthetic* experience. These three traditions do not cover all the positions that have been set forth; the position that Schiller develops in *Letters on the Aesthetic Education of Man* doesn't fit under any of them, nor does that developed by Susanne Langer in various of her writings; but these, I would say, are the three main traditions.

Of these three, it is the aestheticist tradition that has been dominant among analytic philosophers over the past half century. So let me now give specificity to my discussion by looking with you at an example of an instrumentalist account of artistic worth offered by someone in this tradition.

A classic example of such a theory is that developed by Monroe Beardsley. Far more than most instrumentalists in the aestheticist tradition, Beardsley recognized, and tried to face up to, the challenges that confront anyone who tries to develop an instrumentalist account of artistic worth. Nonetheless, instead of looking at Beardsley's theory, I propose looking at a more recent example of this line of thought, viz., the theory of artistic worth developed by Alan H. Goldman in his 1995 book, *Aesthetic Value*.

Goldman distinguishes three ways of evaluating a work of art:

> (1) In terms of the degree to which its strategies satisfy the ideals of the style under the constraints of which it is produced; (2) in terms of its importance in a historical sequence in which it is placed (determined mainly by the first way of evaluating and by its originality); and (3) simply as an artwork, in terms of its overall effects on us and the degree to which it engages and integrates our mental capacities in appreciating it.[5]

The theory that we will be looking at is Goldman's theory concerning the third way of evaluating.

Here, in his own words, is the core of his theory of artistic worth:

> The challenge of great works to our perceptual, cognitive, and affective capacities, and their full occupation and fulfillment in meeting that challenge, removes us entirely from the real world of our practical affairs. It is in the ultimately satisfying exercise of these different mental capacities operating together to appreciate the rich relational properties of artworks that I shall argue the primary value of great works is to be found.[6]

Goldman holds that works of art also have what he calls "subsidiary values," some of these connected in one way or another to what he identifies as their primary value; but their primary value is to be located "in the challenges that great works present to our various mental capacities united in their appreciation and in the pleasure or satisfaction derived from meeting these challenges."[7]

On this occasion, I will refrain from saying anything about the nature of the satisfying experience that lies at the center of Goldman's theory; I want, instead, to focus on another aspect of his account. Goldman speaks in these passages of *us* and of *our* capacities. To whom is he referring? The relative worth of a work of art consists in the degree of satisfaction *we* get from meeting the challenge it presents to *us* of exercising together *our* various mental capacities when *we* appreciate it. Who is the *we* in question?

---

5. Goldman, *Aesthetic Value*, 170.
6. Goldman, *Aesthetic Value*, 8.
7. Goldman, *Aesthetic Value*, 8–9.

Is it each of us, and is Goldman espousing a relativist theory of artistic worth? Is it his view that if some work gives me no satisfaction in meeting the challenge it presents to me in appreciating it, whereas it gives you a great deal of satisfaction when so engaging it, then it is worthless *relative to me* but of considerable artistic worth *relative to you*? That is not Goldman's view. The theory he develops is an ideal observer theory—or rather, as he sometimes describes it, an ideal *critic* view. The artistic worth of a work of art is determined by the satisfaction that an *ideal critic* would experience in meeting the challenges it presents.

And what must a critic or appreciator be like to be ideal? He must be knowledgeable, unbiased, sensitive, and of developed taste.[8] Immediately after first specifying these four traits of the ideal appreciator, Goldman adds that the fact "that critics with these characteristics would react positively to a work suggests that others ought to as well."[9] How exactly this obligation is thought to enter the picture remains obscure to me. Why am I obligated to respond as an ideal critic would respond? But let this pass; reflecting further on the point would be a distraction on this occasion.

As to the *knowledge* that ideal critics must have, this includes, says Goldman, "not only knowledge of the type of work to which O belongs but also of contrasting works and of the historical (social, cultural) milieu in which the work fits."[10] Explaining what he means by saying that ideal critics must be *unbiased*, Goldman says that he does not "mean to rule out preferences in taste or social point of view, only such obvious disqualifications as personal relation to the artist."[11] By requiring that they be *sensitive,* he does not mean, he says, that they must be observant of artistic worth—that would introduce circularity into the theory—but only that they must possess the relevant powers of sensory discrimination. What he means by the fourth requirement, that of *developed taste,* Goldman never really says, so far as I have been able to tell. Whatever he means, it too will have to be understood in such a way that the theory does not become circular; the concept of a critic of developed taste cannot be the concept of a critic who discerns the true artistic value of whatever be the work of art that she is engaging.

I suggest that Goldman's explanation of what he has in mind by an ideal critic falls far short of doing the work that his line of thought requires to be done. Notice that Goldman's explanation refers exclusively to the character traits that the critic must possess. One can press the question of

---

8. Goldman, *Aesthetic Value*, 21.
9. Goldman, *Aesthetic Value*, 22.
10. Goldman, *Aesthetic Value*, 22.
11. Goldman, *Aesthetic Value*, 22.

whether the ideal critic must have other character traits in addition to the four that Goldman has specified. But suppose that those four are sufficient for the critic to be ideal. The critic's possession of those four character traits does not guarantee the ideality that the theory requires.

For one thing, those character traits must also be employed in an ideal way. I may have all the character traits necessary to be an ideal critic for Stravinsky's *Mass*; but if, while listening to the *Mass*, I find myself distracted by the thought of some conflict that has arisen in my department, my satisfaction level might be low even though the Stravinsky *Mass* is one of the finest musical works of the twentieth century. And second: not only must the critic employ ideal character traits in an ideal way; she must employ them in ideal physical circumstances. If someone with ideal character traits is employing them in the ideal way while looking through rippled glass at some painting, whatever satisfaction she gets from doing so is no indicator whatsoever of the artistic worth of the painting. She may get great satisfaction from a work of minor worth and little satisfaction from a work of great worth.

In short, idealizing theories of artistic worth cannot stop with specifying the traits of an ideal critic; they must specify what constitutes an ideal episode of appreciation. And whenever someone points out the possibility of discrepancy between the satisfaction experienced by an ideal critic in an episode of appreciation, as these have been described up to that point, and the worth of some work of art—great satisfaction from a work of minor worth, or minor satisfaction from a work of great worth—the idealizing theorist must add to the specification of ideality so as to prevent the discrepancy between worth and satisfaction.

Now suppose I am right in understanding the idealizing theory as I have just now described it; namely, what drives the idealizing theorist to specify ideality as he does is the attempt to prevent discrepancy between degree of worth and intensity of satisfaction. Then two observations are in order. First, what reason is there to suppose that there is any end to this project of preventing discrepancy by specifying conditions of ideality? The goal is to specify, in a non-circular way, a type of critic and a type of episode of appreciation such that the degree of satisfaction that the critic finds in the episode necessarily matches the worth of the work; that would be the ideal type of critic and the ideal type of episode. The project is daunting, to put it mildly. But more than that: what reason is there to suppose that there is any such type of critic and type of episode of appreciation? May it not be the case that, no matter how these types are specified, if they are specified in a non-circular manner it will always be logically possible that the satisfaction experienced by a critic of that type in an episode of that type does not match the worth of the work?

My second observation concerns an even more fundamental point. There is something misguided about the whole project that the idealizing theorist is engaged in. He approaches the project having already recognized the worth of a good many works of art. What he then tries to do is identify a type of critic and a type of experience such that necessarily the satisfaction of the critic who experiences the work in that way matches the worth of the work. The theorist makes the judgment that works have worth of such-and-such a degree *before* he sets out to identify the type of critic and type of experience whose satisfaction-level will match the worth of the works. If he did not make those prior judgments of worth, he could not determine whether he had been successful in identifying the ideality conditions. But then the worth of works of art cannot consist in the degree of satisfaction that an ideal critic experiences in ideal circumstances.

The dogmatic slumber from which I was awakened by Donald Hall's remark was not merely an instrumentalist slumber; it was, I now think, an instrumentalist slumber of a particularly egregious sort.

The expressivist, the alethic, and the aestheticist traditions are alike in assuming that "engrossed contemplation"—a term that I borrow from Theodor Adorno—is the proper way to engage a work of art. A good deal of my writing about the arts has been devoted to opposing this assumption. There is, so I have argued, an enormous variety of ways in which works of art are meant to be engaged; they are not all meant to be engaged as objects of contemplation. Some are meant to serve as memorials of persons and events from the past whose memory we want to keep alive, some are hymns meant to be sung by a congregation, some are songs meant to function as rhythmic accompaniments to work, some are meant to enhance political protest, and so forth, on and on. And as for those works whose intended or preferred mode of engagement is contemplation, I argued that it was deeply misleading to describe such works as art for art's sake, or to say about them that they are useless—both of these being apothegms that occur frequently in the literature of modern aesthetics. Such works, so I said, are for the sake of satisfaction in contemplation; that is the use for which they are intended. There is no such thing as non-functional art, so I said; all art serves one or another of many different functions, engrossed contemplation being just one of many intended functions. And the worth of a work is to be determined by how well it serves the intended function. In short, mine was a relentlessly functionalist account of art coupled with a relentlessly instrumentalist account of artistic worth.

And now, with the preceding comments about instrumentalist accounts of artistic worth as background, let me lay out for you for the line of thought that Donald Hall's remark initiated in me. I shall approach the matter, as he did, from the side of the artist who makes the art rather than from the side of the public who engage the art. And, for no particular reason, let me formulate what I have to say in terms of music rather than poetry. The application to the other arts of the points that I make will be obvious.

I am not a composer. When it comes to making art, I have done no more than dabble a bit in architecture. So I stand to be corrected in what I say by those who are composers. But it appears to me that at the heart of the activity of composing are three constituent activities: imagining sound patterns, evaluating the sound patterns imagined, and choosing from among the sound patterns imagined on the basis of those evaluations. Works of music, so I suggest, are *traces* of imagining, evaluating, and choosing. Or to use a different metaphor: works of music are imagination, evaluation, and choice *embedded* in sound.

Let me say just a word about the imagination that goes into musical composition. This is not wild and unfettered imagination; it is not whatever some wandering muse happens to whisper in the composer's ear. It is both *schooled* and *guided*. By *schooled* I mean that the composer's imagining of sound-patterns is shaped by the sound-patterns he has previously heard, including especially the sound-patterns of works of music he has heard. Bach did not imagine sound-patterns rather like those in Stravinsky's *Rite of Spring* but discard them on the grounds that he was waiting for something better to come to mind. Given how his imagination had been schooled, he never imagined such sound-patterns—or at least it is most unlikely that he did. By *guided* I mean that the composer will usually not just sit down to compose music but will have requirements or parameters that he wants to satisfy. He wants to compose a piano sonata, he wants to compose a song to fit the words of some poem that moves him, and so forth. And in good measure, his imagination will follow this guidance. I find it both wonderful and mysterious that our human imagination can be guided in this way. A few weeks back I sat down to think about what I would say in this talk that I am presently giving; thereupon, lo and behold, thoughts relevant to the talk came to mind, interspersed, of course, with other stray thoughts.

Let us move on to evaluation and choice. Suppose the composer has resolved to write a piano sonata—that is one of the principal requirements or parameters he has set for himself. Naturally he also wants it to be playable; so he will keep in mind the powers and limitations of the modern piano and the abilities of skilled performers. And he hopes that it will get performed, and that sometimes, when it is performed, there will be an audience that finds it rewarding to listen to. But here is my question: does he make his evaluations and choices by reference to what he expects will give greater satisfaction to anticipated audiences? Does he say to himself that passage A is likely to give greater satisfaction to audiences than passage B, so I'll go with A?

I feel sure that he does very little of this—those of you who are composers will have to tell me if I am wrong—if for no other reason than that the pleasure of audiences is fickle and unpredictable. I suggest that, for the most part, he evaluates and chooses as he does because he wants to compose a good sonata. He chooses this sound-pattern over that one because he thinks it makes for a better sonata. Sometimes he may be able to identify what it is about this sound-pattern that makes it better than that one; often he will not be able to do so. He senses that it is better, but he is not able to say why.

And now for the conclusion of the argument: when the composer evaluates sound-pattern A as making for a better sonata than sound-pattern B, and accordingly chooses A over B as part of his finished sonata, he is, so far as I can see, making a judgment of non-instrumental intrinsic worth. He is not making his evaluation and choice by reference to which of the two options will bring about more aesthetic pleasure.

Imagine a situation somewhat less pure than the one just described. Suppose the composer has accepted a commission from a quirky benefactor who wants him to compose a piano sonata that incorporates his old college fight song as one of its major themes—no different, really, from the long tradition of composers accepting commissions for variations on specified themes. Is the composer, in accepting this requirement and composing in accord with it, producing a work of purely instrumental worth?

Not so far as I can see. Earlier I represented him as resolved to compose a piano sonata; that resolution guided his imagination and entered into his evaluations and choices. I don't see that anything changes if the composer adopts the additional resolution to incorporate the benefactor's college fight song as one of his composition's major themes. His evaluations and choices are now guided by the resolution to compose an excellent piano sonata incorporating that theme. So far as I can see, it makes no difference where the composer's parameters come from—whether he decides all on his own to compose a piano sonata or whether someone commissions him to compose one, whether he decides all on his own to compose a piano sonata incorporating the melody of that fight song or whether someone commissions him to do so.

But, you say, isn't this sort of thing a prime example of what the eighteenth-century writers had in mind by art not come into its own? Isn't this what they had in mind by art in the service of interests extraneous to itself? Maybe. But I don't see that that militates against the conclusion that the composer, after settling on various parameters for what he wants to create—it is to be a piano sonata, it is to include a theme from Handel or from

Count Goldberg or from some quirky benefactor—proceeds then to make his evaluations and choices in terms of the intrinsic comparative worth of sound-patterns that fit the parameters.

In short, the conclusion to which I am led, by these reflections on the practice of composition, is that works of music have intrinsic, non-instrumental worth. If this is correct, then the next question is how we should think of the relation between the worth of works of music and the activity of attentively listening to them. If one rejects the instrumentalist view of artistic worth and holds that, in addition to whatever instrumental worth works of music may have, they also have intrinsic worth, then what is the connection between that worth, on the one hand, and, on the other hand, the satisfaction that is to be found in engrossed contemplation?

Well, if the work of music itself has intrinsic value, then, so it appears to me, the core value of the activity of listening to it does not lie in the *satisfaction* one experiences. Let us say that when a work of music is performed in our auditory presence, it is sonically presented to us. That sonic presentation opens up to us the possibility of perceptually attending to this entity of intrinsic worth, taking perceptual note of that in it which is of intrinsic worth. I think the core of what is worthwhile in the activity of contemplation is just the worth of becoming perceptually aware of something of intrinsic worth and of perceptually recognizing that in it which is of intrinsic worth. Of course, we are not innately capable of perceptually recognizing such worth; this is where music education enters the picture. We have to acquire what the eighteenth-century writers called "taste."

When all goes well in this activity of attending to something of intrinsic worth and taking perceptual note of that in it which is of worth, we experience the love of which Plato wrote in the *Symposium*; "eros" he called it in the original Greek. Love comes in various forms; *eros* is the sort of love that consists of attraction to something of worth. I now think that to describe this experience as "pleasure" is to trivialize it; to describe it as "joy" is only slightly better. I shall never forget the first time I heard a performance of Messiaen's *Quartet for the End of Time*. Was it *pleasure* I felt? Nonsense. *Joy*? I suppose so. But more precisely, it was *eros* I felt, love as attraction. I was drawn in, mesmerized.

My language has been convoluted. I have spoken of the work of music being sonically presented to us and of that sonic presentation opening up to us the possibility of attending perceptually to this entity of intrinsic worth—taking perceptual note of that in it which is of intrinsic worth. Let me explain why I have used such convoluted language.

In various of my writings, I have defended the view that a work of music does not exist only when being performed. Though performance is *basic* in a certain way to the existence of a work of music, there is not a straightforward connection between the existence of a performance and the existence of the work.

When one combines this thesis concerning the existence of works of music with the thesis that works of music have intrinsic worth, then one is naturally led to ask whether it is possible to attend to a work of music, and take note of that in which it is of intrinsic worth, without perceptually attending to a sonic presentation of it. I think the answer to that question is, Yes. After all, that is what is happening when the composer composes his work; he is not hearing a sonic presentation of it. And that is what is happening when those who are skilled at reading music read the score: by reading the score, they become acquainted with the work and aware of that in it which is of intrinsic worth.

I do still want to say that attention to some sonic presentation of the music has primacy among the various ways of engaging the work. But if works of music have intrinsic worth, if they exist even when not performed, and if some of us can gain knowledge of them without listening to performances of them, then I think we have to conclude that there is not some deep divide between attentively listening to some work of music, on the one hand, and reading the score and engaging in a scholarly study of it, on the other. These are different ways of attending to an entity of intrinsic worth. The scholarly study of some work of music, and the attentive listening to a performance, are on the same continuum.

Let me add that we should not assume that everything of intrinsic worth in works of music can be heard. Every now and then one comes across a composer describing what is going on in some passage of his music—obviously regarding this as something good about it—and then adding that probably this cannot be heard, not at least by most listeners; it can only be discerned by looking at the score. If this is correct, then what is intrinsically worthwhile in music goes beyond what can be discerned in perceptual attention. And why should this surprise us? Why should it not be the case that some of the things that are intrinsically good about sound-patterns go beyond the ability of our ears to catch? Sound-patterns have what one might call *intellectual* excellences as well as *auditory*. This, then, is yet another reason for holding that the worth of a work of music does not consist of its utility for bringing about pleasant auditory experiences.

One final point. As I mentioned earlier, the modern and contemporary tradition of philosophical aesthetics has focused almost all of its attention on one way of engaging art, that of engrossed contemplation. And philosophical theories about artistic worth have almost all assumed that the worth of works of art lies in the satisfaction experienced when submitting them to engrossed contemplation. The entities of intrinsic worth are those satisfying experiences, not the works.

I've been asking myself why it was that, until very recently, I went along with this way of thinking about the worth of those works of art intended for engrossed contemplation. I think it was for the following reason. I assumed that, when engrossed contemplation is the intended way of engaging some work of art, then the worth of the work is to be located in how well it serves that way of engaging it. And I assumed, in turn, that how well it serves that way of engaging it is to be determined by how much satisfaction is experienced by those who engage it in this way—with all the provisos that we discussed earlier concerning the right or ideal way to engage it, the right or ideal circumstances in which to do so, and the like.

I now think that this line of thought is fallacious; the assumptions just mentioned are mistaken. From the fact that engrossed contemplation is the intended way of engaging some work of art, it does not follow that its worth is determined by how well it serves as an object of engrossed contemplation; in particular, it does not follow that its worth is determined by how much satisfaction it gives when thus engaged. A way of engaging a work of art is not to be identified with a function that it serves.

An analogy may help. The way to use a hammer is to grasp it rather near the end of the handle and then swing it so that the iron head lands on the head of a nail. That is how a hammer is meant to be used. Its function, by contrast, is to drive nails into wood or some similar substance. One uses it in the intended way so as to achieve that function. And as to the worth of a hammer, that is determined by how well it serves the function when used in the intended way; its worth is most definitely not determined by how much satisfaction one experiences when grasping it rather near the end of the handle and swinging it so that its iron head lands on the head of a nail.

10

Art and the Formation of Just Persons[1]

What role, if any, can art play in the formation of persons who act justly and oppose injustice? That is my topic. Perhaps some of you have read Elaine Scarry's little book, *On Beauty and Being Just*. It is a fine book, engagingly written and handsomely published. Beauty is not the same thing as art. But in the course of discussing the relation of beauty to being just, Scarry says things about the relation of art to being just. Her take on the relationship is very different from mine. So I propose setting the context for the presentation of my own view by presenting hers as an illuminating contrast.

Scarry on Beauty and Being Just

Scarry notes that there has been a widespread banishing of beauty from the humanities in recent decades, and that this "has been carried out by a set of political complaints against" beauty.[2] Her aim in Part Two of her book is to respond to these complaints. "Beauty," she says, "is at the very least innocent of the charges against it, and it may even be the case that far from damaging our capacity to attend to problems of injustice, it instead intensifies the pressure we feel to repair existing injuries."[3]

As Scarry sees it, "the political critique of beauty is composed of two distinct arguments. The first claims that beauty, by drawing our attention, distracts us from attending to unjust social arrangements. It makes us inattentive, and therefore eventually indifferent, to the project of bringing about arrangements that are just. The second argument holds that when we stare

---

1. This essay is the revised text of the Brehm Lecture, given at Fuller Theological Seminary, November 3, 2009.
2. Scarry, *On Beauty and Being Just*, 57.
3. Scarry, *On Beauty and Being Just*, 57.

at something beautiful, when we make it an object of sustained regard, our act is destructive of the object. "This argument is most often prompted when the gaze is directed toward a human face or form."[4]

About these two arguments, Scarry makes the acute observation that whatever merit each has in and of itself, "they are unlikely both to be true since they fundamentally contradict one another. The first assumes that if our 'gaze' could just be coaxed over in one direction and made to latch onto a specific object (an injustice in need of remedy or repair), that object would benefit from our generous attention. The second assumes that generous attention is inconceivable, and that any object receiving sustained attention will somehow suffer from the act of human regard."[5]

Scarry doesn't say much about the second argument. Her attention is focused on the first; so mine will be as well. But I do want to make a few comments about the second argument.

I would state the argument rather differently from how Scarry states it. Her formulation of the argument is that when we stare at something beautiful, our act is destructive of the object. I think the argument is best understood as having two prongs, one prong pertaining to human beings and one to other things.

As it pertains to human beings, the argument is not, I think, that our gaze is *destructive* of the human being at whom the gaze is directed, but that it *wrongs* him or her. Among the examples she gives to make her point, those that make it most powerfully are not those in which our gaze is directed at someone beautiful—though no doubt we do sometimes wrong a beautiful person by staring at him or her—but those in which, often with the aid of a photographer, we subject a human being who is not beautiful to an aestheticizing gaze. The photographs by Diane Arbus, of human beings malformed in various ways, are an example of the point. I think a serious case can be made that these people have been wronged by the combination of Arbus photographing them and you and I now gazing at them in the photographs with aesthetic intent. Speaking for myself, I would strongly dislike being the subject of an Arbus photograph!

The other prong of the argument pertains to those cases in which the aestheticizing gaze finds beauty in trash—photographs taken from a half mile up of a city dump, photographs taken from close-up of peeling paint on a door in a ghetto, that sort of thing. Not infrequently, photographs of dumps taken from a distance, or of a rotted door from close up, are things of beauty. No more than in the first case is the aestheticizing gaze

4. Scarry, *On Beauty and Being Just*, 58.
5. Scarry, *On Beauty and Being Just*, 58–59.

destructive of the object; but neither, in this case, does it wrong the object. What merits concern is rather that the aestheticizing gaze conceals from us the ugliness, conceals from us the fact that this dump is a besmirching of the earth by the human beings whose detritus this is, conceals from us the fact that the ghetto is a place of squalor.

In short, I think that Scarry mis-formulates the second argument and thereby blunts its considerable force. That said, however, I want to focus the remainder of what I have to say on her response to the first argument, which says that attention to beauty distracts us from attending to unjust social arrangements. Her claim is that, to the contrary, beauty, rather than distracting us from justice, "assists us in our attention to justice."[6]

Her defense of this claim is threefold: she argues that there is a *deep analogy* between the *nature* of beauty and the *nature* of justice, she argues that there is a *deep similarity* between our *response* to beauty and our *response* to justice, and she argues that there is an *equivalence* between the *concern* that there shall be beauty in the world and the *commitment* to there being justice in the world. These analogies, similarities, and equivalences have the consequence, so she says, that attention to beauty evokes in us attention to the need for justice.

Let us begin with the *analogy* between the nature of beauty and the nature of justice. Beauty, as Scarry understands it, is grounded in symmetry, or as she often calls it, equality; and justice, so she says, is likewise constituted of symmetry or equality. She regards the phrase, "a symmetry of everyone's relation to one another,"[7] as descriptive of both beauty and justice. In the course of discussing this analogy, Scarry claims the existence of two other analogies in the region. She insists that attention to one instance of beauty exerts on the beholder a pressure to treat other instances of beauty with equal regard, this being analogous to the equal treatment that is a feature of justice; beautiful things, she says, "give rise to the notion of distribution."[8] And she holds that what she calls "the generous availability to sensory perception" of beauty is analogous to the equal distribution that constitutes justice.[9]

Putting these three analogies together, Scarry says that the "pressure" of beauty toward justice "comes from the object's symmetry, from

---

6. Scarry, *On Beauty and Being Just*, 86.
7. Scarry, *On Beauty and Being Just*, 95.
8. Scarry, *On Beauty and Being Just*, 95.
9. Scarry, *On Beauty and Being Just*, 110.

the corrective pressure it exerts against lateral disregard, and from its own generous availability to sensory perception."[10]

As to the *similarity* between our response to beauty and our response to justice, Scarry remarks that "at the moment we see something beautiful, we undergo a radical decentering."[11] "All the space formerly in the service of protecting, guarding, advancing the self (or its 'prestige') is now free to be in the service of something else."[12] Scarry doesn't actually complete the argument by claiming that attention to justice and injustice is likewise decentering; but clearly that is what she has in mind.

And as to the *equivalence* between the concern that there shall be beauty in the world and the commitment to justice, Scarry observes, first, that the former concern is manifested both when one "acts to protect or perpetuate a fragment of beauty already in the world" and when one acts "instead to supplement it by bringing into being a new object."[13] And she then observes that these

> two distinguishable forms of creating beauty—perpetuating beauty that already exists; originating beauty that does not yet exist—have equivalence within the realm of justice, as one can hear in John Rawls' formulation of what, since the time of Socrates, has been known as the "duty to justice" argument: we have a duty, says Rawls, "to support" just arrangements where they already exist and to help bring them into being where they are "not yet established."[14]

So what shall we say about these lines of argument for the conclusion that "beauty, far from contributing to social injustice . . . , or even remaining neutral to injustice as an innocent bystander, actually assists us in the work of addressing injustice"?[15] Let me first observe that what we have here is yet one more re-statement of classic Romantic claims concerning the power of art. With due allowance for the fact that *Romanticism* is by no means a sharply defined category, I think it can fairly be said that the Romantics were the first

---

10. Scarry, *On Beauty and Being Just*, 110.
11. Scarry, *On Beauty and Being Just*, 111.
12. Scarry, *On Beauty and Being Just*, 113.
13. Scarry, *On Beauty and Being Just*, 114.
14. Scarry, *On Beauty and Being Just*, 115. Scarry takes note of a second "feature shared by the kind of creation we undertake on behalf of beauty and the kind of creation we undertake on behalf of justice." This second feature is somewhat more complex than the first; explaining it would not contribute significantly to the reader's understanding of Scarry's line of thought.
15. Scarry, *On Beauty and Being Just*, 62.

to sense that, in the seventeenth and eighteenth centuries, there had emerged in Europe a quite new form of society and culture, call it *modernity*; and that they were also the first to claim that the essence of what was new was that modernity fractured old unities, this fracturing being driven mainly by the relentless and pervasive application of rationality. John Keats said of the new natural science that it "unweaves the rainbow";[16] the Romantics believed that modernity in general unweaves the rainbow.

Art is the exception, the Romantics claimed; art is the social "other." The artist employs imagination rather than rationality; and the work of art is an organic unity rather than a collection of fragments. This social "otherness" of art led the Romantics to ascribe salvific power to art; poetry, someone once remarked to me, "knits together the tattered fragments of our existence." When it came to explaining how, exactly, this salvific power works, the Romantics were always hazy. Somehow or other, engagement with art will energize us to mend the world.

Nothing that Scarry says suggests that she sees herself as standing in the line of the Romantics. But the telltale signs are all there. Injustice is disunity, inequality, asymmetry; beauty is unity, equality, symmetry. Art is thus the social "other." And attention to beauty will awake us to the injustice surrounding us and energize us to struggle against it, until society resembles beauty in its unity, equality, and symmetry. Beauty will save us if we but allow it to.

Let me not pull my punches. Beauty does *not* have the inherent salvific power that Scarry and her Romantic predecessors claim for it; attending to beauty does not inherently energize the beholder to struggle for justice. We have all known people who were intensely attentive to beauty but cared not a fig for justice; we have all heard about people who lived in large beautiful houses and worked in elegant offices but were mean and cruel. Historians tell us that a good many of the Germans who supervised concentration camps during the day attended concerts in the evening and expanded their art collections with paintings plundered from the occupied countries. And let us not forget that many of the artifacts whose beauty now mesmerizes us were created on the backs of indentured labor. Scarry nowhere takes note of this obvious objection to her thesis that attending to beauty has the inherent salvific power of energizing us to pursue justice; I have no idea why she does not take note of it.

I have used the phrase "inherent salvific power" a couple of times. The claims made by Scarry and her Romantic predecessors concerning the salvific power of attending to beauty and art are claims concerning its *inherent*

---

16. In his long poem, *Lamia*.

power. It is *those* claims that I contest, on the ground that they are patently false. Not for a moment do I deny that now and then, here and there, attention to art and beauty does energize us to seek justice. To understand how and why this happens, we have to get down into the trenches. We have to uncover what it is about particular works and types of works that gives them this potential—and what it is about particular viewers and types of viewers that actualizes this potential. We will discover nothing if we remain at the ethereal level of discussing what is inherently the case.

The Role of Certain Works of Art in the Struggle for Justice

Let me now get down into those trenches. Let me call attention to three roles art plays that sometimes energize the struggle for justice; these three are only a few of the many. And let me now re-configure the discussion, so that henceforth it is primarily about art and justice rather than about beauty and justice. My description of each of these roles will be brief—only enough for you to get the idea. Each could be elaborated into an essay, indeed, into a book.

No doubt some people struggle for justice out of a sense of duty; perhaps all of us do this some of the time. And some people struggle for justice because they believe that this is what good and virtuous people do. But if my own experience is any indication, in most people these motivations tend to be weak unless undergirded and reinforced by a quite different motivator, namely, *empathy*. The Samaritan was moved by empathy when he saw the mugged man lying at the side of the road; that is what led him to come to his aid.

And what evokes empathy? Perhaps empathy is evoked in some people by calm and dispassionate newspaper reports of someone's plight; possibly this is true for most of us some of the time. But once again, if my own experience is any indication, what mainly evokes empathy for some person or group of persons is having that person in his predicament, or those persons in their predicament, brought vividly before one. This vivid presentation may take the form of their actually being present to one, so that one sees their faces and hears their voices. Alternatively, it may take the form of seeing vivid photographs or films of them. Or it may take the form of their being made vivid to one by imaginative literature.

By the early 1970s I knew a good deal from newspaper reports about the plight under apartheid of the so-called blacks and coloreds in South Africa; but it was when I attended a conference in South Africa in 1975, and came face to face with so-called blacks and coloreds, that I was moved by empathy to speak and work for their liberation. In the early 1970s I also knew a good deal from newspaper reports about the plight of the Palestinians; but it was when I came face to face with Palestinians at a conference in 1978 that I was moved by empathy to speak and work for their liberation.

In these two cases, it was empathy evoked by face-to-face meetings that energized me to work for justice. But the point I want to make here is that visual representations and imaginative literature also sometimes evoke empathy in us for those who are wronged, and thereby energize us to struggle for justice.

Over the past several years I have made a point of asking people who teach nineteenth-century American literature whether they include Harriet Beecher Stowe's *Uncle Tom's Cabin* in their syllabus. I have learned that a few now do. Only a few, however. The reason *Uncle Tom's Cabin* is not included in the canon is that it doesn't measure up to our current aesthetic standards; it doesn't have enough of the beauty that Scarry talks about. The common charge is that it is too sentimental. Yet the novel was extraordinarily influential in the abolitionist movement. It is easy to see why: it made the plight of the slaves vivid to the reader. I read *Uncle Tom's Cabin* on my own when I was a young teenager; to this day I remember how my heart bled for Uncle Tom and how angry I was at his tormenter, Simon Legree.

Let me move on to a second role art plays whereby it sometimes energizes us to struggle for justice. "Remember Sharpeville" was a cry that echoed for decades in the South African liberation movement. Why so? Well, "Sharpeville" was the name of a village in which the South African police mowed down a large number of blacks who were peacefully protesting against their oppression; the year, as I recall, was 1960. The reason the cry was kept alive is that fundamental to the success of a liberation movement is keeping alive outrage over the injustices being protested; and one way to do that, in turn, is to keep alive the memory of the most egregious examples of those injustices. I must add at once that cries to remember—cries such as "Remember the Battle of the Boyne," "Remember the Alamo," and "Remember Sharpeville"—can also serve to keep alive the memory of merely perceived rather than real injustice, and to serve the cause of vengeance rather than the cause of justice.

To speak more generally: we human beings find it important to keep alive the memory of some person or event from the past—so as to honor that person or event, so as to keep outrage alive, and so forth. But we are forgetful. So we make things and do things as a memorial; we name the capital city "Washington" so as to honor and keep alive the memory of George Washington, we commission a Lincoln Memorial so as to honor and keep alive the memory of Abraham Lincoln, we paint nativity scenes so as to honor and keep alive the memory of the birth of Jesus, and so forth, on and on. And as my examples indicate, art is caught up in this activity of making and doing as a memorial. Many of the things that are made or done as a memorial are works of art, and conversely, many works of art are made or done as a memorial. They are memorial art. It is a role of art that has been almost entirely neglected by the tradition of modern aesthetics; but just a bit of reflection will make clear that it is, in fact, one of the most important and pervasive of all the roles that art plays in our lives.[17]

The point is this: works of memorial art often serve to keep alive the memory of outrageous breaches of justice; often in doing so they energize the struggle against present and future injustice. A work that comes to mind immediately here is Picasso's famous painting, *Guernica*. Another that comes to my mind is a sequence of poems by the contemporary Irish poet Micheal O'Siadhail, entitled *The Gossamer Wall: Poems in Witness to the Holocaust*.[18] Here are a few lines.

> *Destruction turns all their presence into absence*
> *unless some testimony breaks their infinite silence.*
> *In remembrance resides the secret of our redemption.*[19]

And here are just a few more:

> Neat millions of pairs of abandoned shoes
> Creased with mute presence of those whose
> Faces both stare and vanish . . .
> Friedländer, Berenstein Menasche, Blum.
> Each someone's fondled face. A named few.
> Did they hold hands the moment they knew?[20]

Poetry about the Holocaust poses in extreme form the danger I discussed earlier, of aestheticizing the horror and thereby wronging the victims. O'Siadhail is acutely aware of the danger; to my mind, he succeeds admirably in overcoming it.

Now for a third way in which art sometimes energizes the struggle for justice. This being Fuller Theological Seminary, I can safely assume that most of you participate in Christian worship with fair regularity. And knowing what I do about Christian worship, I can also safely assume that your

---

17. I discuss memorial art at some length in Part Four of, Wolterstorff, *Art Rethought*.
18. O'Siadhail, *The Gossamer Wall*.
19. O'Siadhail, *The Gossamer Wall*, 112.
20. O'Siadhail, *The Gossamer Wall*, 122.

participation in Christian worship has at least sometimes included your saying or singing of one or more of the Psalms.

This saying or singing of the Psalms in the liturgy is so familiar that we rarely stop to notice the quite extraordinary nature of what is going on. It is not like reciting a Shakespeare sonnet. In the small Minnesota town in which I grew up it was the practice to have an eighth grader recite Lincoln's Gettysburg Address as part of a program held in the auditorium of the local school on Memorial Day—in those days we called it Decoration Day. When I was an eighth grader, I was chosen for the honor. My saying or singing a psalm in the liturgy is quite unlike my reciting the Gettysburg Address.

In my *Divine Discourse* I developed the idea of saying something by *appropriating* what someone else has said or written, rather than oneself crafting new sentences for the purpose. That is what often happens within Scripture. Over and over St. Paul, for example, says what he wants to say by appropriating sentences from the Old Testament, sometimes altering them a bit. A good many New Testament scholars are bothered by the alterations; they speculate that Paul must have been going by memory rather than looking it up, and that his memory wasn't all that good. And they are bothered by the fact that quite often what Paul uses the sentence to say isn't the same as what the writer or editor of the Old Testament used it to say. Well, yes; that is what happens with appropriation.

When you and I say or sing the Psalms in the liturgy, we are not *reciting* them. We are instead *appropriating* the words of the Psalms to express our own praise, to make our own confession, etc. That often requires changing meanings and references. The name "Jerusalem," for example, rather than naming an ancient Near Eastern city, becomes a metaphor. Though let me add that the required alteration of meaning and reference cannot always be brought off. A Melkite priest in the Galilee, father Elias Chacour, once remarked to me that his congregation no longer used any of the psalms in which the name "Jerusalem" occurs. "Why is that?" I asked. I shall never forget his answer. "Because," he said, "when we come across the name 'Jerusalem,' we can't help but think of the Jerusalem down the road." That was the first time it occurred to me that the strategies required for our liturgical appropriation of the Psalms—treating some terms as metaphors, others as personifications, etc.—cannot always be brought off. There are situations in which we just can't do it, even though we know what has to be done. We don't then *recite* the psalm instead of appropriating it; we just don't say it.

And now for the point. The Psalms are poetry; they are works of art. And what happens in the liturgy when you and I appropriate the poetry of the Psalms for our own worship is that we find ourselves expressing a longing for justice, we find ourselves praying for justice, we find ourselves praising God for God's justice, and so forth. On some Sunday, for example, we find ourselves saying or singing the following words, in appropriation-mode rather than recitation-mode:

> Let me hear what God the LORD will speak,
>   for he will speak peace to his people,
>   to the faithful, to those who turn to him in their hearts.
> Surely his salvation is at hand for those who fear him,
>   that his glory may dwell in our land.
> Steadfast love and faithfulness will meet,
>   Rectitude and peace will kiss each other. (Ps 85:8–10)

For us to appropriate these words for our own worship, very few of the original meanings have to be changed. Indeed, it appears to me that none of the meanings have to be changed, only two of the references. When the psalmist used the words "his people," surely it was Israel that he was referring to. And when he used the words "our land," surely it was the land of Israel that he was referring to. Without even thinking about it, we change the references.

On another Sunday we find ourselves saying or singing the following words:

> Give the king your justice, O God,
>   and your rectitude to a king's son.
> May he judge your people with rectitude,
>   and your poor with justice . . . .
> May he defend the cause of the poor of the people,
>   give deliverance to the needy,
>   and crush the oppressor. (Ps 72:1–2, 4)

When you and I appropriate these words for our own worship we will, again without giving any thought to the matter, use "the king" as a metaphor for *ruler*. So far as I can see, however, that is the only change of meaning or reference that we have to make.

The Psalms are chock full of references to justice and doing right. The examples I have given are just two of many.

What I have said so far is that when we say or sing the Psalms in the liturgy, we appropriate those ancient words for our own worship. That makes it sound as if our modes and ways of worship are already well-formed and we just employ these words to actualize those modes and ways on a given occasion. But that is not how it is. When we appropriate the words of the Psalms in our worship, we are shaped and formed by those words. Our saying and singing of the Psalms shapes us into becoming lovers of justice. There is a subtle interplay between having our selves shaped by our appropriation of these words and our appropriation of these words being the actualization of our selves.

I know, of course, that the shaping into being a lover of justice which is effected by saying and singing the Psalms in the appropriation mode is not all-powerful; many are the dynamics in society and culture that shape us in the opposite way. Thus it is that there are those who say or sing the Psalms in church and are hostile to justice, both in theory and practice. That requires a certain mindlessness in one's saying or singing of the Psalms. But mindlessness in church is not unheard of.

We could discuss yet other ways in which art sometimes energize the struggle for justice—and ways in which it sometimes obstructs the struggle for justice. But I think enough has been said to make my point, and I hope enough has been said to stimulate your own reflections. Attentiveness to art does not *inherently* energize the struggle for justice; it is, rather, the *particular* ways art works that *sometimes* energize the struggle for justice.

A Right to Beauty

Allow me to make one final point, more about the relation of beauty, or aesthetic excellence, to justice than about the relation of art to justice. It is easy for those involved in service organizations to fall into the trap of thinking that to be a human being is to be a food-eater, a clothes-wearer, and a house-dweller; more often than not the people one is dealing with don't have enough food to eat or adequate clothes to wear; and more often than not their housing is squalid or non-existent. Food, clothing, and housing are urgent. Justice requires that we give them priority.

But when one stands back to reflect, it is clear that to be human is more, much more, than to be a food-eater, a clothes-wearer, a house-dweller. To be human is to be a creature who is treated with disrespect if he or she is deprived of education. To be human is to be a creature who is treated with disrespect if he or she is not allowed, to a considerable extent, to set her own course of life rather than having someone else set it for her. And to be human is to be a creature who is treated with disrespect if he or she is forced to live in aesthetic squalor. When social arrangements force some of our fellow human beings to live in poverty, those human beings are wronged, treated unjustly. But it is also true that when social arrangements force some of our fellow human beings to live in aesthetic squalor, those human beings are wronged, treated unjustly. Living in aesthetic decency is not an optional luxury; it is a moral right. Justice requires it.

11

Social Protest Art and the Graphic Art of Georges Rouault[1]

In this essay I will first describe the complex and problematic status of social protest art within the modern art world—more specifically, within the world of so-called *fine art*. I will then offer an analysis of how social protest art works. And I will follow that with some comments about the social protest art of Georges Rouault.

The Complex and Problematic Status of Social Protest Art in the Modern Art World

It is widely agreed that, in the early modern period, revolutionary changes took place in Western Europe in how the arts were engaged, created, and supported, and that those changes in practice both evoked and reflected important changes in how people thought about the arts. As with any such development, different stories can be told about what happened. The standard story, which I endorse, is that the most fundamental changes that took place in the seventeenth and eighteenth centuries were the emergence into prominence of a certain sort of contemplation as a way of engaging those media that we now call "the arts," and the corresponding emergence into prominence, among writers on the arts, of what the literary historian M. H. Abrams calls the *contemplation* model. I have written at length about these

---

1. This essay is the revision of the text of the Duke Initiative in Theology and the Arts Distinguished Lecture, given at Duke University, March 30, 2017, on the occasion of the opening of an exhibition of Georges Rouault's series of graphic art prints titled *Miserere et Guerre*. The exhibition was sponsored by the Duke Initiative in Theology and the Arts.

changes elsewhere.[2] Here, let me describe the two changes very briefly, the change in practice and the change in thought.

In the early modern period there emerged two features of society that enabled the change in practice to occur, namely, the emergence of a sizable middle class with a fair amount of leisure on its hands, and the emergence of a substantial civil society independent of both church and state. It was in the "space" created by these two phenomena, a middle class with considerable leisure on its hands and a substantial civil society, that a certain sort of contemplation came into prominence as a way of engaging works of the arts.

The people of Europe had always had what we now call "the arts." There was folk music and liturgical music, there were plays, there were sculptures on and in the cathedrals. Though some of this was accessible only to the aristocracy and the well-to-do, much of it was accessible to everyone. What was new in the early modern period in Western Europe was not that the arts came into being; the arts had always been there. Also not new was that the arts were engaged as objects of contemplation; that had always been one among the many ways in which they were engaged. What was new, to say it again, was the increasing prominence, among the rising middle class, of a certain sort of contemplation as a way of engaging works of the arts in civil society.

This change in how the arts were engaged gradually gave birth to our familiar modern art world with its public museums, concert halls, and libraries, its art critics and art historians, its market for works of the arts, and so forth.

As for the emergence of a new way of thinking about the arts, M. H. Abrams observes that before the eighteenth century writing about the arts was for the most part focused on practices of making. Writers employed what Abrams calls the *construction* model, offering advice to poets, musicians, painters, architects, and so forth, on how to practice their craft. But then, in the early eighteenth century, the emphasis in writings on the arts shifted from the artist who makes the work to the public who engage it. That was not enough, by itself, to make the contemplation model dominant, since there are many ways in which members of the public engage works of the arts other than as objects of contemplation. In focusing on contemplation, the writers were reflecting the change in practice that was taking place.

Several times over I have said that what was coming into prominence was a *certain kind* of contemplation. Throughout the eighteenth century, writers struggled to explain what kind of contemplation that was. It became common to call it "disinterested" contemplation; but writers had trouble

2. Wolterstorff, *Art Rethought*.

explaining precisely what they meant by "disinterested." The core idea seems clear, however. One's contemplation of something is disinterested if one engages in the act not so as thereby to bring about something other than the act of contemplation but for the sake of the act itself. Contemplating some work of the arts in order to learn something would be an example of contemplation that is interested rather than disinterested. One expects or hopes that one's contemplation will have the effect of expanding one's knowledge.

And why would one listen to some work of music just for the sake of listening, or look at a painting just for the sake of looking? Initially, writers gave a more or less traditional answer to this question: one did so for the experience of apprehending the beauty of the object. But once the concept of *the aesthetic* was introduced in the mid-eighteenth century, it became common to say that one did so for the pleasurable experience of apprehending the aesthetic qualities of the object. The academic discipline of aesthetics was born in the eighteenth century.

What I have done so far is present what I judge to be the standard story of the changes that took place in artistic practice and thought in the early modern period in Western Europe. But in my introductory remarks I said that my aim in this first part of my essay was to describe the complex and problematic status of social protest art in the modern art world; and nothing I have said thus far gives a clue as to the way in which its status is complex and problematic. To see in what way it is, let me now introduce what I call the *grand narrative concerning art in the modern world*. It is this narrative that, from the early nineteenth century until recently, shaped almost all philosophy of art, almost all art theory, almost all art criticism, and almost all art history.

Beginning in the mid-eighteenth century, the standard story of the changes in artistic practice and thought that took place in the early modern period was caught up within a yet-larger story concerning the art-historical and sociological significance of those changes. It is this larger story that I call *the grand narrative*. Let me discuss first the art-historical significance that the grand narrative attributes to the changes in artistic practice that took place, and then the sociological significance.

As for the art-historical significance, writers began to say that the increasing prominence of disinterested contemplation as a way of engaging works of the arts represented progress in the arts; more specifically, represented the arts finally *coming into their own*, finally attaining their historical destiny. The idea was that previously art had been in the service of values extrinsic to art: religious values, political values, educational values, entertainment values, and so forth. Now, at last, artists, along with viewers, listeners, and readers, were increasingly free to be guided in their endeavors by aesthetic values. Hegel makes the point forcefully. We have to rid ourselves, he says, of the "perverse" habit of asking "what is the *use*" of art?

> The perverseness of this [question] lies in the point that the work of art would then be regarded as aspiring to something else which is set before consciousness as the essential and as what ought to be; so that the work of art would only have value as a useful instrument in the realization of an end having substantive importance *outside* the sphere of art.[3]

As examples of aims having "nothing to do with the work of art as such" Hegel mentions "instruction, purification, improvement, pecuniary gain, endeavor after fame and fortune."

That was the art-historical significance that the grand narrative attributed to the changes taking place in artistic practice in the early modern period: the changes represented art coming into its own. Now for the sociological significance. A fundamental theme in the Romantic movement that emerged in the early nineteenth century was the theme of modernization as fragmentation. The Romantics identified what was happening in their day in the Western world as the emergence of a distinctly new period in the history of humankind: the *modern* period. And they said that characteristic of modernity was that tradition was being rejected and the old unities fractured: in politics, in religion, in the economy, everywhere. M. H. Abrams describes very well the Romantic lament.

> [The human being,] who was once well, is now ill, and . . . at the core of the modern malaise lies his fragmentation, dissociation, estrangement, or (in the most highly charged of these parallel terms) "alienation." The individual (so ran the familiar analysis) has become radically split in three main aspects. He is divided within himself, he is divided from other [human beings], and he is divided from his environment; his only hope for recovery (for those writers who hold out hope) is to find his way to a reintegration which will restore his unity within himself, his community with his fellow men, and his companionability with an alien and hostile outer world.[4]

Somewhat later Max Weber would argue that the driving force behind the fragmentation and rejection of tradition that the Romantics regarded as definitive of modernization was the spread of what came to be called *instrumental rationality*, that is, ends/means thinking.

---

3. Hegel, *Introductory Lectures on Aesthetics*, 61.
4. Abrams, *Natural Supernaturalism*, 145.

Most Romantics were of the view, however, that fragmentation was not all-conquering. Art, if created and engaged for pure aesthetic delight, is the exception. In art there is unity rather than fragmentation, imagination rather than instrumental rationality. Art, provided the interests of ordinary life are excluded, is socially other and socially transcendent. Clive Bell, in his 1913 book, *Art*, presented the view in over-the-top rhetoric. After noting that he sometimes found himself distracted from the aesthetic qualities of a work of art and instead attending to what is represented, he says,

> I know very well what has happened. I have been using art as a means to the emotions of life . . . . I have tumbled from the superb peaks of aesthetic exaltation to the snug foothills of warm humanity. It is a jolly country. No one need be ashamed of enjoying himself there. Only no one who has ever been on the heights can help feeling a little crest-fallen in the cosy valleys. And let no one imagine, because he has made merry in the warm tilth and quaint nooks of romance, that he can even guess at the austere and thrilling raptures of those who have climbed the cold, white peaks of art.[5]

Implicit in the art-historical and sociological significance attributed by the grand narrative to the changes in artistic practice taking place in the early modern period is a put-down of social protest art. I understand social protest art to be art created for the purpose of giving expression to, and energizing, protest against social injustice. The creator of social protest art has her eye on some social injustice and creates art that she judges will contribute to the righting of that injustice. She may also concern herself with the aesthetic qualities of her work. But given that she is using art as a means to aid in correcting some social injustice, her art will be regarded by those who embrace the grand narrative as regressive and ensnared in the instrumental rationality characteristic of modernity. There is nothing in principle wrong with such art, so it is said. But it is art in bondage, art not come into its own, art shaped by means/end thinking.

The terms I used to describe the status of social protest art within the modern art world, shaped as it is by those who embrace the grand narrative, were "complex" and "problematic." Nothing I have said so far suggests anything complex or problematic about that status. The grand narrative implies a put-down of social protest art as regressive and ensnared in instrumental rationality. Nothing complex or problematic in that.

So something more has to be said. Those who embraced the grand narrative did not only say that art created for aesthetic contemplation is

---

5. Bell, *Art*, 32–33.

socially other and transcendent; they typically added that such art is inherently critical of society. By virtue of being socially other than, and transcendent to, our fragmented and rationalized society, art points a critical finger at that society. The creator of art for aesthetic contemplation does not have her eye on some social injustice to whose elimination she aims to contribute. Her art is not, in that way, social protest art. It is, nonetheless, critical of what modernization has wrought—inherently critical. Here is how the neo-Marxist Herbert Marcuse made the point in his work, *The Aesthetic Dimension*:

> The radical qualities of art, that is to say, its indictment of the established reality and its invocation of the beautiful image of liberation, are grounded precisely in the dimensions where art *transcends* its social determination and emancipates itself from the given universe of discourse and behavior while preserving its overwhelming presence.... The inner logic of the work of art terminates in the emergence of another reason, another sensibility, which defy the rationality and sensibility incorporated in the dominant social institutions.
>
> Under the law of aesthetic form, the given reality is necessarily *sublimated*: the immediate content is stylized, the "data" are reshaped and reordered in accordance with the demands of the art form, which requires that even the representation of death and destruction invoke the need for hope—a need rooted in the new consciousness embodied in the work of art. Aesthetic sublimation makes for the affirmative reconciling component of art, though it is at the same time a vehicle for the critical, negating function of art.[6]

There is another way in which the status of social protest art within the modern art world is more complex and problematic than would at first appear. Consider Picasso's painting *Guernica*, Benjamin Britten's *War Requiem*, and John Steinbeck's novel *Grapes of Wrath*. Each of these has a secure place within the canon of great twentieth-century art, that is, within the canon of those who embrace the grand narrative. Yet each is, unmistakably, a work of social protest art; each has some specific social injustice in view against which it is protesting.

So what is going on? Given the put-down of social protest art implicit in the grand narrative, how can these works be accepted into the canon of great twentieth-century art?

---

6. Marcuse, *The Aesthetic Dimension*, 6–8.

It is the coming together of two factors that explains the apparent anomaly. First, each of these artists was a celebrated member of the modern art world. As such, each of them would have been aware of the put-down of social protest art by the grand narrative. But each of them also found himself deeply shaken by some social injustice. So they pushed back against the put-down. They refused to be intimidated. And in general, artists themselves have been less in the thrall of the grand narrative than those who think and write about the arts.

The second factor at work, in the acceptance of *Guernica*, *The War Requiem*, and *Grapes of Wrath* into the canon, is that the aesthetic quality of these works is indisputable. No matter that it was clearly Steinbeck's aim to evoke revulsion for the predatory practices of the large companies buying up Oklahoma farmland in the 1930s; the literary qualities of the novel were unmistakable. To those who embrace the grand narrative it is neither here nor there that *Grapes of Wrath* is a social protest novel; its literary qualities call for its conclusion within the canon.

How Social Protest Art Works

In my *Art Rethought* I argue that the grand narrative should be rejected along with its implicit put-down of social protest art. I reject the claim that social protest art is regressive. Here I shall refrain from rehearsing my argument and instead move on to an analysis of how social protest art works. For this, we need some understanding of the basic structure of social justice movements.

Injustice comes in many forms. If I am treated rudely by the receptionist in the health clinic, I am wronged, treated unjustly. Such individual wrongings or injustices, important as they are for the person involved, are not the concern of social justice movements. Social justice movements are concerned with systemic injustices, those injustices that are the result of social practices or laws, or of how laws are enforced or not enforced. The goal of social justice movements is to stop those systemic sorts of injustices, to do what is possible to ensure that they do not happen in the future.

We can distinguish four main stages or components of social justice movements. Often these overlap.

> (1) Members of the public are *awakened to*, or *reminded of,* the fact that certain people are suffering in a certain way.
> (2) Members of the public are given a *social justice analysis and critique* of the situation. They become aware that the cause of the suffering is not misfortune but social injustice.

(3) Members of the public become *emotionally engaged* with the victims and/or the perpetrators: they feel empathy with the victims and anger at those who engage in the practices or uphold or subvert the laws.

(4) Members of the public are *mobilized* to correct the situation. Almost always this includes *bringing pressure* to bear on the perpetrators to stop doing what they are doing.

It is especially to the first three of these components that social protest art makes a contribution: it alerts members of the public to the presence among them of suffering people, it gets them to realize that social injustice is the cause of the suffering, and it evokes emotional engagement with the victims and/or the perpetrators. The question before us is this: how do works of art do these things? How do they alert members of the public to suffering? How do they identify social injustice as the cause of the suffering? How do they evoke emotional engagement with the victims and/or the perpetrators?

I judge that representational art—fiction, drama, film, representational painting and sculpture—works quite differently in these respects from how non-representational art works. What I mean by "representational" art is art in which a world is projected for our imagining—a world containing persons, animals, cities, rivers, events, and so forth. Since Rouault's prints are obviously representational, let me focus on how representational art works as social protest art.

And rather than dealing exclusively in generalities, let me work with a specific example and generalize from there.

Though I have my eye on Rouault's prints, I judge that the workings of social protest art are somewhat easier to identify in the case of novels than in the case of representational visual art. So let me take a novel as my example. *Uncle Tom's Cabin* is indubitably the best known and also the most effective social protest novel ever written; so let me work with it.

All novels project a world for the reader to imagine, a world containing persons, along with houses, animals, rivers, cities, streets, and so forth. They invite and enable us to imagine persons of certain sorts in situations of certain sorts. What gives the novel its peculiar power is that it invites and enables us to sense *what it is like* to be the persons we imagine, what it is like on the inside, as it were. As Martha Nussbaum puts it in her discussion of the novel: the novel "describes the events of life not from an external perspective of detachment . . . but from within, as invested with the complex significance with which human beings invest their own lives."[7] "The inner life of

---

7. Nussbaum, *Poetic Justice*, 27.

each [character] is displayed as having psychological depth and complexity."[8] Good journalism does some of this, but not much.

In the case of social protest novels, the novel invites and enables us to imagine human beings undergoing suffering of a certain sort and to imagine other human beings perpetrating that suffering, doing so in such a way that we sense what it is like to be such human beings. *Uncle Tom's Cabin* invites and enables us to imagine a Mr. Shelby sort of person; we sense what it is like to be a slave owner who is willing to sell off his most prized slaves in order to keep his farm afloat. It invites and enables us to imagine an Uncle Tom sort of person; we sense what it is like to be ripped away from one's family and put up for sale on an auction block. It invites and enables us to imagine a Simon Legree sort of person; we sense what it is like to be sadistically cruel.

Most readers of *Uncle Tom's Cabin* at the time of its publication automatically identified the suffering experienced in the world of the work as caused by social injustice. The moral convictions and sensitivity they brought to their reading of the novel led them to make that judgment without even thinking about it. And so it is in general: for a novel to work as a social protest novel, readers must bring to their reading of the novel moral convictions and a moral sensitivity that leads them to judge that the suffering depicted is the result of social injustice. John Steinbeck's *Grapes of Wrath* worked as a social protest novel because readers readily identified as unjust the way in which large corporations in the world of the work were buying up farmland in Oklahoma and causing mass poverty.

What has to be added is that almost always there will be some readers of a social protest novel who do not bring to their reading the requisite moral sensitivity. The response of some readers to *Uncle Tom's Cabin* was that, though the suffering depicted was certainly regrettable, there was nothing to be done about it that would not make matters worse. Stowe has some characters in the novel defend the institution of slavery in exactly those terms. For such readers, the novel did not work as a social protest novel.

To function as a social protest novel *Uncle Tom's Cabin* had to do something more as well, namely, evoke emotional engagement with the persons imagined: empathy, pity, and the like with those who were suffering; anger, revulsion, and the like at those causing the suffering. The novel was extraordinarily successful in this regard. A writer of the time, William Lloyd Garrison, described his response this way: "we confess to the frequent moistening of our eyes and the making of our heart grow liquid as water, and trembling every nerve within us, in the perusal of incidents and scenes so

---

8. Nussbaum, *Poetic Justice*, 27.

vividly depicted in her pages."⁹ And here is how a historian writing recently, David Reynolds, summarized the response of readers at the time:

> Sympathetic readers of *Uncle Tom's Cabin* were thrilled when the fugitive slave Eliza Harris carried her child across the ice floes of the Ohio River and when her husband George fought off slave catchers in a rocky pass. They cried over the death of the angelic little Eva and were horrified by the fatal lashing of Uncle Tom, the gentle, strong enslaved black man. . . . They sneered at the selfish hypochondriac Marie St. Clare and loathed the cruel slaveowner Simon Legree.[10]

My argument thus far has been that a novel functions as a social protest novel by inviting and enabling us to imagine suffering human beings and perpetrators of suffering whom we engage morally and emotionally, empathizing with the former as victims of injustice, feeling anger toward the latter as perpetrators of injustice.

We must now add a quite different consideration to our analysis. Social justice movements aim to end some injustice in the actual world, not some injustice in the projected world of a work of art. If a work of fiction is to serve the cause of social justice, the reader's moral and emotional engagement with the persons in the projected world of the novel must somehow shape her moral and emotional engagement with persons and their doings in the actual world.

Specifically, given, as we saw earlier, that moral empathy with the victims of injustice in our actual world is crucial to social justice movements, moral empathy with the victims of injustice in the projected world of the novel must somehow evoke or enliven moral empathy with flesh-and-blood victims of injustice in the actual world. And given that moral anger at the perpetrators of injustice in our actual world is crucial to social justice movements, moral anger at the perpetrators of injustice in the projected world of the novel must somehow evoke or enliven moral anger at flesh-and-blood perpetrators of injustice in the actual world. *Transference*, as I call it, must take place: transference of emotional and moral engagement from imagined persons in the projected world of the work to real persons in the actual world.

What accounts for such transference? The combination of two phenomena. First, the projected world of the novel must be substantially true to reality with respect to the suffering depicted and the causes thereof; and second, readers must believe that it is substantially true to reality in those

9. Quoted in Reynolds, *Mightier Than the Sword*, 130.
10. Reynolds, *Mightier Than the Sword*, xi.

respects. This combination, of the projected world of the work being substantially true to reality in the relevant respects and the reader believing that it is, awakens the reader to features of the actual world of which she was previously unaware, or heightens her sensitivity to those features in case she was already somewhat aware of them. It is this awakening and enlivening of sensitivity that results in moral and emotional transference from the projected world to the actual world.

The original readers of *Uncle Tom's Cabin* empathized with the victims of slavery in the projected world of the novel and felt moral anger at those, in the world of the work, who operated and benefited from the system. Believing that slavery in the projected world of the novel was substantially true to slavery in the American South of the time, they were awakened or newly sensitized to the realities of real-life slavery. Thereupon they found themselves feeling moral empathy for the victims of slavery in the actual world and moral anger at those who operated and benefited from the system.

Rouault's *Miserere et Guerre* as Social Protest Art

I turn now to Rouault's powerful series of fifty-eight prints, *Miserere et Guerre*.[11] That this is social protest art is unmistakable. Yet the series was meant to be displayed in museums and art galleries; today they are to be found in the print collections of museums. Thus Rouault's series joins Picasso's *Guernica*, Britten's *War Requiem,* and Steinbeck's *Grapes of Wrath*, as a push-back against the put-down of social protest art by the grand narrative. The series has what I called the "complex and problematic status" of being created to express and evoke social protest while being accepted into the canon of early twentieth-century graphic art on aesthetic grounds.

The fifty-eight prints are a unit, a whole. Individual prints can, of course, be viewed in isolation; many of them, when so viewed, are deeply moving. But they illuminate each other and acquire their distinct power only when viewed together. Plate #5, "Alone in this life of pitfalls and malice," and plate #6, "Are we not slaves?" are powerful in their own right: moving depictions of two sorrowing human beings. But when we move on to the next print, plate #7, "Believing ourselves kings," we interpret #5 and #6 in the light of #7. The persons depicted in #5 and #6 are not just unfortunate; they are victims, victims of the person so bitingly depicted in plate #7 and of others like him, victims of injustice. Conversely, we interpret plate #7 in the light of plates #5 and #6. Viewing plate #7 all by itself, we don't know quite what to make of its ferocity. Is it hatred of royalty that

11. Images of Rouault's prints are readily accessible on the internet.

is being expressed? Perhaps. But if so, why? Viewing #7 after #5 and #6 we know how to interpret it: this is the perpetrator of injustice. Throughout the series, images of sorrow and suffering alternate with images of arrogance, viciousness, and self-satisfaction, the former interpreting the latter and the latter interpreting the former.

Another distinctive feature of the series is that images of sorrowing and suffering human beings alternate with images of Christ suffering, in this case too, the former interpreting the latter and the latter interpreting the former (#20, #21, #57). This is not the Jesus meek and mild of the late Romantics, nor is it the Christ all-powerful of Eastern Orthodox iconography. This is Christ suffering, suffering along with those who suffer, sharing in their suffering. Their suffering has religious import. This is both social protest art and religious art, each interpreting the other.

When one first looks at plate #30, John baptizing Jesus, one thinks that here we have an image of Jesus from which suffering is absent. But then one reads the title, a quotation from Paul's letter to the Romans, "as many of us as were baptized into Christ Jesus were baptized into his death," and a cloud is cast over the otherwise serene scene: Christ's death is in prospect. The next plate, plate #31, depicts the crucifixion.

Not only do the images interpret each other; the titles Rouault has attached to the plates also interpret the images. Philosophers of art have debated whether the title of an artwork is part of the work. I think the answer in some cases is yes and in some cases is no. The words "Symphony No. 5," written at the top of a composer's score, are not part of the work; they are nothing more than a label attached to the score for ease of reference. By contrast, the titles Rouault has attached to his prints are, in each case, part of the work; they interpret the image.

I mentioned that the title of plate #30, "as many of us as were baptized into Christ Jesus were baptized into his death," casts a cloud over what would otherwise be seen as the serene depiction of Jesus' baptism. The title of the next plate, plate #31 depicting the crucifixion, is likewise significant. The cross is flanked on both sides by people in postures of devotion and the title is, "love one another." Now we know what to make of the multiple images of Jesus suffering: it is out of love that Jesus suffers with the suffering.

When discussing plates #5, #6, and #7, I noted that when we interpret the images in plates #5 and #6 in the light of the image in plate #7, we interpret them not just as sorrowing and suffering human beings but as victims of injustice. The titles of #5 and #6 already suggested that interpretation, however. The title of #5 is: "Alone, in the life of pitfalls and malice." Note well: not just "pitfalls," but "pitfalls and malice." The title of plate #6 is: "Are we not slaves?" These are victims of malice and oppression. And now we know how to interpret more precisely the face in plate #7: this is a face of malice, more specifically, the face of arrogant malice. The sarcastic title is: "Believing ourselves kings."

The images in *Miserere et Guerre* are confrontational. In most cases, the image consists of just one human being, usually with no background, thus nothing to distract from the figure, drawn with broad black brush strokes, very little detail, often filling the space of the print. The power of the images comes, in good measure, from this up-front, confrontational style, a style very much like that of the German artist Käthe Kollwitz in the prints depicting human suffering that she produced between the two world wars.

In my analysis of how a novel functions as social protest art, I suggested that it does so by virtue of three things taking place in the interaction between persons in the world of the work and the reader: the novel invites and enables the reader to imagine human beings of a certain sort in certain kinds of situations, it evokes moral and emotional engagement with those imagined human beings, and transference of moral and emotional engagement takes place from persons in the projected world of the work to persons in the actual world by virtue of the world of the work being true to reality in relevant respects and the reader believing that it is. Rouault's prints function as social protest art in the same way.

Return to print #5. I described the image there as the image of a sorrowing and suffering human being. I described it that way because that is what the image invites and enables me to imagine. The title, "Alone, in this life of pitfalls and malice," also invites me to imagine such a human being. But before I read the title I was already imagining a sorrowing and suffering human being. The image by itself did the work. How so? By depicting how such a human being looks: bent over, stooped, sagging.

Let me flesh out a bit how this works. Thomas Reid, the eighteenth-century Scots philosopher, has a fascinating discussion in one of his books of what he called "natural signs" of the body. Natural signs are "certain features of the countenance, sounds of the voice, and gestures of the body, [which] indicate certain thoughts and disposition of mind."[12] "Nature hath established a real connection" between these.[13]

The question that interested Reid was: What enables us to interpret these natural signs? Do we acquire the ability from extended experience, as we learn that smoke is a sign of fire? Or is the ability, in its basic contours, innate? Reid argued for the latter account. "When I see the features of an expressive face, I see only figure and color variously modified. But,

12. Reid, *Inquiry into the Human Mind*, V.iii.
13. Reid, *Inquiry Into the Human Mind*, VI.xxiv.

by the constitution of my nature, the visible object brings along with it the conception and belief of a certain passion or sentiment in the mind of the person."[14] I think Reid was right about that. But whether or not he was right, we do have the ability to infer states of the self from signs of the body. That is what is going on when I interpret the slumping sagging body depicted in plate #5 as that of a sorrowing, suffering human being. And it is worth noting how many of the images in *Miserere et Guerre* are of slumping, sagging, drooping bodies.

What supports my interpreting the "natural signs" of the body in plate #5 as that of a sorrowing, suffering human being is the formal expressive qualities of the image. Suppose one momentarily ignores the image in plate #5, attending just to the contour of the lines, and then asks oneself whether this is expressive of joy or of sorrow, I think everyone would say, "of sorrow."

Once one has imagined a sorrowing, suffering human being, I think one would have to be hard-hearted indeed not to become emotionally engaged, not to feel at least a twinge of pity and empathy—especially given what I have called the "confrontational" character of this and other images. The person is right in front of me, not off in the distance somewhere. Philosophers have written at length trying to explain why it is that we respond emotionally to imagined fictional characters; it remains a puzzle. But nobody doubts that we do respond emotionally.

As for what it is that effects the moral analysis and judgment that what is depicted is not just an unfortunate human being but one who is the victim of injustice, in part this response is evoked by the title: "Alone, in this life of pitfalls and malice." But as I observed earlier, when we move along in the series to plate #7, with its image of a huge leering face, it is impossible not to interpret the person depicted as the perpetrator of the suffering we have just seen in plate #5.

What remains to consider is how transference of moral and emotional engagement takes place. But before I get to that, let me make just a few remarks about the images in Rouault's prints of nasty, arrogant, self-satisfied human beings. In these cases, too, it is our reading of the natural signs of the body, reinforced by the formal expressive qualities of the image, that does the work. In each case, the people depicted are standing straight, holding their heads high. In some cases the body language is that of arrogance; in some cases, that of self-importance; in some cases, that of cruelty. Those are the sorts of persons that the images and the titles invite and enable one to imagine. One would have to be morally obtuse not to condemn them, emotionally impaired not to feel revulsion.

14. Reid, *Essays on the Intellectual Powers of Man*, VI.v.

Now for the matter of transference. Rouault drew the images for most of the prints in the years 1914 to 1918. The images were then laboriously transferred to copper plates, the printing finally completed in 1927. In an edition that I own of reproductions of the series there is a preface by Rouault in which he speaks of "these times of bitterness and offence in which we seem to live today." I don't know much about the state of French society between 1914 and 1927, but I know enough to know that they were indeed "times of bitterness and offence." There was widespread suffering, social injustice was rampant, judges were corrupt, clowns were mocked. It would have been as natural for viewers of Rouault's prints at the time to make the transference of moral and emotional engagement from imagined persons in the projected worlds of the prints to persons in actual world as it was for readers at the time of publication of *Uncle Tom's Cabin* to make the transference from projected world to actual world.

Our time and place—the US in 2017—are very different from France in the early decades of the twentieth century. So the question arises: have the prints in the series lost their function as social protest art? Have they now been fully absorbed into the art world, to be enjoyed for their aesthetic qualities and treated as an episode in the history of stylistics?

It is possible that there are some aesthetes of the Clive Bell type whose engagement with these prints is purely aesthetic. But I would guess that my response is typical. I find myself deeply moved when looking at these prints, moved to empathy when looking at those depicting suffering, moved to revulsion when looking at those depicting arrogance and cruelty. I do take note of, and enjoy, their aesthetic qualities. But for me, a purely aesthetic engagement is impossible.

Notice that this does not, however, answer our question, as to whether they have lost their function as social protest art. For these prints to function as social protest art, transference, as I call it, has to take place, transference of moral and emotional engagement with imagined persons in the worlds of the prints to moral engagement with live persons in the actual world. The fact that I feel empathy and revulsion for the persons in the projected worlds of these works does not establish that transference takes place.

I judge that, for many of us, transference does take place. Though American society today is quite different from French society in the early twentieth century, nonetheless there are also deep similarities, so that the way in which the prints depict human beings is very nearly as true to social reality in our place and time as it was to social reality in Rouault's place and time, and most of us know that it is. So we come away from our viewing feeling intuitively that we have been viewing a visual expression of injustice in our society and finding ourselves newly sensitized to such injustice.

Liturgy

12

Sacrament as Action, Not Presence

Sign-Agency in Aquinas and God-Agency in Calvin

Consider a standard medieval explanation of what constitutes a sacrament—for example, that of Thomas Aquinas. A sacrament, says Aquinas, is a *sign of a sacred reality*. He adds, by way of elaborating a few of the assumptions behind that formula, that "the term 'sacrament' is properly applied to that which is a sign of some sacred reality pertaining to men; or—to define the special sense in which the term 'sacrament' is being used in our present discussion of the sacraments—it is applied to that which is a sign of a sacred reality inasmuch as it has the property of sanctifying men."[1] Now compare that to the definition of sacrament which John Calvin gives at the opening of his discussion of sacraments in the *Institutes:* a sacrament, says Calvin, "is an outward sign by which the Lord seals on our consciences the promises of his good will toward us in order to sustain the weakness of our faith; and we in turn attest our piety toward him in the presence of the Lord and of his angels and before men."[2]

Though the differences between these two definitions are striking, some of those differences do not really make any difference. Sacraments are for the purpose of sustaining the weakness of our faith, says Calvin. Aquinas would have no disagreement with that—not, at least, if he understood Calvin's understanding of *faith;* he just happens not to build it into his definition of "sacrament". Then there is Calvin's claim that the sacraments are, secondarily, attestations of piety. Though I do not think Aquinas would quite want to endorse that, he would have no objection to saying something similar.

---

1. Aquinas, *Summa Theologiae*, 3a.60.2.
2. Calvin, *Institutes*, IV.xiv.1.

Where my interest lies in this essay is a desire to call attention to, and reflect on, a difference between the two accounts which does not strike us at first, because it belongs to the underlying conceptuality of the definitions rather than to the details I have emphasized in the previous paragraph. Let me rephrase the definitions just a bit so as to highlight the difference I have in mind. A sacrament, says Aquinas, is a sign that both signifies a sacred reality and effects sanctification in human beings, or to adapt an Augustinian formula, which was a favorite of the tradition: a sacrament is a sign that effects in human beings that sacred reality which it signifies. Now, by contrast, Calvin: a sacrament is a sign whereby God seals God's promises to us so as thereby to sustain our weakness. Or as he would also be willing to put it: a sacrament is a sign whereby God effects in us the promise which God seals to us with that sign. Speaking specifically of the Eucharist, Calvin says that in "the sacred mystery of the Supper," God "inwardly fulfills what he outwardly designates."[3]

You see the difference: in Aquinas it is *the sign* that is the agent: the sign inwardly effects what the sign outwardly signifies. In Calvin, it is *God* who is the agent: God inwardly fulfills by way of the sign what God outwardly designates with the sign.

Now I do not by any means wish to contend that Calvin never used the language of sign-agency in his discussion of sacraments, that he always and only used the language of God-agency. Though the God-agency language is clearly dominant, he does, not at all surprisingly, every now and then speak of the signs as doing things. Furthermore, immediately after he has given the definition I cited, along with another briefer one that seems to me very unsatisfactory for his purposes, he says:

> Whichever of these definitions you may choose, it does not differ in meaning from that of Augustine, who teaches that a sacrament is "a visible sign of a sacred thing," or "a visible form of an invisible grace," but it better and more clearly explains the thing itself. For since there is something obscure in his brevity, in which many of the less educated are deceived, I have decided to give a fuller statement, using more words to dispel all doubt.[4]

Calvin strikes me as somewhat disingenuous here, probably out of respect for Augustine. He represents himself as merely clarifying points left obscure in Augustine's definition. He was indeed clarifying points left obscure. I suggest, however, that he was at the same time altering the

---

3. Calvin, *Institutes*, IV.xvii.5.
4. Calvin, *Institutes*, IV.xiv.1.

fundamental conceptuality of thinking about the sacraments from a sign-agency conceptuality to a God-agency conceptuality.

This use of the God-agency conceptuality, as I am calling it, became standard fare in the Reformed confessions. Let me give you a sampling. You will have to put up with some sixteenth-century verbosity! The Reformed Gallican Confession of 1559, apparently written by Calvin himself, begins its account of the sacraments [§34] ambiguously, but then resolves the ambiguity in the God-agency direction. The account runs like this:

> the sacraments are added to the Word for more ample confirmation, that they may be to us pledges and seals of the grace of God, and by this means aid and comfort our faith, because of the infirmity which is in us, and that they are outward signs through which God operates by his Spirit, so that he may not signify any thing to us in vain.[5]

The Scots Confession of 1560, going rather aggressively out of its way to repudiate the accusation of Zwinglianism, says that the sacraments

> were instituted by God . . . to exercise the faith of his children, and by participation of the same sacraments, to seal in their hearts the assurance of his promise, and of that most blessed conjunction, union and society, which the elect have with their Head, Jesus Christ. And thus we utterly damn the vanity of they that affirm sacraments to be nothing else but naked and bare signs. No, we assuredly believe . . . that in the Supper rightly used, Christ Jesus is so joined with us, that he becomes very nourishment and food of our souls.[6]

The Second Helvetic Confession of 1566, at the beginning of the chapter dealing with the sacraments says:

> Sacraments are mystical symbols, or holy rites, or sacred actions, ordained by God himself, consisting of his Word, of outward signs, and of things signified: whereby he keeps in continual memory and recalls to mind, in his Church, his great benefits bestowed upon man; and whereby he seals up his promises, and outwardly represents, and, as it were, offers unto our sight those things which inwardly he performs unto us, and therewithal strengthens and increases our faith through the working of God's Spirit in our hearts; lastly, whereby he does separate us from all other people and religions, and

---

5. Schaff, *The Creeds of the Evangelical Protestant Churches*, 378–79.
6. Schaff, *Creeds*, vol. 3, 467–68.

> consecrates and binds us wholly unto himself and gives us to understand what he requires of us.[7]

And the Belgic Confession of 1561:

> our gracious God, on account of our weakness and infirmities, hath ordained the sacraments for us, thereby to seal unto us his promises, and to be pledges of the good will and grace of God towards us, and also to nourish and strengthen our faith, which he hath joined to the word of the gospel, the better to present to our senses, both that which he signifies to us by his Word, and that which he works inwardly in our hearts, thereby assuring and confirming in us the salvation which he imparts to us. For they are visible signs and seals of an inward and invisible thing, by means whereof God worketh in us by the power of the Holy Ghost.[8]

Later, in its article on the Holy Supper this same Confession gives the most crisp expression of the God-agency conceptuality that I know of when it says that God "works in us all that he represents to us by these holy signs."[9] Lastly, in the Heidelberg Catechism, though the Catechism was a compromise document, and is non-committal on the question of whether God effects by sacraments what God promises thereby, the God-agency conceptuality is there as in all the others: "The sacraments are visible, holy signs and seals, appointed of God for this end, that by the use thereof he may the more fully declare and seal to us the promise of the Gospel."[10]

The linguistic pattern is clear. The question is what, if any, significance is to be attached to the fact that Calvin, and those influenced by him in the sixteenth century, were so strongly inclined to use the language of God-agency rather than the language of sign-agency in their discussions of the sacraments.

Not a Difference over Causal Principles

The thought that comes first to mind is that Calvin and the Calvinists were *occasionalists* in their thought—occasionalism being the doctrine that only persons, divine and human, have causal powers. On the occasionalist view, fire does not cause wood to be consumed by burning; fire has neither that

7. Schaff, *Creeds*, vol. 3, 285 (my translation).
8. Schaff, *Creeds*, vol. 3, 474.
9. Schaff, *Creeds*, vol. 3, 429.
10. Schaff, *Creeds*, vol. 3, 328.

causal power nor any other. Rather, God causes wood to be consumed by burning, and does so *on the occasion of* the wood being brought into contact with fire. But I think it is very clear that Calvin was not an occasionalist. In fact, Calvin both formulated a very occasionalist-sounding objection to his account and proceeded to answer the objection. He states the objection thus: "the glory of God passes down to the creatures, and so much power is attributed to them, and [God's glory] is thus to this extent diminished." He answered the objection as follows:

> we place no power in creatures. I say only this: God uses means and instruments which he himself sees to be expedient, that all things may serve his glory, since he is Lord and Judge of all. He feeds our bodies through bread and other foods, he illuminates the world through the sun, and he warms it through heat; yet neither bread, nor sun, nor fire, is anything save insofar as he distributes his blessings to us by these instruments. In like manner, he nourishes faith spiritually through the sacraments, whose one function is to set his promises before our eyes to be looked upon, indeed, to be guarantees of them to us.[11]

"We place no power in creatures," says Calvin. But in saying this he is obviously not expressing occasionalism but a thorough-going form of theistic instrumentalism. Bread, sun, fire—all are instruments of God's beneficent actions toward us. That presupposes that bread has the causal power of nourishing us; otherwise God could not make it available to us for the beneficent purpose of nourishing us. And so forth.[12]

But now the contrast between Aquinas and Calvin that I claimed to see, and that I expressed as the contrast between the use of a sign-agency conceptuality in thinking about the sacraments and a God-agency conceptuality, seems to be slipping away from us. For Aquinas affirms exactly what I have just quoted Calvin as saying. It appears that we have only a verbal contrast—a *purely verbal* contrast. Aquinas also addresses an occasionalist-sounding objection, which he phrases thus: "some, however, assert that the sacraments are not the cause of grace in the sense of actually producing any effect, but rather that when the sacraments are applied God produces grace in the soul." Aquinas replies that "we have it on the authority of many of the

---

11. Calvin, *Institutes*, IV.xiv.12.

12. Thus I strongly disagree with Kilian McDonnell's comment that "the Scotistic and Occamist philosophies, together with the mystical movement and the *devotio moderna* piety, are important for the general background to Calvin's eucharistic doctrine. ... They manifest themselves in a flight from secondary causality, and ... in a reassertion of the sovereignty of God as the only cause." McDonnell, *John Calvin, the Church and the Eucharist*, 37.

saints that the sacraments of the New Law not merely signify but actually cause grace. Therefore we must adopt a different approach based on the fact that there are two kinds of efficient causes, principal and instrumental." It is the latter of these, the concept of *instrumental cause,* that is relevant here:

> An instrumental cause . . . acts not in virtue of its own form, but solely in virtue of the impetus imparted to it by the principal agent. Hence the effect has a likeness not to the instrument, but rather to that principal agent, as a bed does not resemble the axe which carves it but rather the design in the mind of the carpenter. And this is the way in which the sacraments of the New Law cause grace. For it is by divine institution that they are conferred upon man for the precise purpose of causing grace in and through them. . . . [N]ow the term "instrument" in its true sense is applied to that through which someone produces an effect. This is why we are told in Titus, *He saved us by the washing of regeneration.*[13]

If there really is, on the point I have been emphasizing, a difference of conceptuality between Aquinas and Calvin, and not merely a difference of language, that difference cannot consist in Calvin embracing occasionalism and Aquinas resisting it. Both reject occasionalism.

A Symbol System or Discourse System

I am not at ease, however, with letting the unsatisfactoriness of this first thought be the end of the matter. The difference of linguistic pattern is so dominant and so striking as to make me reluctant to conclude that there is nothing more to it than a fortuitous difference of linguistic emphasis. So let me pursue another way of construing how Calvin was thinking, in the hope that this will illuminate why he speaks as he does. Perhaps it will also explain why Calvin thinks he has answers to two objections that have repetitively been lodged against him ever since he first published his thoughts on the sacraments.[14]

I have in mind the charge that, on his account, nothing new happens in the sacrament, and the charge that, on his view, the sacraments cannot possibly effect what they signify. The "nothing new" charge arises from the fact that the promise that God supposedly seals by way of the sacrament is something that God has already made and that the recipient of the

---

13. Aquinas, *Summa Theologiae,* 3a.62.1.
14. See the discussion in the recent book by Gerrish, *Grace and Gratitude.*

sacrament, as a hearer of the preached word and a person of faith, is already acquainted with and has already accepted. The matter, that is, the content, of the preached word is Jesus Christ; but Jesus Christ is also the matter of the sacrament. The "no effect" charge arises from the fact that the bread and wine not only remain bread and wine in substance, but do not acquire any new causal powers. Perhaps God *on the occasion of* the sacrament works the effect in the recipient of uniting him or her more closely with Christ; but how could God possibly work that effect *by way of* the sacrament? Though Calvin may profess instrumentalism, doesn't his resistance to acknowledging any substantial or causal change in the bread and wine force him into that quite other doctrine of occasionalism?

We are all by now familiar with Ferdinand Saussure's distinction between language and discourse—between *langue* and *parole*. A language as such is just a code: words and grammar. To understand the role of language in human society we have to add to the code the use of that code in discourse. For all the familiarity of Saussure's distinction, however, it is clear that a wide and deep stream in contemporary philosophy of language would not accept it—or more precisely, would not accept it as marking a *fundamental* distinction. Everybody would agree that there is more than just the code; not everybody would agree that, at the deepest level, what must be added to the code is discourse. One party would agree that it is discourse that must be added. But the other party would say that what must be added is what might be called, following Nelson Goodman, *symbol systems*, in which the signs belonging to the system are assigned denotations, which those signs then designate.[15] Those combinations of the signs that are well-formed sentences are then true or false depending on how the denotations of the terms are related in reality.

Of course, the discourse party is willing to speak of signs as having designations, and of sentences as being true or false; but it regards those attributions as parasitic on the phenomena of persons referring to entities with signs and of persons using sentences to say things that are true or false. Correspondingly, the symbol-system party is willing to speak of persons as referring to things with terms and of persons saying true and false things with sentences; but it regards such speech as grounded ultimately on the phenomena of terms designating in symbol system and of sentences being true or false. It should be added that a given thinker's use of one of these conceptualities rather than the other is not always grounded on the conviction that it truly is more fundamental; even less often is it grounded on the *argued* conviction that it is more fundamental. And in fact I know

15. Goodman, *Languages of Art*.

of no discussion which thoroughly and systematically compares the powers of the two conceptualities.

My initial suggestion is that a good many of the differences between Aquinas' account of the sacraments and Calvin's stem from the fact that Aquinas was thinking in terms of symbol systems whereas Calvin was thinking in terms of discourse. More must be said about discourse, however, if we are fully to understand Calvin's thought.

A Discourse of Assured Promise

On the contemporary scene there are, broadly speaking, three ways of thinking about discourse. One is the Romantic expressivist way: discourse consists, at bottom, of the speaker using signs to express his or her inner life. Another is the quasi-behaviorist way: discourse consists at bottom of using signs to produce effects in auditors or readers. On the quasi-behaviorist way of thinking, communication rather than expression is viewed as the essence of language. The third way of thinking about discourse prominent on the contemporary scene is the speech-action way, pioneered by J. L. Austin.[16]

At the heart of the speech-action way of thinking is the distinction, to use Austin's terminology, between *locutionary* actions, *illocutionary* actions, and *perlocutionary* actions. Let me explain. Suppose I relieve your anxiety by promising that I will buy new tires for the car, and that I do so by leaving a note for you on which I have inscribed the words, "I will buy new tires for the car this afternoon." In that case, my locutionary act is the act of inscribing the words, "I will buy new tires for the car this afternoon." My illocutionary act is the act of promising you that I will buy new tires for the car this afternoon; my act of inscribing those words *counts* as my act of making that promise. And my perlocutionary act is my act of relieving your anxiety by making that promise to you. Of course, my performing that perlocutionary act presupposes that I have also performed another perlocutionary act, the act, namely, of communicating to you *what and that* I have promised.

It would be comically anachronistic to suggest that Calvin was thinking about the sacraments in term of speech-action theory. Such prescience was not his! So let me instead state the suggestion I want to pursue like this: the best model for understanding how Calvin was thinking about the sacraments is the model of speaking proposed by speech-action theory. Let us try out this suggestion by thinking in accord with the model for a while. Naturally there are many facets of Calvin's thought about the sacraments

---

16. Austin, "Performative Utterances," 133–252. A subject developed in Austin, *How to Do Things with Words*.

that I will not be able to say anything about. In particular, I will confine my discussion to the sacrament of the Eucharist.

The prying apart of illocutionary actions from locutionary actions is a crucial part of the model. Once we have that distinction in hand, then immediately we notice that the same sorts of actions that are illocutionary actions—and in many cases not just the *same sorts* of actions but *the very same* actions—can be performed not only by uttering or inscribing words, and not only by doing such other things with words as pointing to them or, signing them, but can be done without using words at all, using instead pictures, semaphore signals, gestures, and so forth. Of course, in these latter cases they would not, strictly speaking, be *illocutionary* actions, since they would not be performed by way of locutionary actions; nonetheless they would belong to the same ontological category. Thus we can make sense at once of Calvin's insistence that, in spite of the difference in medium between sacrament and preaching, it should "be regarded as a settled principle that the sacraments have the same office as the Word of God: to offer and set forth Christ to us, and in him the treasures of heavenly grace."[17]

We should understand Calvin as saying, in that passage, that the *content* of the sacraments is the same as the *content* of the preached word; both of them present to us the promise of our redemption in Jesus Christ. What Calvin emphatically wants to say, however, is that the illocutionary act—the illocutionary *stance,* as Austin sometimes called it—is different. Calvin himself over and over uses the metaphor of a seal: by way of the sacrament God presents to us the promise made in Jesus Christ and seals, confirms, or ratifies, that promise: "the seals which are attached to government documents and other public acts are nothing taken by themselves, for they would be attached in vain if the parchment had nothing written on it. Yet, when added to the writing, they do not on that account fail to confirm and seal what is written."[18]

The metaphor obviously appealed strongly to Calvin's followers; it is used in all the Reformed confessions. But if I at all understand what Calvin is getting at here, and how a seal on a document functioned, the metaphor is not a wholly felicitous one. A document does not count as the discourse of the official until the seal—or nowadays the signature—of the official has been attached. *Then and there,* when the seal is attached, the official says whatever the document makes him say. But that is not at all analogous to Calvin's thought. God's promise of redemption was already made in Jesus Christ, and is proclaimed by Scripture and preaching. It is

17. Calvin, *Institutes,* IV.xiv.17.
18. Calvin, *Institutes,* IV.xiv.5.

not made episodically when and where the sacrament is celebrated. Calvin's thought—if I may make so bold as to offer an improvement on what he says—Calvin's thought is rather this: by way of offering the sacrament, God *here and now* assures the assembled that God's promise to redeem them remains in effect. In the sermon God tells us, by way of the words of the preacher, of the promises already made in Jesus Christ. In the sacrament God does not so much *tell* us of those promises made in Christ as *here and now assure us* that they remain in effect.

This especially is a point that symbol-system theory leaves obscure, but that discourse theory of the speech-action sort can clarify. The promise is not made *here and now*. Nor is it just the case that it is *here and now said* that the promise *was* made; that is the fundamental function of the proclamation. What in the sacrament is done *here and now* is the *issuing of the assurance* that the promise once made remains in effect. That is what is new, or part of what is new: the assurance of which, as Calvin sees it, we frail human beings are so very much in need. Sacraments, he says, "are like seals of the good will that [God] feels toward us, which by attesting that good will to us, sustain, nourish, confirm, and increase our faith."[19]

Promise Clearer in the Sacrament Than in Preaching

What is also true for Calvin is that the *medium* of the sacraments is of indispensable importance. Though the promise presented in Scripture and preaching, and presented in the sacraments and confirmed as remaining in effect, is the same promise, it is not at all true that the sacramental medium is dispensable. Calvin is convinced, for one thing, that assurance by way of the sacramental medium is more reassuring in its effects than is the presentation of the promise by Scripture and preaching. "The sacraments, therefore, are exercises which make us more certain of the trust-worthiness of God's Word." They make us more certain because God "attests his good will and love toward us more expressly than by word."[20]

It is not a point most of us would have expected Calvin to make! Yet there it is: the sacraments present the promises of God to us in Jesus Christ more clearly than does "the word, because they represent them for us as painted in a picture from life."[21] So "the Lord here not only recalls to our memory . . .the abundance of his bounty, but, so to speak, gives it into

19. Calvin, *Institutes*, IV.xiv.7.
20. Calvin, *Institutes*, IV.xiv.6.
21. Calvin, *Institutes*, IV.xiv.5.

our hand and arouses us to recognize it."[22] By way of the sacrament, God graphically presents to us the promise made in Jesus Christ, and in so doing assures us that the promise remains valid. God dramatically represents closer union with the body and blood of Christ and in so doing assures us that the promise to secure such union for us remains valid.

Let us allow Calvin to develop the point in his own words:

> ... from the physical things set forth in the Sacrament we are led by a sort of analogy to spiritual things. Thus, when bread is given as a symbol of Christ's body, we must at once grasp this comparison: as bread nourishes, sustains, and keeps the life of our body, so Christ's body is the only food to invigorate and enliven our soul. When we see wine set forth as a symbol of blood, we must reflect on the benefits which wine imparts to the body, and so realize that the same are spiritually imparted to us by Christ's blood. These benefits are to nourish, refresh, strengthen, and gladden. For if we sufficiently consider what value we have received from the giving of that most holy body and the shedding of that blood, we shall clearly perceive that those qualities of bread and wine are, according to such an analogy, excellently adapted to express those things when they are communicated to us.[23]

The gestural metaphor of being offered bread and wine is open-ended in meaning, however; so much so that after following out the meaning for a while we come to a point where we can no longer say what the metaphor means. It points beyond our grasp, to mystery. Yet we *experience* what it means, experience it without understanding it. Or so, at least, Calvin described his own case:

> Now, if anyone should ask me how this takes place, I shall not be ashamed to confess that it is a secret too lofty for either my mind to comprehend or my words to declare. And, to speak more plainly, I rather experience than understand it. Therefore,

---

22. Calvin, *Institutes*, IV.xvii.37.

23. Calvin, Institutes, IV.xvii.3. Given this probing by Calvin of the import of the dramatic representation, I find it very strange that McDonnell would say that, on Calvin's view, God "uses bread as a means because he chooses to use bread, and though the bread is an apt symbol of nourishment, the significance of the means is not so much that it is bread, as that it is chosen. There is something almost accidental in the choice of this particular means" (McDonnell, *Calvin, the Church, and the Eucharist*, 166). Of course Calvin believes that God *could* have worked by other means: *all* theologians in the Christian tradition have believed the same. But Calvin was very far indeed from thinking that the choice of sacramental elements was accidental; to be united with the body of Christ, we must meditate on the import of these very elements.

> I here embrace without controversy the truth of God in which I may safely rest. He declares his flesh the food of my soul, his blood its drink. I offer my soul to him to be fed with such food. In his Sacred Supper he bids me take, eat, and drink his body and blood under the symbols of bread and wine. I do not doubt that he himself truly presents them, and that I receive them.[24]

Earlier I remarked that the prying apart of illocutionary acts from locutionary acts characteristic of speech-action theory enables us to illuminate several aspects of Calvin's thought on the sacraments. Let me point to one more such aspect. When we are introduced to the distinction between locutionary and illocutionary acts, it is natural to have in mind the situation in which a *given person* performs an illocutionary act by performing a locutionary act—asserts something by speaking, makes a promise by writing something on a sheet of paper, and so forth. But in fact the agent of the two acts need not be the same. The president may come down with an attack of laryngitis just before he is slated to give his State of the Union address. Someone else may then read his speech for him; if so, then by that person's uttering the words, the president makes his proposals. That is how we must think of the sacramental case before us. By the appointed minister of the church uttering the words and performing the actions of the sacrament, God presents the promise made in Jesus Christ and assures us that the promise remain in effect. The minister does not do it, *God* does it. God is the agent. With hammering insistence, the Reformed confessions assert that *God* is the one who signifies and seals the promises.

For Aquinas Bread Acquires an Additional Causal Power

The main thing remaining is to consider how our model illuminates some of what Calvin says about the perlocutionary effect of God's discourse in the sacrament. Here I think it will help to have, as a foil, some of what Aquinas says on the matter of sacramental effect, for he remarks that "the sacraments of the New Law are designed to produce two effects, namely, to act as a remedy against sins, and to bring the soul to its fulness in things pertaining to the worship of God in terms of the Christian life as a ritual expression of this."[25] The first effect Aquinas calls "grace"; the sacraments are an instrumental cause of grace. The second he calls "sacramental

---

24. Calvin, *Institutes*, IV.xvii.32.
25. Aquinas, *Summa Theologiae*, 3a.63.1.

character"; the sacraments are an instrumental cause of sacramental character. The question is how these instrumental effects come about. Given the causal powers of bread, wine, water, and oil, how can God bring about those effects? Hammers and saws do not build houses; we human beings have to build houses by using hammers and saws as instruments. But our doing so presupposes a definite set of causal powers on the part of hammers and saws. The causal powers of an egg, for example, are quite irrelevant to cutting boards or sinking nails. Aquinas states the application of the general point to the sacramental case thus: "once we assert that a sacrament is an instrumental cause of grace it is straightway necessary to assert also that there is a certain kind of instrumental power in the sacrament designed to produce the sacramental effect."[26]

In order to help us think about the instrumental causation that takes place in the sacraments, Aquinas offers some analogies. Here is one:

> ... cutting is proper to an axe in virtue of the sharpness intrinsic to it, whereas the function of making a bed belongs to it only inasmuch as it is an instrument used in a craft. So too it is with the sacraments. They touch the body and so produce upon it the sort of effects which are connatural to them as physical entities. But in the very act of doing so they also operate as instruments, producing effects upon the soul in the power of God. For instance the water of baptism, by the very fact of washing the body of its own connatural power, washes the soul too in virtue of being an instrument of the divine power.[27]

The analogy, though it may in a general way enhance our understanding of instrumental causation, does not help us understand what goes on in the sacrament. It is the natural sharpness of an axe that makes it useful to us in making a bed; but how is God enabled, by using water with its physical cleansing properties to infuse grace (and sacramental character) into the soul of the one dipped in the water of baptism?

So Aquinas offers another analogy:

> ... there is nothing to prevent a spiritual power being in a body provided it is instrumental—in other words in virtue of the fact that a body can be impelled by some spiritual substance to produce some spiritual effect. Thus too in the human voice itself as perceptible to the senses a certain spiritual power resides to arouse the mind of the hearer in virtue of the fact that it proceeds from a mental concept, and in this way there is a spiritual

26. Aquinas, *Summa Theologiae*, 3a.62.4.
27. Aquinas, *Summa Theologiae*, 3a.62.1.

power in the sacraments inasmuch as they are ordained by God to produce a spiritual effect.[28]

Here Aquinas goes beyond the axe and bed analogy. Sounds made by the human voice have "a certain spiritual power" to arouse the mind of the hearer which they do not have as such; they acquire that causal power, under certain circumstances. Nothing like that happens in the case of the axe; the axe does not acquire any additional causal powers. So this second analogy comes closer to Aquinas' thought about the sacraments than does the first. But it, too, will not quite do; Aquinas does not think that bread and wine acquire the causal power to infuse grace in the way in which the sounds of the human voice acquire the causal power to arouse the mind of someone. The analogy remains distant.

So let us try again, moving on from Aquinas' general discussion of sacraments to his particular discussion of the Eucharist. He observes:

> It is not because of the natural power of the water that any spiritual effect is caused in Baptism, but because of the power of the Spirit which is in the water. . . . But what the power of the Spirit is to the water of Baptism, that the very body of Christ is to the appearances of bread and wine. They are operative only because of the very body of Christ that they contain. A sacrament is so called because it contains something sacred. A thing can be sacred in two ways; in itself absolutely, and in relation to something else. The difference between the Eucharist and other sacraments having a material element is this: whereas the Eucharist contains something that is sacred in itself absolutely, namely, Christ, the water of Baptism contains something that is sacred in relation to something else, that is, it contains the power of sanctifying us.[29]

Now the point is becoming clear: the water used in baptism has acquired special causal powers, spiritual powers, in addition to its ordinary physical powers. Likewise, in the Eucharist special causal powers come to be associated with the bread and wine. The dynamics are somewhat different between the two sacraments, however. The bread and wine do not themselves acquire additional causal powers. Rather, the bread is transubstantiated into the body of Christ and the wine into the blood of Christ; and those inherently have spiritual powers. The accidents of the bread and wine, that remain after the alteration of substance, retain the ordinary

---

28. Aquinas, *Summa Theologiae*, 3a.62.4.
29. Aquinas, *Summa Theologiae*, 3a.73.2.

causal powers of bread and wine. By contrast, the water of baptism really does have new spiritual powers.

When and how does this drastic alteration of substance, and this acquisition, of new causal spiritual powers, take place? In and by the consecration of the elements:

> in the other sacraments [than Eucharist] the consecration of the matter consists merely in a certain blessing, as a result of which the consecrated matter receives an instrumental spiritual power; this derives from the minister who is a living instrument able to reach to inanimate instruments. But in this sacrament the consecration of the matter consists in a miraculous change of the substance, which only God can bring about. So it is that the minister has no other act in effecting this sacrament than to pronounce the words.[30]

Calvin's judgement on this whole theory of transubstantiation and acquisition of additional causal powers is clear: he wants nothing to do with it. God has not attached to the sacramental elements "some sort of secret powers."[31] It is an error to "think that a hidden power is joined and fastened to the sacraments by which they of themselves confer the graces of the Holy Spirit upon us as wine is given in a cup."[32]

Calvin's Very Different Account: The Promise Appropriated

But how then do the sacraments gain their effect, of strengthening in faith—which for Calvin is the same as uniting us more closely with the divine-human person, Jesus Christ? For that they do have this effect, Calvin repetitively insists. There are two parts to Calvin's answer.

In the first place, if we are to be united more closely with Christ by God's sacramental presentation of the promise and assurance that that promise remains in force, then we must *understand* that God is presenting that, and is assuring us of that, by this sacrament. The fundamental function of the sacramental words is to bring about such understanding. Calvin expresses his agreement with his opponents that a sacrament, strictly speaking, "consists of the word and the outward sign" together. But then he immediately adds: "we ought to understand the word not as one whispered without meaning

---

30. Aquinas, *Summa Theologiae*, 3a.78.1.
31. Calvin, *Institutes*, IV.xiv.14.
32. Calvin, *Institutes*, IV.xiv.17.

and without faith, a mere noise, like a magic incantation, which has the form to consecrate the element. Rather, it should, when preached, make us understand what the visible sign means."[33] So he says: "accordingly, when we hear the sacramental word mentioned let us understand the promise, proclaimed in a clear voice by the minister, to lead the people by the hand wherever the sign tends and directs us."[34]

In short, the perlocutionary effect of the sacrament, if we may call it that, is not produced simply by the uttering of the sacramental words and the performance of the sacramental actions—any more than the perlocutionary effect in speech is produced simply by the sound or the look of the words. It occurs only when the recipients discern the illocutionary acts performed—only when they discern that God is assuring them that the promise made in Jesus Christ remains in effect for them. If your anxiety is calmed by the note I leave on the kitchen table, that is because you do not merely see the words but discern what I was saying with those words.

On the other hand, we saw earlier that the perlocutionary effect of the sacrament is also not produced simply by discerning the assurance; the *signs* whereby the assurance is made are also of fundamental importance. It is God's assuring us that the promise remains in effect *by offering us this meal* that unites us more closely to Christ. To use the jargon of our model: it is this illocutionary act produced by this locutionary act that produces this perlocutionary act.

But more is needed than meditation on the dramatic representation, and understanding of what God is saying thereby, if the sacraments are to work their intended effect. Receptivity on the part of the recipient is also necessary and that comes about by the work of the Holy Spirit within us; we do not just do it on our own.

> [God] illuminates our minds by the light of his Holy Spirit and opens our hearts for the Word and sacraments to enter in, which would otherwise only strike our ears and appear before our eyes, but not at all affect us within.... [T]he sacraments properly fulfill their office only when the Spirit, that inward teacher, comes to them, by whose power alone hearts are penetrated and affections moved and our souls opened for the sacraments to enter in. If the Spirit be lacking, the sacraments can accomplish nothing more in our minds than the splendor of the sun shining upon blind eyes, or a voice sounding in deaf ears.[35]

33. Calvin, *Institutes*, IV.xiv.4.
34. Calvin, *Institutes*, IV.xiv.4.
35. Calvin, *Institutes*, IV.xiv.8–9.

What immediately follows this passage in the text of the *Institutes* is a great flowering of metaphors for the work of the Spirit in the recipient of the sacrament. What I find fascinating is that all of them are metaphors for the Spirit's making us receptive in heart and mind. Here are some of the metaphors:

> just as the eyes see by the brightness of the sun, or the ears hear by the sound of a voice, so the eyes would not be affected by any light unless they were endowed with a sharpness of vision capable of being illumined of themselves, and the ears would never be struck by any noise, unless they were created and fitted for hearing. But suppose it is true ... that what sight does in our eyes for seeing light, and what hearing does in our ears for perceiving a voice, are analogous to the work of the Holy Spirit in our hearts, which is to conceive, sustain, nourish, and establish faith. Then both of these things follow: the sacraments profit not a whit without the power of the Holy Spirit, and nothing prevents them from strengthening and enlarging faith in hearts already taught by that Schoolmaster.[36]

In summary: "what increases and confirms faith is precisely the preparation of our minds by [the Spirit's] inward illumination to receive the confirmation extended by the sacraments."[37] When that happens, then "the believer, when he sees the sacraments with his own eyes, does not halt at the physical sight of them, but by those steps (which I have indicated by analogy) rises up in devout contemplation to those lofty mysteries which lie hidden in the sacraments,"[38] thus becoming united with Jesus Christ, the God-man.

Personal Action: The Awesome Impact of Ordinary Bread and Wine

There you have it: a philosopher's attempt to use the model provided by speech-action theory to illuminate Calvin's doctrine of the sacraments! There are many aspects of Calvin's doctrine about which I have said nothing. Perhaps some of those could also be illuminated by thinking about them in accord with the speech-action model. I hope, though, to have said enough to help us decide whether thinking of Calvin's account along these lines proves

---

36. Calvin, *Institutes*, IV.xiv.9.
37. Calvin, *Institutes*, IV.xiv.10.
38. Calvin, *Institutes*, IV.xiv.5.

illuminating—and in particular, whether it makes his account less elusive than it has proved to most readers ever since it was first published.

Let me close by mentioning two overall impressions that I am left with. What strikes me, in the first place, is something about the understanding of the liturgy that emerges from Calvin's account. To enter the liturgy, as Calvin understands it, is to enter the sphere not just of divine *presence* but of divine *action*. God, in Calvin's way of thinking, is less a presence to be apprehended in the liturgy than an agent to be engaged.

What strikes me, in the second place, is the extraordinary significance that Calvin assigns to God's offering us these material elements of bread and wine and our eating and drinking them. I know, of course, that Calvinism is often thought to be a highly rationalistic form of Christianity; no doubt it has often been that. But just ordinary bread and ordinary wine— no special causal powers: Calvin believes that by way of these, dramatically presented and understandingly and receptively received, God strengthens our faith by uniting us more closely to the humanity as well as the divinity of Jesus Christ. Never, to my knowledge, has ordinary material stuff been freighted with such momentous significance.

Kilian McDonnell, imbued with the Thomistic conviction that the sacramental elements are infused by God with special spiritual powers, is struck by the freedom from material means which God enjoys on Calvin's view, as he understands that. In his book, *John Calvin, the Church and the Eucharist*, he says that on Calvin's view,

> God uses bread to nourish us because he chose to do so, but he does not in any sense remain bound to objects even after having chosen them. Nor does he give to them a power which is proper to himself. To feed man unto salvation is a work of God and the sacraments never possess this as an immanent power. The Eucharist is never an object, but a personal instrument. The Eucharist does not have, either from nature or from God, a power of nourishing spirituality which it possesses in a definitive sense. There is no power given to the eucharistic bread so that the bread possesses that power now and need not again, and ever again, receive the power to nourish spiritually.[39]

McDonnell considerably overstates and even distorts the Thomistic view which he professes to embrace. Let us take the case of baptism, since, as we have seen, its structure is somewhat less complex, on Aquinas' analysis, than that of the Eucharist. It was Aquinas' view that the water used in baptism is in fact "ever and again" infused with special spiritual powers, by

---

39. McDonnell, *Calvin, the Church and the Eucharist*, 167.

consecration; water does not possess "in a definitive sense" the power of cleansing us spiritually. Further, Aquinas was as eager as was Calvin to say that the Eucharist is not "an object, but a personal instrument." And on the Thomistic view as well as on the Calvinistic—indeed, on every Christian view—God is not "bound to" objects after choosing them.

All that pertains, however, to the view that McDonnell uses to contrast with Calvin's; it is, I contend, a very distorted version of Thomism. As to Calvin's view itself: it wears to my eye a very different appearance from that which it wears to the eye of McDonnell: God took the risk of trusting ordinary bread and ordinary wine, when devoutly and meditatively received under the power of the Spirit in the sacrament, to unite us more closely with Jesus Christ. It is true that that does not imply that God is bound by bread and wine. But it certainly does imply that God places on these humble, eminently material, stuffs an awesome load of significance. Or perhaps the more accurate thing to say is that the *drama* of God offering us bread and wine as a sign and assurance of Christ offering us his body and blood, and our then eating that bread and wine—it is on that simple dramatic representation performed with ordinary bread and ordinary wine that God places an awesome load of significance. Never has dramatic representation been freighted with such awesome import.

13

Preaching the Word of God

In the Episcopal liturgy for the ordination of a priest, the bishop says to the person who has just been ordained, "receive this Bible as a sign of the authority given you to preach the Word of God and to administer God's holy sacraments."[1] In the liturgy of the Reformed Church in America for the ordination of a minister, the ordaining minister asks of the person to be ordained, "will you, with the help of God, strive to fulfill all the duties of a minister of Christ, preaching the Word of God in sincerity, administering the holy sacraments in purity?"[2] The same terminology, "to preach the Word of God" (or "preaching the Word of God"), is found in the liturgies for ordination of many other denominations as well. What is someone doing when he or she preaches the Word of God? That is the question I will address in this essay.

I addressed the question in two previous publications. I addressed it in the chapter of *The God We Worship* titled "God as One Who Speaks." But I spent most of my time in that chapter expounding and arguing against Karl Barth's understanding of preaching rather than developing my own understanding. I also addressed the question in the chapter of my *Acting Liturgically* titled "God as Liturgical Agent." But there, too, I did so briefly, in the context of a general discussion concerning the various ways in which God acts liturgically.[3]

Of course, not everybody agrees that what the preacher does is preach the Word of God. Some would insist that everything about preaching is purely human. Whether or not there is or was any such thing as *the Word of God*, preachers don't preach the Word of God, not literally, anyway. The preacher shares with the congregation some edifying thoughts for the day, perhaps

---

1. *The Book of Common Prayer*, 534.
2. *The Liturgy of the Reformed Church in America*, 97.
3. I regard what I say in this present essay not only as an expansion of what I said previously but also as an improvement and, in places, a correction.

thoughts about the Scripture passage read. That is all. If the preacher's discourse was especially edifying, someone who embraced this understanding of preaching might say, "he really preached the Word of God this morning." But that would be speaking metaphorically.

I will not undertake, on this occasion, to argue against this reductionist understanding of preaching. I will assume that the preacher does in fact do something that can rightly be called, speaking literally, "preaching the Word of God." My question is, what is a preacher doing when he or she preaches the Word of God?

How God Might Speak

If the preacher preaches the Word of God, then there is such a thing as the Word of God. And if there is such a thing as the Word of God, then God speaks—then God did do, and/or God does do, something that can appropriately be called *speaking*. How might that happen?

In my *Divine Discourse*, I developed an account of how that might happen. Fundamental to my account was the distinction, introduced by speech-act theory, between *locutionary* acts and *illocutionary* acts. A locutionary act is an act of uttering or inscribing a sentence with a certain meaning in mind. The distinction between such acts and illocutionary acts can best be explained with an example. By uttering the sentence "it is sunny today" in a situation of a certain sort, I can perform the other distinct act of asserting that it is sunny today. On account of performing the locutionary act of uttering that sentence (in that situation), I am to be reckoned as having performed the illocutionary act of making that assertion. My uttering that sentence *counts as* my making that assertion.

The reason for holding that these are indeed two distinct acts is that a person can perform one without performing the other. I can offer the sentence simply as an example of a well-formed English sentence, in which case I do not make that assertion. Conversely, I can make that assertion by uttering a sentence in some other language.

Once one has the idea of an illocutionary act in mind, it becomes obvious that we can and do perform illocutionary acts in other ways than by performing locutionary acts. One can assert something by smoke signals, for example, by signing one's name to a document, or by winking at one's partner in a card game. In the philosophical literature on these matters there is no general term for those acts—whatever the sort—whereby some illocutionary act is performed. One could stipulate that one will use the term "locutionary act" for all such acts.⁴ But I fear that the meaning of the word "locution" is so clear that readers will forget that the application of "locutionary act" has been expanded in this way. So I shall use the rather clumsy term, *counting-as acts*. So too, the act that one is to be reckoned as performing by performing some counting-as act need not be a speech-act—that is, need not be an illocutionary act. It might, for example, be an act of selling some property. I shall call those acts in general that are performed by some counting-as act, *counted-as acts*—again, a clumsy term.

After borrowing from speech-act theory the distinction between locutionary and illocutionary acts, and then generalizing the distinction to that between counting-as acts and counted-as acts, I went on, in *Divine Discourse*, to introduce the idea of *double-agent* discourse. The image that dominates speech-act theory is that of one and the same person performing a locutionary act and thereby performing some illocutionary act. But it need not be the same person. When a lawyer possesses the power-of-attorney for his client on certain matters, it is the lawyer who performs the counting-as act of signing certain documents whereas it is his client who performs the counted-as act of selling some property, making some declaration, or whatever. The lawyer signs on behalf of his client. So too, an ambassador may be authorized to speak on behalf of his head of state—deputized to do so.

There is another way in which double-agent discourse can occur, namely, by what I call "appropriation." I can extend birthday greetings to a friend by buying a greeting card in a gift shop and sending it off to my friend. In this case, the counting-as act is that of sending to my friend the card I purchased. But I did not myself perform the locutionary act of inscribing those words; the company that produced the card did that. I appropriated the inscription the company produced—that being the content of its locutionary act.

When a greeting card company prints a birthday card, nobody is thereby greeting anybody. Nothing more is going on than that words appropriate for greeting are being printed. But suppose I send greetings to a friend by posting a poem I came across. Then, in most cases, I am not only appropriating the words of the poem but also appropriating what the poet was saying with those words—I am appropriating the content of the poet's illocutionary act.

For our purposes in this essay it is important to note that what I thereby say to my friend need not be the same as what the poet said—the content of my illocutionary act need not be a restating of the content of the poet's illocutionary act. What I am saying might be only indirectly related

---

4. In some of my writings, I have done this.

to what the poet said, and my friend might be baffled for quite some time as to the point I was making in sending him this poem. I might have to explain it to him. If he did eventually figure it out on his own, it would be because he had extensive personal knowledge of me and had acquired some of the skills of literary interpretation. Those who don't know me well, or don't have such skills, will remain baffled. Or I might send him one of Aesop's lesser-known fables without the moral and let him guess what I want to say to him, namely, the moral.

I employed this idea of double-agent discourse to develop an account of how God might speak—that is, how God might perform illocutionary acts of asserting, questioning, consoling, commanding, promising, and the like. Of course, God might perform some illocutionary act by Godself performing some counting-as act—by causing some words to appear on a wall, for example, by producing the sound of a still small voice, or by causing someone to "hear words." But a full account of how God speaks has to reckon with the fact that, in Scripture, God is often represented as speaking by way of what some human being says or said.

God might speak by way of appointing some human being to speak on God's behalf—to speak in the name of God. That is how the prophet was understood in certain passages in the Old Testament and how the apostles appear to have been understood in certain passages in the New Testament. When the prophet addressed certain words to his fellow Israelites, God was to be reckoned as speaking to them. Alternatively, God might speak by way of appropriating words produced by some human being, or by appropriating the content of an illocutionary act performed by some human being. As to how it might be that God appropriated Christian Scripture as a whole, in all its widely diverse genres, as the medium of God's speech, I said that what seemed to me the best way to think of it was that it was by leading the church to treat the texts comprising Christian Scripture as its canon that God appropriated these texts as the medium of God's speech.[5] God continues to lead the church to treat these texts as its canon.

---

5. Though this is what I intended to say in *Divine Discourse*, it is not what I actually did say. I said that God appropriated the text as a whole by way of *the church* treating these texts as its canon, not by way of *God leading the church* to treat these texts as its canon.

Interpreting Preaching in Light of the Acclamation, "This Is the Word of the Lord"

With this theoretical framework in hand, let us now turn to the main question of this essay: what is someone doing when he or she preaches the Word of God?

In almost all Christian liturgical enactments, the preaching of the sermon or homily is preceded by the reading aloud of one or more passages from Scripture. In many liturgical traditions this reading is followed by the acclamation, spoken by the reader, "This is the Word of the Lord." Obviously, our interpretation of the claim that the preacher, in delivering the sermon, is preaching the Word of God has to fit with our understanding of the acclamation, "This is the Word of the Lord." So let us approach our analysis of the nature of preaching by considering the force of the acclamation.

What is the force of the acclamation, "This is the Word of the Lord"? In particular, what does the pronoun "this" refer to? *What* is being referred to as the Word of the Lord?

Let us set certain reductionist understandings off to the side at once. What is referred to as the Word of the Lord in the acclamation cannot be the act of reading aloud the words of the biblical passage, nor can it be the words themselves. It has to be something God said—the content of some illocutionary act on God's part. And neither the act of reading aloud the words, nor the words themselves, are that.

Might it be that what is referred to as the Word of the Lord in the acclamation "This is the word of the Lord" is what God said to certain persons in ancient times by way of someone in ancient times addressing those persons by uttering or inscribing these words?[6] If this were the correct interpretation of the acclamation, then *preaching* the Word of God would presumably consist of drawing lessons, applicable to us today, from what God said to those people of ancient times by way of these words.

Quite clearly this, too, is not the correct interpretation of the acclamation. It has some plausibility for certain parts of Scripture—for much of the prophetic literature of the Old Testament, for example, and for at least some of the epistolary literature of the New Testament. But for the rest, the literary genre of the text militates against this interpretation. The Psalms, for example, are addressed to God, not to certain human beings. And the historical literature of the Old Testament is not addressed to anyone. No doubt the original writers and editors of the historical writings had an intended readership in mind; but they did not *address* their composition to those

---

6. More precisely: the words of which these are the translation.

people, or to anyone else. So too, though I have a readership in mind for this present essay, there is no one to whom I am addressing it.

The account I offered in *Divine Discourse* of how it might be that God appropriates the entirety of Christian Scripture as a medium of God's speech, namely, by moving the church to treat these texts as its canon and by continuing to lead the church to do so, suggests a different interpretation of the acclamation. Perhaps what the "this" in "This is the Word of the Lord" refers to is what God said and continues to say by guiding the church to adopt and retain the passage read as part of its canon.[7]

To whom does God say what God says in this way? To the church in general, down through the ages. And, for some passages, to human beings in general, down through the ages. To each and all God says what each and all have to hear as relevant to all.

On this understanding of the acclamation, *preaching* the Word of God is most naturally understood as the preacher identifying what God is saying to each and all in the passage read, putting that in his or her own words, and explaining how that applies to the people assembled here and now. Preaching the Word of God, so understood, is not to be identified with interpreting what the biblical author or editor was saying when he composed the passage read. What God was and is saying by way of this passage may or may not be the same as what the biblical writer was saying. A sermon is, for that reason, not a Bible study. Preaching so understood does, however, require and presuppose careful and responsible biblical exegesis.

When I say, "putting in his own words," I have in mind some comments of Karl Barth about preaching. Preaching, he wrote, is not some new word devised by the preacher but a "repetition of the divine promise." Barth then explains that this repetition "cannot consist in the mere reading of Scripture or in repeating and paraphrasing the actual wording of the biblical witness. This can be only its presupposition." The preacher "must be ready to make the promise given to the Church intelligible in his own words to the men of his own time."[8]

It is my clear impression that this is how the liturgical reading of Scripture and preaching have often been understood. The reading presents to us certain teachings, certain warnings, certain imperatives, and the like, that God addresses to the church in general, or to human beings in general, these typically clothed in the particularities of ancient times. The preacher then undertakes to extract those general teachings, warnings, imperatives, and the

---

7. In chapter 10 of Wolterstorff, *Acting Liturgically*, I introduce the concept of a *continuant illocution* (in contrast to an *occurrent illocution*), and I analyze this understanding of the Word of the Lord as an example of such an illocution.

8. Barth, *Church Dogmatics*, I.1, 59.

like from the particularities of ancient times in which they are clothed, to put them in his own words so that the people assembled grasp them, and to explain how they apply to the lives of the particular people assembled.

Call this interpretation of liturgical Scripture reading and sermon, *Interpretation A*. Before considering how we should appraise this way of understanding these activities, let me introduce another interpretation. Call this, *Interpretation B*. This alternative way of understanding is strongly suggested by some other words of Barth, words that appear to me to fit poorly, or not at all, with those quoted above. This is what Barth wrote: "wherever and whenever God speaks to man its content is a *concretissimum*. God always has something specific to say to each man, something that applies to him and to him alone. The real content of God's speech or the real will of the [person speaking] of God is not in any sense, then, to be construed and reproduced by us as a general truth."[9]

What these sentences suggest is that, by way of the liturgical reading of Scripture, God is saying something quite *specific* to the people assembled. The situation is not that, by the reading of Scripture, we are presented with some of what God says to the church in general or to human beings in general, and that the preacher then undertakes to identify, and to state in his own words, that general teaching and to explain how it applies, concretely and specifically, to the lives of the people assembled. The situation is rather that, by the liturgical reading of Scripture, God speaks, specifically and concretely, to the people assembled. It is not left to the preacher to speak specifically and concretely. *God* speaks specifically and concretely. The "this" in the acclamation "This is the Word of the Lord" refers to that concrete and specific speech of God. What the preacher then does, presumably, is to undertake to put in his own words, so that the people "get" it, what God was saying, specifically and concretely, to the people by way of the reading of Scripture. The preacher does not *apply* what God says. The application is, as it were, built into what God said. The preacher simply undertakes to repeat in his or her own words, in such a way that the people grasp it, what God was saying to the congregants by way of the reading. If the preacher is more or less successful in this undertaking, then he or she has preached the Word of God.

There is no inconsistency in holding that, by way of the liturgical reading of some passage of Scripture, we are presented *both* with something God says to the church in general (or to human beings in general) *and* with what God is saying, concretely and specifically, to the people assembled. Indeed, by way of the Scripture reading, God might here and now be reiterating or

---

9. Barth, *Church Dogmatics* I.1, 140.

underscoring what God says in general with this passage. Barth appears to think otherwise. He writes, "the real content of God's speech" is never "to be construed and reproduced by us as a general truth."

I find it inexplicable that Barth would make this claim. Over and over, so it appears to me, he does what he says we should never do, namely, construe the content of God's speech "as a general truth." Barth holds that by becoming incarnate in Jesus Christ, God speaks, issuing both a command and a promise. As for the promise, Barth says, "the promise given to the Church in this Word is the promise of God's mercy which is uttered in the person of Him who is very God and very Man and which takes up our cause when we could not help ourselves at all because of our enmity against God. The promise of this Word is thus Immanuel, God with us."[10] The promise, *God with us,* is given to the church in general!

Which Interpretation Is to Be Preferred?

We now have before us what seem to me the two main contenders for understanding the delivery of the sermon as preaching the Word of God, these two understandings corresponding to two different interpretations of the acclamation, "This is the Word of the Lord." Before we consider which is to be preferred, let us briefly review.

On Interpretation A, what the acclamation refers to as the Word of the Lord is what God was saying and is saying all along to everybody by way of appropriating this text. The preacher then undertakes to identify that, to put it in his own words, and to explain how it applies, concretely and specifically, to the people assembled.

On Interpretation B, what the acclamation refers to as the Word of the Lord is what God is saying here and now to the people assembled by way of the reading of the passage. The reading does not simply present what God has been saying all along by way of appropriating this passage—though it does do that. By way of the reader's reading of the passage, God says a new thing here and now to the people assembled—not an entirely new thing, of course, but a new thing. The preacher then undertakes to identify what God was saying, concretely and specifically to the people assembled, by way of the reading and to repeat that in his or her own words.

On interpretation A, God does not speak here and now by way of the reading of the passage; on Interpretation B, God does speak here and now by way of the reading. On Interpretation A, God is not a liturgical agent by way of the reading of Scripture; on Interpretation B, God is.

10. Barth, *Church Dogmatics* I.1, 107–8.

Which of these interpretations is to be preferred? I see no decisive reason for preferring either to the other. There is, however, a consideration that inclines me to prefer B to A.

Running throughout Christian liturgical enactments are the conviction, the expectation, and the prayer that God will engage here and now with the people assembled. When the bread and wine of the Eucharist are distributed, the presider declares that Christ offers himself here and now to the recipients. When the people address God in praise, thanksgiving, confession, and petition, they do so in the expectation that God will listen here and now to what they are saying. When the presider prays, "Almighty God, cleanse the thoughts of our hearts by the inspiration of your Holy Spirit, that we may perfectly love you, and worthily magnify your holy name," he or she does so in the expectation that God will listen and reply favorably here and now. I could go on.

Given the pervasiveness of God's action in the liturgy, it would be strange indeed if, when Scripture is read, God were not active here and now by way of the liturgical act of reading. That would introduce a strange dissonance into the liturgy. If there were a good reason for holding that God is not active here and now by way of this liturgical act, then so be it. But I fail to see any such good reason.

Does God Also Speak by Way of the Preacher's Preaching?

An important question remains to be addressed: is there more to preaching the Word of God than we have thus far identified? Does God also speak here and now, *hic et nunc,* by way of the *preacher's preaching*? On Interpretation A, the preacher undertakes to identify what God says to the church in general by way of the passage read, to put that in his or her own words in such a way that the people grasp it, and to explain how that applies specifically to the people assembled. Assuming that the preacher is more or less successful in that undertaking, is it then the case that *God,* by way of the preacher's speaking, says something specific to the people assembled? Though God, on this interpretation, is not saying something here and now by way of the liturgical act of *reading Scripture,* may it be that God is saying something here and how by way of the liturgical act of *preaching*—saying more or less what the preacher is saying? If so, then we must add that to our understanding of what it is to preach the Word of God on Interpretation A. Some terminology will again be helpful. Let us call Interpretation A plus the denial that God speaks by way of the preacher's speaking, *Interpretation A.1*; and let us call

Interpretation A plus the claim that God speaks by way of the preacher's speaking, *Interpretation A.2*.

On Interpretation B, the preacher undertakes to identify what God was saying here and now by way of the Scripture reading to the people assembled and to put that in his or her own words in such a way that the people grasp it. The preacher undertakes to repeat, in his or her own words, what God was saying. Assuming that the preacher is more or less successful in that undertaking, is God then also speaking by way of the preacher's speaking, saying again what God already said specifically to the people assembled by way of the reading of Scripture—saying it now by way of the words of the preacher rather than by way of the words of Scripture? If so, then we must add that to our understanding of what it is to preach the Word of God on Interpretation B. Let us call Interpretation B plus the denial that God speaks by way of the preacher's speaking, *Interpretation B.1*; and let us call Interpretation B plus the claim that God speaks by way of the preacher's speaking, *B.2*.

Is there a reason for preferring A.2 over A.1 and B.2 over B.1? That is, is there a reason for holding that God does speak here and now by way of the preacher's speaking? Well, the same consideration that led us to prefer B to A also leads us to prefer A.2 to A.1 and B.2 to B.1. Given the pervasiveness of God's action in the liturgy, it would be strange indeed if God were not active here and now by way of the preacher's speaking. That would introduce what I called "a strange dissonance" into the liturgy.

There is a biblical passage that is worth considering as well.[11] Paul, Silvanus, and Timothy are identified as the writers of the first letter to the Thessalonians. In the opening two chapters they praise the Thessalonians for their devotion, for the hospitality they have shown them, and for their receptivity to their preaching. In 2:13 they write,

> We also constantly give thanks to God for this, that when you received the word of God that you heard from us, you accepted it not as a human word but as what it really is, God's word, which is also at work in you believers.

The writers understand themselves as having spoken the word of God and understand the Thessalonians as having received that word. By "the word of God" they cannot have meant the message of the canonical Christian Scriptures since there were as yet no canonical Christian Scriptures. Interpretation A of the acclamation "This is the Word of the Lord" does not apply.

---

11. I thank Edwin van Driel for calling this biblical passage to my attention.

Might they have meant something that God spoke previously to someone and that they, in their preaching, had handed on to the Thessalonians? Three considerations seem to me to militate against that interpretation. If that was how they were thinking, one would expect them to have written "the word of God that we *passed on* to you" rather than "the word of God that you *received from* us." Second, in 1:5 they describe the content of their preaching not as some previously spoken word of God but as "our message of the gospel" (and in 2:8 as "the gospel of God"). And third, they speak of the word of God that they preached as "at work" in believers. (In 1:5 they wrote, "Our message of the gospel came to you not in word only, but also in power and in the Holy Spirit and with full conviction.")

I think the most plausible interpretation of what they are saying here is that they understood their preaching as an instrument of God's speaking. By way of their preaching to the Thessalonians, God was speaking to the Thessalonians. That they regarded God as speaking by way of present human action is confirmed by what they say in 1:8:

> For the word of the Lord has sounded forth from you not only
> in Macedonia and Achaia, but in every place your faith in God
> has become known, so that we have no need to speak about it.

Are we justified in extrapolating from their understanding of their preaching to our understanding of what those are doing who have been authorized by the church to preach the word of God? Might they have thought that the theology of preaching to which they allude in his letter to the Thessalonians applies not only to those who were chosen by Jesus as his apostles—plus Paul, who was chosen specially. I think we are justified in that extrapolation. The letter is explicitly said to be from Paul, Silvanus, and Timothy—not just from Paul. The pronouns throughout are "we" and "us." "We constantly give thanks," "the word of God that you received from us." It is significant that at one point Paul makes a point of speaking for himself: "we wanted to come to you—certainly I, Paul, wanted to again and again—but Satan blocked our way" (2:18). Silvanus and Timothy were not specially chosen in the way Paul was. So the thought of the writers cannot have been that God speaks by way of what the preacher says only if the preacher is Paul or an apostle.

Liturgical Theology on God Speaking by Way of the Preacher's Preaching

There is a significant strand in the tradition of liturgical theology—not prominent, but also not obscure—that holds that God does indeed speak by way of the preacher's preaching. *The Apostolic Tradition*, an anonymous writing from (probably) the late second century CE, contains a considerable number of liturgical texts and a good many comments about the liturgical practices of the time. Among the comments is this one: "if . . . there is an instruction on the word of God, everyone should go to it gladly. He will reflect in his heart that he is listening to God speak through the mouth of the one giving the instruction."[12]

Speaking of the ecclesiastical office of minister, John Calvin wrote, God "uses the ministry of men to declare openly his will to us by mouth, as a sort of delegated work, not by transferring to them his right and honor, but only that through their mouths he may do his own work—just as a workman uses a tool to do his work." God "declares his regard for us when from among men he takes some to serve as his ambassadors in the world, to be interpreters of his secret will and, in short, to represent his person."[13] A bit later Calvin refers to the minister as "a puny man risen from the dust [who] speaks in God's name."[14]

The twentieth-century Swiss Reformed liturgical scholar J. J. von Allmen follows Calvin in speaking of the minister as an "ambassador" of God and as "representing" God.[15] Karl Barth, after describing what happens in preaching as a "miracle," writes that the miracle consists in the fact that by means of the human words of the preacher, "God speaks about Himself."[16] "When the Church speaks of God, God Himself will and does speak of Himself."[17] And in my copy of the contemporary Catholic liturgy, the following explanation is given of how the homily is to be understood: "God's word is spoken again in the homily. The Holy Spirit speaking through the

---

12. Deiss, *The Springtime of the Liturgy*, 150–51. Deiss attributes *The Apostolic Constitution* to Hippolytus. That attribution has now been discredited.

13. Calvin, *Institutes*, IV.iii.1.

14. Calvin, *Institutes*, IV.iii.1.

15. von Allemen, *Worship*, 142. In Wolterstorff, *The God We Worship*, 128–30, I question whether, when he put together everything von Allmen says about the sermon and the Word of God, von Allmen really does mean that by way of the preacher preaching, God speaks here and now. Though von Allmen is a very perceptive and imaginative liturgical scholar, he is not always as precise as one would wish.

16. Barth, *Church Dogmatics*, I.1, 94.

17. Barth, *Church Dogmatics*, I.2., 759.

lips of the preacher explains and applies today's biblical readings to the needs of this particular congregation."[18]

This last passage seems to me quite clearly to express the understanding of preaching that I called "Interpretation A"; the others are ambiguous as between Interpretation A and B. In his discussion of preaching von Allmen says, "in the hands of God, the sermon is a basic means by which there takes place a direct prophetic intervention in the life of the faithful and of the Church. . . . [Preaching] prevents the petrifaction of the Word of God in the *illic et tunc* of the event in which it was enshrined, of its coming in Jesus Christ, and makes that *illic et tunc* newly operative in the *hic et nunc*."[19] I judge this to be ambiguous as between interpretations A and B.

Awesome

Preaching, when understood in any of the four ways I have delineated, is an awesome undertaking. It is, of course, especially awesome if one understands God as speaking here and now to the people assembled by way of one's preaching. But even apart from that, it is awesome. Let me focus my comments on preaching as understood on Interpretation B; what I say can easily be adapted to Interpretation A.

It is truly awesome to undertake to present to the congregation what God was saying to them by way of the Scripture reading and to do so in such a way that the congregation "gets it." It requires, on the one hand, spiritual discernment to identify what God was saying and, on the other hand, the ability and willingness to present that to the people in a way that "speaks" to them. These two aspects of what is required for the preacher to succeed in the undertaking are nicely expressed in one of the prayers in the form for ordination of the Reformed Church in America: "we pray thee to qualify this servant more and more, by thy Holy Spirit, for the ministry to which thou hast chosen and called him. Enlighten his understanding to comprehend thy holy Word. Give him utterance that he may boldly make known thy Gospel. Endow him with wisdom and courage."[20] Both wisdom and courage are required.

There is much that can and should be said on how the preacher should go about discerning what God says to the congregation by way of the reading of the biblical passage appointed for the day. It requires knowing God and knowing what God has said previously, and it requires the skills of

18. *Sunday Missal*, 17.
19. *Sunday Missal*, 143.
20. *Sunday Missal*, 99.

biblical interpretation. To know what a friend is saying to me when he sends me the text of a message he came across that was addressed to someone quite different from me, and in a situation quite different from mine, I have to employ my knowledge of my friend and of other things he has said, and I have to apply my skills of literary interpretation to the text he sent. Only by bringing together that knowledge and those skills can I discern what he might be saying to me by sending me this text.

But rather than developing this point, let me instead call attention to the fact that whereas a preacher is ordained to preach the Word of God, I have described what the preacher actually does as *undertake* to preach the Word of God. My reason for describing it this way is, of course, that the preacher may fail to preach the Word of God—may fail to present to the congregation, in such a way that they "get" it, what God was saying to them by way of the reading of Scripture. The preacher may completely miss what God was saying, attributing to God something quite different, or may discern only a small bit of what God was saying. Or he may discern what God was saying but fail to present that to the congregation in such a way that they "get" it—perhaps because he fears that, if they do get it, they will be enraged, or perhaps because his attempts at oratorical eloquence get in the way of his message, or perhaps because he has so many annoying tics that everybody's attention is distracted. For these reasons, and a good many others, the preacher may fail to communicate to the congregation what he discerned God to be saying, and in that way fail to preach the Word of God.

Of course, some preachers do not even undertake to preach the Word of God. They undertake to share some edifying thought about the passage read. Or maybe not even that. They may find the biblical passage embarrassing and undertake to talk about something else. If they were ordained to preach the Word of God they would, in so doing, be violating their ordination vows. I once listened to a sermon, ostensibly on the passage about "the massacre of the innocents" in Matthew's Gospel, which the preacher introduced by saying that we had just listened to a description of an episode of severe child abuse. Since there was also child abuse in our society, he would preach about that.

It should be noted that even if the preacher rejects the idea of preaching the Word of God, God might nonetheless speak to one or more members of the congregation by way of what the preacher says. St. Augustine overheard a child saying, in a singsong tone of voice, *tolle lege, tolle lege,* "take and read, take and read," and understood God to be telling him to take up the copy he had at hand of Paul's epistles and read whatever his eye fell on.

Listening to the Preaching of the Word of God

Let me now, in concluding this essay, discuss the sort of listening that is called for when, as a member of the church, one listens to the sermon of someone who has been ordained to preach the Word of God and who is now undertaking to do so. In its distinctive blend of receptivity and activity, there is no other form of listening quite like it.

In many Christian denominations, before the one who is preaching was ordained, he or she was examined extensively by officers or appointees of the church to discern whether he or she had the gifts necessary for preaching the Word of God and whether they had received the training necessary. In the ordination ceremony itself they are then asked whether they believe they are called to the office of priest or minister and whether they commit themselves to faithfully filling that office. In the Episcopal ceremony, the words are these:

> *Bishop*: My brother [sister], do you believe that you are truly called by God and his Church to this priesthood.
>
> *Answer*: I believe I am so called.
>
> *Bishop*: Do you now in the presence of the Church commit yourself to this trust and responsibility?
>
> *Answer*: I do . . .
>
> *Bishop*: Will you endeavor so to minister the Word of God and the sacraments of the New Covenant, that the reconciling love of Christ may be known and received?
>
> *Answer*: I will . . .[21]

After making a number of additional commitments, the ordinand is then consecrated as a priest.

The fact that the person to whom I am listening was judged by the church to be gifted and trained for preaching the Word of God, that at her ordination she committed herself to doing so, and that she has undertaken to do so in preaching this sermon, requires, as its counterpart on my part, a distinct sort of listening. She is not an upstart standing on a street corner thundering divine judgment on passers-by. I have to take seriously what she is saying, in a way that I do not have to take seriously what the self-appointed street-corner prophet is saying. I have to listen in an attitude of receptivity—open to the likelihood that she is presenting to us what God said to us by way of the reading of Scripture. She has been judged gifted

---

21. *Sunday Missal*, 531–2.

and trained to preach the Word of God, she has meditated on the passage in the course of the week, read commentaries, taken note of what is happening in the life of the congregation and the church at large, in the city, the nation, the world. I listen in the expectation that I will hear from her lips the Word of God.

Given the nature of ordination, receptive listening is not only appropriate but obligatory. I began this essay with a sentence from the Episcopal liturgy for ordination. After the ordinand has been consecrated as a priest, he or she is given a Bible "as a sign of the authority given you to preach the Word of God and to administer his holy sacraments." Not only does the ordinand commit herself to preach the Word of God after being declared fit to do so. She is given *the authority* to do so, she is *authorized* to do so. Though not all ordination liturgies declare explicitly that the ordinand is given the authority to preach the Word of God, nonetheless, I judge that that is, in fact, what takes place in all of them. In addition to the church declaring the ordinand fit to preach the Word of God, and in addition to the ordinand declaring that she believes she is called to do so and committing herself to doing so, the church does this other distinct thing: it bestows on her the authority to do so.

How exactly such authority should be understood requires and merits an extensive discussion. Here is not the place for that. What is relevant for our purposes here is that, whenever someone is authorized to do something, that authorization carries with it the obligation on the part of others to honor and respect that authorization in whatever ways are appropriate. If someone is authorized to move into the White House, then the rest of us are obligated, as a minimum, to permit him or her to do so.

In the form for ordination of the RCA, the presiding minister, immediately after the ordination, turns to the congregation and says, "Beloved in the Lord, inasmuch as this most solemn procedure involves obligations and duties on your part toward him whom you have called to minister to you in holy things, I ask you before God and our Lord Jesus Christ . . . ."[22] The presiding minister then mentions obligations of the congregation, and asks whether they promise to accept those obligations, among them being the obligation "to receive the word of truth from his [the ordinand's] lips with meekness and love."[23]

Listening to an ordained preacher who has undertaken to preach the Word of God requires another, and deeper, form of receptivity as well. One is not just receptive to the likelihood that one is hearing the Word of God

---

22. *Sunday Missal*, 99.
23. *Sunday Missal*, 99.

preached. If one discerns that the Word of God is indeed preached, one is then receptive to that Word of God itself. One takes it in, receives it. One listens *to* the Word of God.

An attitude of receptivity is not sufficient, however, for listening to a sermon. One has to engage in *active* listening. For one thing, usually some of what a preacher says in the course of a sermon is not meant as a presentation of what God said. The preacher shares some news of the congregation, takes note of events in the nation, explains why they are singing a certain hymn, reports what some commentator said about the scriptural passage read, etc. Listeners have to discriminate between those parts of the sermon where the preacher is undertaking to preach the Word of God and those parts where he or she is doing something else.

Making this sort of discrimination is usually not difficult. Much more difficult is the active listening required by the fact that the preacher may fail in his or her undertaking to preach the Word of God. I noted, above, that this failure may take either of two forms. The preacher may have failed to discern what God was saying by way of the reading and may thus have attributed something quite different to God, or discerned only a small bit of what God was saying, missing most of it. Or the preacher may have discerned what God was saying but failed, partially or totally, in undertaking to present that to the congregation in such a way that they grasp it. Either way, the sort of active listening called for at this point is *listening for* the Word of God. In one of the Presbyterian worship books, the reading of Scripture is preceded by the reader's saying, "Listen for the Word of God!"[24] That, I suggest, is also what we are to do when we listen to the sermon.

Preachers fail to communicate for many different reasons: flowery speech that obscures the thought, silly jokes that distract, self-revelations that embarrass, theological jargon that most listeners don't understand, obscure ways of expressing himself. When we actively listen *for* the Word of God, we do our best to get past all such obstacles so as to discern what it is that the preacher is trying to say. We strain to catch that.

Suppose we have overcome the obstacles and grasped what the preacher is presenting to us as what God was saying by way of the reading of Scripture. What form does our active listening for the Word of God take when we keep in mind that the preacher may be mistaken in claiming that it was mainly such-and-such that God was saying? Do we listen to the preacher with a critical attitude?

Before I answer that question, let us take note of what makes it possible for us to judge that the preacher got it wrong—or got it mostly wrong. If

---

24. *The Worship Book*, 28.

someone claims to be telling me what someone else said whom I don't know at all, I have no reliable way of judging whether the speaker is correctly reporting what that other person said. I may know that the speaker is not very reliable; nonetheless, he may have gotten it right in this case. And I may judge it quite unlikely that a person of the sort referred to would say what is being attributed to him; nonetheless, he might have.

It is different when we listen to the sermon for the Word of God. Though few of us may have the gifts for spiritual discernment that the preacher has, nonetheless, most of us have some knowledge of God and of what God has said previously. And though few of us received the theological and biblical training that the preacher has, most of us have some knowledge of theology and some ability to interpret Scripture. It is because we too possess that knowledge and that ability that we can judge whether the preacher did or did not discern what God was saying.

Back to the question: do we then listen to the preacher with a critical attitude? We do not. In our listening, we are open to concluding that the preacher is mistaken. But we do not listen critically. Our underlying attitude remains that of receptivity. We remind ourselves that most of us are at least as fallible in discerning what God says as the preacher is.

I said that, in our listening, we are "open to concluding" that the preacher is mistaken in what he or she presents as the Word of God. Something stronger needs to be said. The church is *obligated*—as a body, not individually—to be open to concluding that the preacher is mistaken. Listening without being open to that conclusion is dangerous listening.

If we are successful in *listening for* what God was saying—if we have heard what God was saying—we then *listen to* what God was saying.[25]

---

25. I thank Terence Cuneo and Edwin van Driel for critical comments on a previous draft of this essay.

14

Knowing God by Liturgically Addressing God

> "The right worship of God is essential because it forms the mind to a right understanding of God."
> —Pastor Ames, speaking in Marilynne Robinson's novel *Gilead*.

The thesis I will develop in this essay is that participating in liturgical enactments is a way of gaining, deepening, and sustaining knowledge of God. More specifically, the thesis I will develop is that participating in the liturgical practice of *addressing God* is a way of gaining, deepening, and sustaining knowledge of God. By engaging God in the mode of address, we can come to know, and to know better, the one whom we address. We can become *attuned* to God, and remain attuned.[1]

There is, of course, more to liturgical participation than addressing God. In addition, there is listening when one is *being* addressed—for example, listening to the reading of Scripture and listening to the sermon. And these, too, contribute to one's knowledge of God. Indeed, most people will think of these when reflecting on liturgical participation as a way of gaining, deepening, and sustaining knowledge of God. They think of addressing God liturgically not as a way of gaining, deepening, and sustaining knowledge of God but as a way of expressing knowledge of God acquired in some other way.

Imagine a liturgical enactment that consists exclusively of the people addressing God; at no point are the people addressed. Enactments of the Orthodox liturgy sometimes come close to that. I hold that participating in

---

1. I addressed this same topic in my essay "Knowing God Liturgically," 1–16. My treatment of the topic in this present essay is very different from and, in my judgment, a vast improvement over what I wrote there.

such a liturgical enactment is a way of gaining, deepening, and sustaining knowledge of God. We will see how that works.

The sort of liturgical participation I have in mind is *fully compliant* participation. A person's participation is fully compliant if she performs all the verbal, gestural, and auditory acts prescribed for her and thereby also performs all the acts of worship prescribed to be performed thereby. What I have to say applies to many forms of participation that are not fully compliant. It applies, for example, to someone whose only abstention from doing what is prescribed is that she doesn't kneel or stand when those are prescribed. But our discussion will be much less cumbersome if, throughout, we have fully compliant participation in mind.

Types of Knowledge

Knowledge comes in a number of fundamentally different types. The type that has received far and away the most attention from philosophers in recent decades is knowledge that consists, at its core, of believing something—call it *doxastic* knowledge, from the Greek *doxa*, meaning belief. I say, "consists at its core." Not every belief is a case of knowledge; obviously a false belief is not. And many true beliefs are also not cases of knowledge; a correct guess, for example. Philosophers have spilled much ink trying to identify what else is necessary for a true belief to count as knowledge.

There are two types of doxastic knowledge. One type is knowledge of the form, *knowing that so-and-so*—for example, knowing that Lansing is the capital of the state of Michigan. Since what is known in knowledge of this form is commonly called by philosophers a *proposition*, knowledge of this sort is commonly called *propositional* knowledge, sometimes, *de dicto* knowledge.

The other type of doxastic knowledge is knowledge of the form, *knowing, about something, that it is such-and-such*—commonly called *de re* knowledge. For example, knowing, about Lansing, that it is the capital of the state of Michigan.

A question that will come to the mind of some readers is whether *de dicto* and *de re* knowledge really are two different forms of knowledge, as opposed to two different ways of expressing the same item of knowledge. Isn't what one knows, when one knows that Lansing is the capital of the state of Michigan, the same as what one knows when one knows, about Lansing, that it is the capital of the state of Michigan?

It is not the same. Suppose that one is in the city of Lansing and is reliably told that the city in which one finds oneself is the capital of the state of Michigan, but one doesn't know that the city is Lansing, nor does one know the name of the city that is the capital of Michigan. Then one knows, *about* the city in which one finds oneself, namely, Lansing, that it is the capital of the state of Michigan, but one doesn't know *that* Lansing is the capital of the state of Michigan.

It is likely that some readers will find the distinction between *de dicto* and *de re* knowledge arcane and not easy to wrap one's mind around. I introduce it not out of a love for distinctions but because we will need the concept of *de re* knowledge in our subsequent discussion.

A form of knowledge that has also received considerable attention from philosophers in recent decades, though much less than doxastic knowledge, is *knowledge-how*—knowing how to do something, how to play the violin, for example, or how to lay bricks. Such knowledge is commonly called *practical knowledge*. A question that has received considerable attention by philosophers is the relation between practical and doxastic knowledge. No doubt practical knowledge often incorporates some doxastic knowledge. But might it be the case that practical knowledge is nothing but a species of doxastic knowledge?[2]

In recent years, a third form of knowledge has caught the attention of some philosophers, namely *knowing some entity*: some person, some animal, some stuff, some object, some way of acting, etc. Such knowledge is now commonly called *objectual knowledge*.[3] Knowing a person—let me call it *person-knowledge*—is a species of objectual knowledge. In some languages—Dutch to name just one of many—objectual knowledge is marked off from doxastic and practical knowledge by distinct terms, in Dutch, *kennen* for objectual knowledge and *weten* for doxastic and practical knowledge.[4]

When I say that participating in the liturgical practice of addressing God is a way of gaining, deepening, and sustaining knowledge of God, the type of knowledge I have in mind is person-knowledge. I realize that, in classical Christian doctrine, God is *three* persons—a trinity of persons, rather than *a* person. The concept of *person* employed in this theological formula is obviously different from our ordinary concept of *person*. God is a personal being in three persons. I think no confusion will result from my saying that the sort of knowledge I have in mind, as gained, deepened, and sustained by liturgical participation, is *person-knowledge* of God.

---

2. For an example of the attempt to analyze practical knowledge as a species of doxastic knowledge, see Stanley and Williamson, "Knowing How," 411–44.

3. Some philosophers have argued that practical knowledge is a species of objectual knowledge. See Bengson and Moffett, "Nonpropositional Intellectualism," 161–95.

4. For additional linguistic markers, see Benton, "Epistemology Personalized," 813–34.

Whereas in recent years there has been an extraordinarily rich discussion of doxastic knowledge of God by philosophers of religion, I know of only four contemporary philosophers and one theologian who have discussed person-knowledge of God at any length: the philosophers William Alston in *Perceiving God*, Matthew A. Benton in his essay, "God and Interpersonal Knowledge," Terence Cuneo in his essay "Ritual Knowledge," and Eleonore Stump in *Wandering in Darkness*; and the theologian Sarah Coakley in her essay "'Beyond Belief': Liturgy and the Cognitive Apprehension of God." None of these five writers has taken note of gaining, deepening, and sustaining person-knowledge of God by participating in the liturgical practice of addressing God.

Practical Knowledge as Yielding Objectual Knowledge

Before I address my topic—gaining person-knowledge of God by participating in the liturgical practice of addressing God—I think it will help to have in hand a clear example of practical knowledge yielding objectual knowledge. Let me choose James Elkins's fascinating description, in *What Painting Is*, of coming to know paint by painting. There is, need I say, little similarity between paint and God! Nonetheless, in Elkins's description of coming to know paint by engaging in the practice of painting, we have an illuminating adumbration of several important points in our subsequent description of the person-knowledge of God that can be gained, deepened, and sustained by participating in the social practice of liturgically addressing God.

Elkins is an art historian; but before taking up art history he was a painter. He writes that he knows "from experience how utterly hypnotic the act of painting can be, and how completely it can overwhelm the mind with its smells and colors, and by the rhythmic motions of the brush."[5] I will focus first on what he says about the practical knowledge that the painter acquires, and then on what he says about the objectual knowledge of paint that this practical knowledge yields. In Elkins' discussion, these topics are interwoven; to some extent they will unavoidably be interwoven as well in my presentation of his thought.[6]

---

5. Elkin, *What Painting Is*, 6.

6. One of the most fascinating features of Elkins's discussion is his use, throughout the book, of alchemy to illuminate painting. Alchemy, he says, "despite all its bad press, and its association with quackery and nonsense, . . . is the best and most eloquent way to understand how paint can *mean*: how it can be so entrancing, so utterly addictive, so replete with expressive force, that it can keep hold of an artist's attention for an entire life-time. Alchemists had immediate, intuitive knowledge of waters and stones, and

The practice of painting, says Elkins, "takes place outside science and any sure and exact knowledge. It is a kind of immersion in substances, a wonder and a delight in their unexpected shapes and feels."[7] "Its materials are worked without [scientific] knowledge of their properties, by blind experiment, by the feel of the paint. A painter knows what to do by the tug of the brush as it pulls through a mixture of oils, and by the look of colored slurries on the palette. . . . Artists become expert in distinguishing between degrees of gloss and wetness—and they do so without knowing how they do it, or how chemicals create their effects."[8] Elkins shows no interest in the chemistry of paint.

On Elkins' description, only a small part of the know-how of the painter consists of *de re* beliefs about paint or painting. Most of it is subdoxastic, located primarily in his eye and the muscles of his fingers, wrist, and arm. It is located in his acquired ability to make fine intuitive discriminations in the look and feel of paint and in his ability to interpret the significance of those differences. Such knowledge "can just barely be taught, and it can never be written down."[9]

Elkins notes that it was traditionally thought that there were rules for painting and that those rules could be taught; it was the project of art academies to teach the rules to novices. Painting, on Elkins' account, is beyond the reach of any "routine education." It is not that there is nothing about the know-how of painting that can be taught by routine education; rather, much, if not most, of the know-how of the painter does not consist of following rules that were formulated and taught him by some teacher.

Let us move on from Elkins' description of the practical know-how of the painter to his description of the artist's objectual knowledge of paint that his know-how gives him. "Painters learn substances," says Elkins. "Long years spent in the studio can make a person into a treasury of nearly incommunicable knowledge about the powderiness of pastels, or the woody feel of different marbles, or the infinitesimally different iridescences of ceramic glazes. That kind of knowledge is very hard to pass on, and it is certainly not expressed well in books on artist's techniques. . . . But it is a form of knowledge."[10]

---

their obscure books can help give voice to the ongoing fascination of painting" (Elkins, *What Painting Is*, 7). I will have to neglect Elkins's description of alchemy.

7. Elkins, *What Painting Is*, 193.
8. Elkins, *What Painting Is*, 9.
9. Elkins, *What Painting Is*, 18.
10. Elkins, *What Painting Is*, 22–23.

"Painters know paint by their bodies," he says, "'body' is a standard painter's term for the heft of the paint, its resilience and sturdiness. Paint that has no body is 'thin' or 'lean,' and apt to disappear into the crevices of the weave. . . . Other paint is called 'fat,' and it adheres to the canvas in lumps and pats, reminding even the most absentminded viewer that the object is a painting, and not a landscape."[11]

"There is so much to learn about even the simplest substances," says Elkins.[12] "Each paint [has] its particular feel, its quirks and idiosyncrasies, or it cannot take its place in the mixtures and blendings" of the painter.[13] Elkins offers a flurry of detailed descriptions of what it is about paint that painters learn. The common thread in these descriptions is that the knowledge of paint that painters acquire is knowledge of the distinctive character of different paints: what different paints are like, how different paints act and react, their causal powers and dispositions. But words cannot capture what it is that a painter knows when he knows what is distinctive of a certain paint. Poetic though many of Elkins' descriptions are, one does not, by reading them, come to know paint as Elkins knows paint. His objectual knowledge of paint, like his practical knowledge of how to paint, is largely sub-doxastic. Many of those who take painting lessons in the hope of becoming painters never acquire the requisite know-how and consequently never get to know paint, except in the most elementary way. Knowing paint eludes them. So they beat their head against the wall, or give up and do something else.

Before moving on, let me give a simple personal example of sub-doxastic practical knowledge yielding sub-doxastic objectual knowledge. I know how to type using all ten fingers and without looking at the keyboard. This knowledge-how does not consist of applying beliefs that I possess about how to type; the knowledge is embedded in the muscles of my fingers. The fact that I know how to type implies that I also possess objectual knowledge of the layout of the keyboard. But I am unable to describe or sketch the layout; I do not possess the *de re* beliefs concerning the relative location of the keys that would enable me to do that. When learning to type, I must have formed beliefs about the layout; I would then have had *de re* doxastic knowledge of the relative location of the keys. But if so, that memory disappeared long ago. My objectual knowledge of the layout of the keyboard is now entirely sub-doxastic, lodged in the muscles of my fingers.

---

11. Elkins, *What Painting Is*, 104.
12. Elkins, *What Painting Is*, 34.
13. Elkins, *What Painting Is*, 67.

Gleaning from Elkins

I remarked that in Elkins' description of coming to know paint by painting we have an adumbration of several important points in our subsequent description of coming to know God by liturgically addressing God.

First, and most important, in Elkins' description of coming to know paint by painting we have a clear example of practical knowledge yielding objectual knowledge. Elkins came to know paint by engaging in the practice of painting. So too, I claim, one can come to know God by participating in the practice of liturgically addressing God.

Second, learning how to paint, as Elkins describes it, does not consist of learning how to apply beliefs about the properties of paint acquired by reading books or listening to lectures on the chemistry of paint. Elkins did, of course, have beliefs about the properties of paint. But many of those beliefs were acquired by engaging in the practice of painting; the practice preceded the beliefs rather than the beliefs preceding the practice. And much of his knowledge of paint was ocular and muscular knowledge, knowledge embedded in his eyes and in the muscles of his fingers, wrist, and arm, sub-doxastic knowledge, not knowledge in the form of *de re* beliefs about the properties of paint. Probably some of it did not even reach the level of awareness.

So too, I will argue, learning to participate in the practice of addressing God liturgically does not consist of learning how to apply beliefs about God that one acquired in some other way. One acquires beliefs about God by engaging in the practice; and a good deal of the knowledge of God acquired by engaging in the practice is not in the form of *de re* beliefs but is sub-doxastic.

Third, the knowledge of paint that Elkins acquired by painting was acquired by bodily interaction with paint: seeing it, smelling it, mixing it, feeling it on one's brush. It was, in that way, very different from the knowledge of paint that a chemist has. So too, the knowledge of God acquired by liturgically addressing God is different from the knowledge of God articulated by theologians.

Fourth, the knowledge of paint that Elkins acquired by painting was not just a smattering of items of knowledge; that would not count as *knowing paint*. What he gained was a sense of the *character* of paint, or rather, of different kinds of paint—a sense of what is distinctive of paint of different kinds. So too, the knowledge of God acquired by liturgical participation is knowledge of what is distinctive of God. A point implicit in Elkins's discussion is that the sense a painter acquires of the distinctives of different kinds of paint comes in degrees; one can know a certain paint very well, or not very well. So, too, with liturgically acquired knowledge of God.

Knowing a Person

To make my case, that knowledge of God can be gained, deepened, and sustained by participating in the liturgical knowledge of God—that we can thereby become attuned to God—it will be necessary to spend some time discussing person-knowledge in general; the understanding that the typical reader brings to the discussion will not be sufficient.

Only recently have philosophers devoted sustained attention to objectual knowledge in general, and to person-knowledge in particular. I regard the two articles by Matthew A. Benton already mentioned ("God and Interpersonal Knowledge" and "Epistemology Personalized"), in which he develops an analysis of person-knowledge in the context of a thorough acquaintance with the recent literature on the topic, as a state-of-the-art discussion of the issues. So rather than striking out on my own, let me present, respond to, and appropriate elements of Benton's analysis. Benton's discussion is rich and detailed. Here, I must neglect that richness and confine myself to presenting its highlights.

Strictly speaking, what Benton offers is not an analysis of what it is for one person to know another but of what it is for two persons to know each other; *interpersonal* knowledge he calls it. Benton's focus on interpersonal knowledge is not incidental on his part. He affirms a principle that he calls "symmetry":

SYMMETRY: S knows R, only if R knows S.[14]

It is not clear to me why Benton holds this principle of symmetry. Though most of the cases he cites are examples of interpersonal knowledge, it seems clear to me that, in general, S can have person-knowledge of R without R having person-knowledge of S. Accordingly, with an eye on my subsequent analysis of our liturgical knowledge of God, I will delete, from my presentation of Benton's thought, the interpersonal component. Participating in the liturgical practice of addressing God is a way for the participants to gain knowledge of God; it is not a way for God to gain knowledge of the participants.

Benton's discussion is shaped by the distinction between knowing *a person* and having *de re* doxastic knowledge *about* that person—for example, knowing, about a person, *who* she is, so that one can identify her.[15] He observes

---

14. Benton, "God and Interpersonal Knowledge," 425.

15. Benton offers a number of considerations in favor of the conclusion that person-knowledge is not a species of doxastic knowledge ("Epistemology Personalized," 814–19). I find his arguments compelling. Rather than rehearsing them here, I refer the interested reader to his discussion.

that our ordinary English term "knows so-and-so" is ambiguous on this point. He writes, "the 'S knows NP' construction can take a propositional use and an interpersonal use."[16] He holds—rightly, in my judgment—that the locution "S knows so-and-so personally" is not ambiguous in this way; it consistently refers to what I have been calling "person-knowledge." It makes sense to say: "I know Rebecca, though I don't know her personally."

What, then, is Benton's analysis of *knowing someone personally*? He writes, "two people might have excellent knowledge of each other by working in the same institution and learning about each other from web research, or internal literature, or from the say-so of colleagues. They recognize each other's faces, they might go to the same committee meetings and hear each other offer suggestions, and so on."[17] Nonetheless, they might not know each other personally. What is missing? Referring to the epistemologist Ernest Sosa's discussion of person-knowledge, Benton writes, "Sosa notes that knowing a person requires an acquaintance-like perceptual contact."[18] The requirement of "acquaintance-like perceptual contact" is satisfied in the case Benton imagines. So what, then, is still missing?

What is missing, says Benton, is an "encounter" of a certain sort. He highlights three features of this encounter. First, knowing someone personally "requires treating another subject *as a subject*, that is, as an 'I' treats an individual 'you,' . . . for example in the language of address or in joint attention to objects or topics of conversation."[19] If two people have "never addressed each other in conversation or properly met, it would seem they don't yet know each other personally."[20]

Second, the encounter must yield a meeting of minds. In knowing someone personally, "the mind of the known subject itself [is brought] right into the subjective life of the knower's mind."[21] Knowing each other personally—interpersonal knowledge—is "a state of minds meeting."[22] Whereas knowledge-that "is a state of mind consisting in a subject's attitude to a (true) proposition, . . . interpersonal knowledge [is] a state of mind*s* [plural], involving a subject's attitude to another (existing) mind."[23]

---

16. Benton, "Epistemology Personalized," 818.
17. Benton, "God and Interpersonal Knowledge," 423.
18. Benton, "Epistemology Personalized," 822.
19. Benton, "Epistemology Personalized," 821.
20. Benton, "God and Interpersonal Knowledge," 423.
21. Benton, "Epistemology Personalized," 823.
22. Benton, "Epistemology Personalized," 823.
23. Benton, "Epistemology Personalized," 813.

Third, the "acquaintance-like perceptual contact" must function essentially in bringing about this meeting of minds. Knowing someone personally requires perceptual contact with the other person in which one "[learns] facts from them first-hand," that is, "not mediated by transmission through someone else's mind."[24] This contact need not be "in the flesh perceptual contact."[25] It might be "technologically mediated" and still be a "meeting of the minds." "Thus, two people could interpersonally know each other entirely as pen pals or phone pals or chat room pals."[26] Such technologically mediated knowledge would be deficient in that the two persons would have little or no "qualitative knowledge of mannerisms, facial expressions, mood patterns, and so on,"[27] and little or no knowledge of who the other person is, that is, little or no knowledge that enables one to identify the other person by, for example, visual recognition. "For mature subjects, interpersonal knowledge typically brings with it some knowledge-who by which the known person can be individuated."[28] But that is not essential to knowing someone personally. What is essential is that one gain some of one's knowledge of the other person *directly from the other person* without the mediation of another person's mind. "Some of what one learns about [the other] is learned from, because it is given to one by, the [other person]."[29]

Such knowledge comes in degrees. "Through personal encounters, people can progress from being mere acquaintances to being friends, to close friends, to intimates or lovers. Increase in personal encounters, once there are enough of them, makes for interpersonal knowing."[30] There is probably "a context-sensitive threshold for how well S knows R, or how often S and R have had personal interactions in order for S to count, in a given context, as knowing R personally. In some contexts knowing someone interpersonally requires more than just having met once. . . . In other contexts, even when one hasn't met someone multiple times, one can in principle still count as knowing someone: 'Do you know R?' 'Yes, I just met her for the first time yesterday.'"[31]

---

24. Benton, "Epistemology Personalized," 822.
25. Benton, "Epistemology Personalized," 21.
26. Benton, "Epistemology Personalized," 824.
27. Benton, "Epistemology Personalized," 824.
28. Benton, "Epistemology Personalized," 824–25.
29. Benton, "Epistemology Personalized," 822.
30. Benton, "God and Interpersonal Knowledge," 425.
31. Benton, "Epistemology Personalized," 825.

Appraising Benton's Analysis

Though Benton places a great deal of emphasis on his claim that knowing someone personally requires having treated them as a subject by, for example, addressing them as "you," that claim seems to me mistaken. I must, of course, *regard* them as a person. But I might know someone personally without ever having had occasion to address them, or in some other way to *treat* them as a person. It is not true, so far as I can see, that if two people have "never addressed each other in conversation or properly met, it would seem they don't yet know each other personally."[32]

That leaves us with two core intuitions on Benton's part as to what constitutes knowing someone personally, both of which seem to me essentially correct. To know someone personally, I must have some "acquaintance-like perceptual contact" with them, and/or with their speech or actions. That contact need not be face-to-face, in-the-flesh, contact; it may be technologically mediated. Her appearance may be mediated to me by television or Skype, what she says may be mediated to me by phone or by texting. But in one way or another, she must be presented to me, given to me, revealed to me; and at least some of my knowledge of her must be "anchored" in that.

Second, I must acquire, in this way, a sense of her mind, says Benton. "Mind" seems to me too restrictive, at least when interpreted as it ordinarily would be interpreted. In knowing someone personally, one acquires a sense not only of how they think but of how they feel, of what they love, of what they invest themselves in. One acquires a sense of their character, of what is distinctive of them, of what makes them "tick."

It turns out that knowing someone personally has the same fundamental structure as knowing paint in the way that Elkins came to know paint: to have an Elkins-like knowledge of a certain paint, one must have a sense of its character, its distinctives, acquired by perceptual contact with the paint.

Beyond Benton

Suppose that I have never met Reuben. Nor have I ever seen him, either in person or on any electronic medium such as television, Skype, and the like. Neither have I heard him speak, neither when in his presence nor by way of telephone and the like. Nor have I read anything he has written. But Jennifer, a good friend of both of us, has been with him often and talked with him at length. Her personal knowledge of him is deep. And she has transmitted to me so much of what he is like that I feel I know him well,

---

32. Benton, "God and Interpersonal Knowledge," 423.

better than I know a good many of my friends. I know what drives him, how he thinks, what makes him tick.

I would hesitate to say that I know Reuben *personally*, perhaps because, to use Benton's terminology, my knowledge has been "mediated" through "another person's mind." But if asked whether I know Reuben or just know some things about him, I would unhesitatingly say that I know *him*. I have a good sense of his character, and I have acquired my sense of his character by way of someone who knows him well personally transmitting her sense of his character to me. Though I myself don't have perceptual acquaintance with Reuben, nonetheless, by way of Jennifer's transmission I have a sense of his character that is *anchored in* perceptual acquaintance with him—anchored in *her* perceptual acquaintance. That is why I know *him*, and don't just have *de re* knowledge of things *about* him. Though I don't know him personally, I nonetheless have person-knowledge of him.

An Unusual Example of Getting to Know a Person

I now invite the reader to imagine an example of a quite unusual way of getting to know a person. Imagine someone—let us call her Hannah—who has emigrated from the old country with her parents and her siblings except for one brother, Jurian, who declines to emigrate because he has just landed a high position in the secret service of the government. He tells Hannah, before she leaves, that he is eager to receive frequent letters from her, but that his position makes it impossible for him to reply on any regular basis. On occasion, she may receive a message from him by way of a courier. And every now and then he will send a gift.

Hannah writes Jurian faithfully, interweaving news about her doings in the new country with expressions of her ardent love for him, reminiscences about their good times together in the past, her pride in him for the high position he has secured, praise for what he is doing, according to reports that occasionally come her way, requests of various sorts, concerns of hers that she hopes he can do something about, etc.

Hannah marries and has children. When the eldest of her children, Ben, is in his early teens, Hannah notices him watching intently as she writes to Jurian. One day he asks whether he can also write to Jurian—for him, it is *Uncle* Jurian. Hannah says, "of course." But she has never told him anything about Jurian, other than that Jurian is an uncle of his in the old country and that Jurian loves to receive letters but cannot answer them on any regular basis. She has not shared with him the few communications she has received from Jurian, nor the reports that have come her way about his doings. Though she gladly allows Ben to look over her shoulder when she is writing to Jurian, for reasons she doesn't explain, she never talks to Ben *about* his uncle. So what is Ben to write?

"Why not copy what I write," says Hannah; your uncle will love getting a letter in his nephew's handwriting. So that is what Ben does: he copies his mother's letters to Uncle Jurian. On occasion, Hannah varies the practice. Sometimes she says aloud the next sentence, and they write it down together. Now and then she dictates a letter for Ben to write to his uncle. Where "I" in his mother's letters refers to her, the "I" in Ben's letters refers to him, of course.

Ben finds much in his mother's letters to Uncle Jurian that is very striking, especially the reverential tone that she adopts toward Jurian, the ardent love for her brother that she expresses, and the range of concerns that she seems to think he can do something about. When his mother writes "I love you," he faithfully copies the sentence even though he isn't entirely sure that he does love his uncle. After some time, he is quite sure he does. Writing to his uncle whom he loves him has ignited in him love for his uncle.

Gradually Ben gets the hang of how to address his uncle in a way that befits his uncle's high position, and the hang of which sorts of things it is appropriate to tell him and ask him. Ben begins to interpolate a few sentences of his own into the letters of his mother that he copies. Then, one day, he asks whether he can write his own letter. His mother says, "go ahead." Before he sends it off, he shows her what he has written. "That is fine," she says.

My question now is this: has Ben, in this curious way, gotten to know his Uncle Jurian? Has he gained a sufficient sense of his uncle's distinctiveness, and has he gained that knowledge in the right way, for his knowledge to count as person-knowledge of his uncle? I would say that he has, or may well have. Hannah knows Jurian from having grown up with him. In the curious way described, she has transmitted much of what she has long known of her brother to Ben. What she transmits is anchored in her perceptual acquaintance with Jurian. Not all of what she knows in this way can be transmitted, of course. Some of it cannot be captured in words: the way he walks, for example, the way he gestures, the timbre of his voice. But as we saw above, one can gain a sense of someone's distinctiveness sufficient for knowing the person without oneself having perceptual acquaintance with the person. Over time, Hannah has transmitted to Ben much of what can be put into words that she knows, by acquaintance, of Jurian's distinctiveness. And that may be enough to count as Ben having person-knowledge of his uncle. Should he someday meet his uncle and engage him in conversation, he might well respond: "Uncle Jurian is just as I expected him to be!"

Knowing God by Participating in Liturgically Addressing God

It is time to employ what we have learned about person-knowledge in general to the topic of this essay, namely, gaining, deepening, and sustaining knowledge of God—becoming attuned to God—by participating in the liturgical practice of addressing God. Just as Ben learned how to address his uncle by engaging in the scripted action of following the example of his mother, so one learns how to address God by engaging in the scripted action of participating in the liturgy.[33] And just as Ben came to know his uncle by learning, in the way described, how to address him, so one comes to know God by learning how to address God liturgically.

There may be some people who have never participated in any liturgical enactment but have come to know God by reading Scripture. Such a person might, at a certain point, decide to address God in a way that accords with his biblically acquired knowledge of God. Or he might look around for an assembly of believers who address God in a way that accords with his biblically acquired knowledge of God and, if he finds such an assembly, join them in their worship. This person knows God before he addresses God. For him, addressing God is a way of putting into practice, or expressing, his knowledge of God. Among the things he has come to know of God is that God is worthy of praise. Now he puts that knowledge into practice by praising God for what God has done and is doing.

That is not how things go for most worshippers. They don't first come to know God and then participate in liturgical enactments in order to express the knowledge of God they have already acquired. In good measure, they come to know God by participating in liturgical enactments. Some of the knowledge of God gained by liturgical participation is acquired by listening to what is said when they are addressed by the reader of Scripture and by the preacher; but much of it is acquired by participating in the scripted action of addressing God.

A central component of Christian conviction is that God has spoken by way of the prophets, by way of Christ and the apostles, and by way of Christian Scripture, and that, by listening to what God has said in these ways, we learn what is distinctive of God. God is creator of heaven and earth, God is love, and so forth. The sort of liturgy I have in mind—when I say that knowledge of God can be gained, deepened, and sustained by participating in liturgically addressing God—is liturgy that is anchored in, and shaped

---

33. I discuss scripted action in general in chapter 1 of my *Acting Liturgically*, and scripted *liturgical* action in particular in chapter 2.

by, God's revelation. Assuming that God has in fact revealed Godself in the way Christians claim God has, such liturgies are, one might say, *reliable* with respect to the understanding of God explicit and implicit within them.[34] And they are *communitarian* with respect to that understanding. A liturgy devised by an individual to express his own haphazardly acquired personal "take" on God is neither reliable nor communitarian.

Knowing God by Taking for Granted, in Addressing God, God's Distinctiveness

Let us identify some of the aspects of liturgy that account for the fact that one can gain, deepen, and sustain knowledge of God by participating in the liturgical practice of addressing God. Over and over in Christian liturgical enactments the people address God as *You*: "we bless You, O God," "we worship You," "we praise You," "we thank You," "we confess to You," "we petition You." The participants engage God in second-person address. In doing so, they take for granted that God is the sort of being whom it is appropriate to engage in that way. They take for granted that God is a subject. The thought that God is a subject never crosses the mind of most of them; nowhere in the liturgy does anyone declare God to be a subject. They just address God as "You" and, in so doing, take God to be a subject—the sort of being whom it is appropriate to engage in second-person address. Some of them, at some point in their lives, may form the explicit belief that God is a subject. Most of them do not; *being a subject* is not a component in their conceptual repertoire.

Add, now, that God is in fact a subject. Then, by participating in the scripted liturgical practice of addressing God as "You" they acquire some sense of what is distinctive of God. They gain some person-knowledge of God. Practical knowledge yielding person-knowledge.

In liturgically addressing God the participants also take for granted that God is capable of listening, that is, capable of cognitively apprehending what they say to God. Otherwise, addressing God as "You" in the way they do makes no sense.[35] The thought that God is a listener also never crosses

---

34. In employing the concept of reliability at this point I am, of course, gesturing toward reliability theories of propositional knowledge.

35. In Wolterstorff, *The God We Worship*, I distinguish what I call "strong address" from what I call "weak address." In strong address, one takes one's addressee to be capable of apprehending what one is saying; in weak address, one does not. An example of weak address would be a child saying to his goldfish, "You sweet little things." When one considers the full range of liturgical address to God, it is obvious that such address is strong address.

the mind of most participants; nowhere in the liturgy does anyone declare God to be a listener. In addressing God as they do, the participants just take for granted that God is a listener. Add, now, that God is in fact capable of listening. Then, by participating in the scripted liturgical practice of addressing God, they acquire some sense of what is distinctive of God. They gain some person-knowledge of God.

"We worship You, O God," say the participants, "we praise You," "we thank You." In addressing God in this way, the participants take for granted not just that God is a subject capable of listening but that God is a listening subject of a distinct sort, namely, one who is worthy of worship, praise, and thanks. In some liturgies there is an explicit declaration that God is worthy of worship, praise, and thanks; in many, there is not. When there is not, the thought that God is this sort of being probably doesn't cross the mind of most participants, certainly not of those who are young. In how they address God, they just take for granted that God is that sort of being.

Add, now, that God is in fact worthy of worship, praise, and thanks. Then by engaging in the liturgical practice of addressing God in these ways they gain some sense of what is distinctive of God. They acquire some person-knowledge of God.

In the enactment of all Christian liturgies the participants also address to God their confession of individual and communal sins and ask God for forgiveness. The point of doing so is that our sins are sins *against* God; they are wrongings of God. In addressing one's confession of sin to God and asking God's forgiveness, one is taking God to have been wronged, and thus to be the sort of being who can be wronged. Only the person that one wronged can forgive one for the wrong one did them. In no Christian liturgy that I know of is it explicitly declared that God is the sort of being who can be wronged; the participants just take it for granted in addressing to God their confession of sin.

Add, now, that God is in fact the sort of being who can be wronged. Then, by engaging in the liturgical practice of confessing one's sins to God and asking forgiveness, one gains some sense of God's nature, God's distinctiveness. One acquires some person-knowledge of God. At some point in one's life one may form the explicit belief that God is the sort of being who can be wronged. Then again, the thought may never cross one's mind. This aspect of one's knowledge of God may remain sub-doxastic.

My general point will now be obvious; it would be tedious to analyze additional examples. To participate in the liturgical practice of addressing God in accord with the script of some reliable Christian liturgy is to take God to be a subject who is capable of listening, who is worthy of worship, praise, and thanks, who can be and has been wronged, etc. If God is as one takes God to be in one's address to God, then, by engaging in the liturgical practice of addressing God in these various ways, one comes to know God in those respects—or to deepen and sustain one's knowledge. For most participants, the knowledge of God acquired in this way is almost entirely sub-doxastic.

We have been touching here on a phenomenon that pervades our lives, the phenomenon of gaining knowledge of certain aspects of reality by engaging in activities in which one takes for granted that aspect of reality. Every human being who lives past infancy has been socialized, this socialization consisting, in good measure, of being taught when and how to perform certain actions and when and how to participate in certain social practices. Anyone who performs those actions and participates in those practices takes for granted a great number of things about the world, herself, and her fellow human beings. If those things are as we take them to be, then, in taking those things for granted in what we learn to do, we gain objectual knowledge of the world, ourselves, and others.

An example: our objectual knowledge of the physical world includes knowing that the world existed before we were born. But nobody in the course of our socialization bothered to tell us that the world existed before we were born. We just learned to perform a wide variety of actions in which one takes for granted that the world existed before one was born. Another example: objectual knowledge of the physical world includes knowing that, in fundamental ways, the future will be like the past as we have experienced it. But nobody in the course of our socialization told us this. We just took it for granted in a wide range of actions that we learned to perform.[36]

Much of what we take for granted in what we do is never explicitly believed by the ordinary person. It is *sub-doxastic* knowledge. It never crosses the mind of most people that the world existed before they were born. If the question were put to them whether or not they believe this, they would say they do—with the possible exception of a few highly sophisticated philosophers.[37] But most people are never asked. I am not aware that any philosopher has ever articulated an analysis of what it is to take something for granted in what one does. But clearly any such analysis would have to be

---

36. I have adapted these two examples from Ludwig Wittgenstein's scattered remarks, on taking things about reality for granted in what we do, in his little book *On Certainty*. He argues that to say that we know that the world existed before we were born and that we know that the future will be more or less like the past is a strained use of the word "know," if not incorrect. I do not find his argument on that point persuasive.

37. Those highly sophisticated philosophers who say they do not believe this might nonetheless take it for granted in their everyday lives. Not only do we all take things for granted that we do not hold as beliefs; one can believe the negation of something that one takes for granted.

compatible with the fact that one can take something for granted in what one does without then, or ever, explicitly believing it.

Before we move on, let it be noted that it is by no means only when addressing God that liturgical participants take God to be a certain way. In closing their eyes and kneeling for the prayers, they take God to be a certain way. In receiving the Eucharistic elements, they take God to be a certain way. And so forth. Whatever they take God to be in performing the actions of some reliable liturgy, if God is in fact that way, then, by performing those actions they gain, deepen, or sustain knowledge of God as being that way. One of the tasks of liturgical theology is to bring to the level of explicit belief such knowledge of God.

An Interruption

Let me interrupt my train of thought for a moment. I said that there are probably many worshippers who confess their sins to God and ask God for forgiveness, thereby taking for granted that God can be wronged, without ever having the thought, then or later, that God can be wronged. However, there might also be some who do have the thought but reject it. A good many philosophers and theologians have explicitly rejected the proposition that God can be wronged. What we take for granted about God, in confessing our sins to God and asking God for forgiveness, is contradicted in a good many philosophy and theology classrooms.

Now suppose that the philosopher or theologian who claims that God cannot be wronged participates in the liturgical actions of confessing his sins to God and asking God for forgiveness. He does not just say the words without performing any illocutionary act thereby, nor is he a revisionist who does something else when he utters those words than confess and ask for forgiveness. He is a fully compliant participant; he follows the script. He says the words that the script prescribes and thereby performs the actions of worship that the script prescribes to be performed thereby. He confesses and asks for forgiveness by saying the words. Does he or does he not possess the liturgically acquired knowledge of God as one who can be wronged? Can his explicit belief to the contrary inhibit his knowledge of God in that respect?

I think not. Recall an example I gave earlier. I know the standard layout of a typewriter (or computer) keyboard; the knowledge is in the muscles of my fingers. At present I cannot, however, diagram the layout. Suppose I do my best to visualize the layout and diagram what I think it is, but get it partly wrong. Do I, or do I not, know the keyboard layout? I would say that I do, notwithstanding my false beliefs on the matter. The proof of the fact that I do know the layout is that I don't make mistakes in my typing—except for mistakes caused by the fact that my fingers are not as nimble as they once were.

And so, I think, it is in general. If, in performing some action, we really do take for granted that reality is a certain way and reality is that way, then we know reality as being that way even if we explicitly believe that it is not. The philosophical skeptic who has brought himself around to believing that the world did not exist before he was born nonetheless knows that it did. His knowledge that it did does not have the form of a contrary belief; it has the form of sub-doxastic objectual knowledge embedded in his actions.

I am reminded here of the mocking treatment of the philosophical skeptic by the eighteenth-century Scots philosopher Thomas Reid. Imagine that I am a skeptic about the existence of an external world.

> I resolve not to believe my senses. I break my nose against a post that comes in my way; I step into a kennel; and, after twenty such wise and rational actions, I am taken up and slapped into a mad-house.... If a man pretends to be a skeptic with regard to the informations of sense and yet prudently keeps out of harm's way as other men do, he must excuse my suspicion, that he either acts the hypocrite, or imposes upon himself.[38]

Participating in some liturgical enactment is, of course, very different from employing one's senses to get around in the world, and denying that God can be wronged is very different from denying the existence of an external world. But it is true in general, so it appears to me, that the objectual knowledge one has of some aspect of reality, on account of taking that aspect of reality for granted in what one does, is not inhibited by holding a belief to the contrary.

Gaining Knowledge of God from the Basis-Specifications of Liturgical Address to God

Participants in liturgical enactments do not just declare, "we worship You, O God"; they specify *for what it is* that they worship God: for God's wisdom, God's power, God's love, whatever. They specify the basis of their worship. And they do not just declare, "we praise You, O God"; they specify the basis of their praise of God. So too for their declarations of gratitude;

---

38. I discuss Reid's treatment of the skeptic in chapter 8 of Wolterstorff, *Thomas Reid and the Story of Epistemology*.

they specify the basis of their gratitude. Let me call these specifications, *basis-specifications*. The basis-specifications of liturgical address to God are a second aspect of liturgy accounting for the fact that one can gain, deepen, and sustain knowledge of God by participating in the liturgical practice of addressing God.

Eucharistic prayers provide a rich body of examples of basis-specifications. One example will suffice. Here are some lines from one of the Eucharistic prayers of the people in the *Book of Common Prayer*. The prayer is spoken by the celebrant.

> God of all power, Ruler of the Universe, You are worthy of glory and praise.
>
> At your command all things came to be: the vast expanse of interstellar space, . . . and this fragile earth, our island home.
>
> From the primal elements you brought forth the human race and blessed us. . . . You made us rulers of creation. But we turned against You. . . .
>
> Again and again, You called us to return. . . . And in the fullness of time You sent your only Son . . . to open for us the way of freedom and peace.
>
> Therefore we praise You, joining with the heavenly chorus, with prophets, apostles, and martyrs.[39]

If the basis-specifications in this prayer apply to God, then, by participating in this prayer, one learns many of the specifics of what God has done that make God worthy of praise. One gains person-knowledge of God.

The hymns that the people sing are another rich body of examples of the point. One example will again suffice.

> For the beauty of the earth, for the glory of the skies,
> for the love which from our birth over and around us lies. . . .
>
> For the joy of human love, brother, sister, parent, child,
> friends on earth, and friends above, for all gentle thoughts and mild. . . .
>
> For Yourself, best gift divine, to the world so freely given,
> agent of God's grand design, peace on earth and joy divine. . . .
>
> Christ, our Lord, to You we raise, this our hymn of grateful praise.[40]

---

39. *Book of Common Prayer*, 370.
40. #19 in Borger, Tel, and Witvliet, eds., *Lift Up Your Hearts*.

The hymn consists entirely of basis-specifications. A new-comer to Christianity who participates in singing this hymn may not understand everything she is singing. But if she continues to participate in singing this hymn and others like it, and gradually comes to understand what the words refer to, then, assuming the basis-specifications apply to God, she increases in her person-knowledge of God.

The Psalms, which the people sing, chant, or recite, are another rich body of examples. Here are the opening lines of Psalm 147:

> Praise the LORD!
> How good it is to sing praises to our God;
> > for the LORD is gracious, and a song of praise is fitting.
>
> The LORD builds up Jerusalem,
> > and gathers the outcasts of Israel.
>
> The LORD heals the brokenhearted,
> > and binds up their wounds.
>
> The LORD determines the number of stars,
> > and gives to all of them their names.
>
> Great is our LORD, and abundant in power,
> > with understanding beyond measure.
>
> The LORD lifts up the downtrodden,
> > and casts the wicked to the ground.
>
> Sing to the LORD with thanksgiving.[41]

Assuming that the basis-specifications in this psalm apply to God, by participating in voicing this psalm, one's knowledge of what God has done that makes God worthy of praise is deepened and enhanced.[42]

A point that is important to add here is that, in learning the basis-specifications of liturgical address to God, one not only comes to know God but also learns to see history and reality, including oneself, in a distinctive way. One learns to see the beauty of the earth and the glory of the skies as God's handiwork. One learns to see the joy of human love as God's gift. One learns

---

41. NRSV, adapted to remove gendered pronouns for God.

42. An unusually exuberant example of the point we are making here is the prayer in the Orthodox liturgy that occurs at the opening of the Anaphora:

"It is meet and right to sing praises unto thee, to bless thee, to magnify thee, to give thanks unto thee, to worship thee in all places of thy dominion. For thou art God ineffable, unknowable, incomprehensible, the same from everlasting to everlasting. . . . Thou didst bring us up from non-being into being; and didst raise us up that were fallen away; and left naught undone till thou hadst lifted us to heaven, and hadst bestowed upon us thy kingdom to come. For all these things we give thanks unto thee."

to see human beings as turning against God and as called to return to God. One learns to see history as the arena in which God opens up for us the way to freedom and peace. One learns to see the righting of injustice as a manifestation of God's love and a sign of the coming of God's kingdom.

It is in the assembly, by participating in the liturgy, that one learns to see reality and history in these ways. But one's seeing things in these ways does not cease when one leaves the assembly. It carries over into one's life in the everyday. That is because that for which one gives God thanks and praise is mainly not for what God does in the assembly but for what God does in history and reality in general.

When the way of seeing history and reality that one has acquired liturgically carries over into one's life in the everyday, it often comes into conflict with alternative ways of seeing history and reality that are prominent in our culture and that powerfully impinge themselves upon us. The result, for many, is that their way of seeing things is bifurcated and unstable. They regard all human beings as possessing the ineradicable dignity of bearing the image of God. But they also regard some human beings as just scum. These two ways of regarding their fellow human beings compete for dominance in their minds without either one ever winning out.

In this section I have said nothing, thus far, about that form of address to God that consists of petitioning God to do something. Just as the worshippers do not content themselves with declaring "we praise You, O God," but go on to give specificity to their praise, so also they do not content themselves with declaring "we petition You, O God," but go on to give specificity to their petition.

The specificity is different in this case, however. When praising God, the worshippers give specificity to their praise by specifying the *basis* of their praise—by specifying what it is about God and God's doings that God is to be praised for. When petitioning God, they may also specify what it is about God and God's doings that is the basis for their petition. But, mainly, the specificity of their petitionary prayers consists of specifying what it is that they are petitioning God to do. By participating in these prayers, they learn the sorts of things for which it is appropriate to petition God; and from this, in turn, they learn something of what is distinctive of God. They advance in their knowledge of God. Most liturgies include the people praying the Lord's Prayer. By participating in praying this prayer, they gain, deepen, and sustain knowledge of God. They become more attuned to God.

Gaining Knowledge of God from the Addressee-Specifications of Liturgical Address to God

There is a third aspect of liturgy that accounts for the fact that one can gain, deepen, and sustain knowledge of God by participating in the liturgical activity of addressing God. Just as the participants in liturgical enactments go beyond declaring that they worship, praise, and thank God to specify the basis for their worship, praise, and thanks, so also they go beyond identifying as *God* the one whom they are addressing to specify more fully what is distinctive of their addressee: "almighty," "creator of heaven and earth," merciful," and so forth. These terms can be used to make declarations about God. But that is not how they are used when they are incorporated into address to God; they are used to specify the nature and identity of the one addressed. Let me call them, *addressee-specifications*. By employing these addressee-specifications in their address to God, liturgical participants gain, deepen, and sustain knowledge of God.

Let us have a few examples. In the present-day Catholic mass liturgy, the confession opens with the priest and the people saying, "I confess to almighty God ...." When saying these words, the priest and the people are not *declaring that* God is almighty; they are using the addressee-specification term "almighty God" to *specify* the one to whom they are addressing their confession.

In "The Holy Eucharist: Rite One" of the Episcopal Church, one of the options for the prayer of confession, spoken by the priest and the people together, opens with the words, "Almighty God, Father of our Lord Jesus Christ, maker of all things, judge of all men ...." When saying these words, the priest and the people are not *declaring that* God is almighty, Father of our Lord Jesus Christ, maker of all things, and judge of all men. They are using these addressee-identification terms to *specify* the one to whom they are addressing their confession. Thereby they become more attuned to the one whom they are addressing.

In the Orthodox Liturgy of St. John Chrysostom, the prayer the priest offers just before the public liturgy begins incorporates a flurry of addressee-specification terms: "O heavenly King and Comforter, Spirit of truth, Who art in all places and fillest all things; Treasure of goodness and Giver of life: come and abide in us, and cleanse us from all that defileth."[43] When saying

---

43. This flurry pales, however, before the flurry of addressee-identification terms in the anaphora of the so-called *Testamentum Domini* (probably fifth century): "Holy God, strengthener of our souls, giver of our life, treasure of incorruptibility, Father of your only-begotten, our Savior." The prayer then addresses Christ: "[G]race of the nations, knowledge, true wisdom, the exaltation of the meek, the medicine of souls,

these words, the priest does not *declare that* God is in all places and fills all things; he *specifies* the addressee of the prayer as one who is in all places and fills all things. Parenthetically, what these examples show is that the addressee-specification terms incorporated into liturgical address to God come in a number of different grammatical forms. Some are adjectives: "almighty," "merciful." Some are nouns: "Father," "King." Some are verbal nouns: "creator of heaven and earth," "giver of life." Some are who- or that-clauses: "who art in heaven," "that takest away the sins of the world."

The prayer of the Trisagion in the Orthodox liturgy is an unusually flamboyant example of the last of these grammatical forms:

> O Holy God, Who restest in the holies, unto Whom the seraphim sing the thrice-holy song; Whom the cherubim glorify, . . . Who didst bring into being all that exists; Who didst create man in Thine own likeness, . . . Who givest wisdom and understanding to him that asked, . . . Who hast deemed us, Thine humble and unmeritable servants, worthy at this hour to stand before the glory of Thy holy altar.

Suppose, now, that the addressee-specification terms employed in some liturgical address to God do in fact fit God; then, in participating in addressing God in that way, one becomes more attuned to God. One gains, deepens, and sustains one's person-knowledge of God. If one of the addressee-specification terms employed is "creator of heaven and earth" and that term fits God, then, by participating in the liturgical practice of addressing God in that way, one's knowing God as creator of heaven and earth burrows more deeply into one's soul.

I am assuming, of course, that the person who shares in using the terms "almighty," "creator of heaven and earth," etc., in addressing God has some grasp of what those terms mean. If she shares in voicing the words but has no grasp of what they mean—because she is a small child, or because she doesn't know English—her knowledge of God is not deepened.

Grasping the meaning of the terms "almighty" and "creator of heaven and earth" comes in degrees, as does grasping the meaning of most terms. One has a better grasp as an adult than as a child; one adult has a better grasp than another. A liturgical neophyte learns to employ the term "creator

---

the confidence of us who believe, . . . the strength of the righteous, the hope of the persecuted, the haven of the buffeted, the illuminator of the perfect, the Son of the living God." The prayer then returns to addressing God the Father with an additional flurry of addressee-identification terms: "founder of the heights, king of the treasuries of light, visitor of the heavenly Zion, king of the orders of archangels, of dominions, praises, thrones, vestures, lights, joys, and delights, father of kings." Quoted from Jasper and Cuming, *Prayers of the Eucharist: Early and Reformed*, 139.

of heaven and earth" in addressing God. At first, the knowledge of God that she acquires thereby is shallow. As she understands better what he is saying, her knowledge of God as creator of heaven and earth deepens. The better one understands the meaning of the addressee-specification terms used when addressing God liturgically, the deeper one's knowledge of God—assuming that the terms fit God.

In Conclusion

Let me make three brief remarks in conclusion. First, there is a certain artificiality about my discussion. As I noted earlier, liturgical participants do not gain, deepen, and sustain knowledge of God only by participating in addressing God; they also do so by attentively listening to the reading of Scripture, to the sermon, to the declaration of God's forgiveness and blessing. In practice, these two ways of becoming attuned to God—by addressing God and by attentive listening—are intertwined. I have abstracted the former from its intertwinement with the latter in order to get clearly in view this way of becoming more attuned to God.

If one holds, as I do, that by the reading of Scripture and by the preaching of the sermon God speaks to the people assembled,[44] and if one grants that, by attentive listening to what God says, one becomes more attuned to God, then liturgical knowledge of God is gained, deepened, and sustained both by God addressing the people and the people listening, and by the people addressing God.

Second, the clue to how it is that one becomes more attuned to God by participating in addressing God liturgically in a reliable liturgy is that liturgical activity is scripted activity. If, following no script, one just addresses God as one pleases, one is not, in so doing, advancing in one's knowledge of God—not even if one's way of addressing God happens to be right and proper.[45] One may be *expressing* one's knowledge of God, assuming that one's understanding of God is in fact knowledge, but one is not *gaining* or *deepening* in knowledge. In following a reliable liturgical script, one is *being taught* how to worship God. One is *submitting* to being taught. It is a distinctive form of being taught, consisting not in being taught by someone—though one may receive some coaching along the way—but in being taught by the script.

---

44. See Wolterstorff, "Preaching the Word of God," 247–69.

45. There is the possibility, however, that the *Holy Spirit* uses this activity on one's part to enhance one's knowledge of God.

Third, because throughout my discussion I have had reliable liturgies and fully compliant worshippers in mind, I have said nothing about situations in which one should resist the formative influence of liturgy. But, of course, there are such situations. When should one allow liturgical practice to form one's understanding of God and when should one, instead, allow one's understanding of God to govern one's liturgical practice? When addressing this question, it might prove interesting to explore the similarities and differences between gaining knowledge of God by participating in the liturgy and gaining knowledge of God by accepting testimony. These are similar in that, in both of them, there is a "handing on." In recent years, philosophers have begun identifying and analyzing the situations in which one is entitled to accept (or warranted in accepting) what is handed on to one in testimony and those in which one is not. Are the latter situations similar to the situations in which one should not participate in what is handed on to one for one's liturgical participation?

To Those Who Yearn

There are a number of different ways of gaining knowledge of God, whether it be doxastic *de re* knowledge or person-knowledge: by reading Holy Scripture, by revelatory experiences of various sorts, by testimony, by following the arguments of natural theology. Over the centuries, philosophers and theologians have discussed, at great length, these ways of gaining knowledge of God. They have not, to the best of my knowledge, discussed gaining knowledge of God by participating in liturgically addressing God. I'm not sure why that is. Perhaps it is because they have assumed that, in addressing God, one expresses one's knowledge of God acquired in some other way.

There are many in our society who are confident that they know God very well. There are others who are confident that there is no God to be known. And then there are those who are inclined to believe that God does exist and who yearn to know God, and to know God better. The advice to be gleaned from our discussion is this: consider participating in addressing God, with whatever degree of compliance one can muster, within some rich liturgical practice that seems reliably grounded in divine revelation. Over the centuries this has proved to be, for many, one way of becoming attuned to the divine reality one yearns to know.[46]

---

46. I thank Matthew Benton, Kelly Clark, Terence Cuneo, Stephen Wykstra, and Jennifer Zamzow, for very helpful comments on successive drafts of this essay.

15

Art and Liturgy[1]

In all places and at all times the Christian church has broken out into music, poetry, architecture, visual design, and visual representation; it cannot restrain itself. And in many places and at many times it has been mired in controversies over music, poetry, architecture, visual design, and visual representation. The church has neither been able to live without the arts nor to live peaceably with the arts. The contemporary American church is no exception. In recent years, at least as many congregations have been torn apart by controversies over music as by controversies over theology.

My goal in this essay is to present a framework for thinking about the relationship between liturgy and art. Such a framework will not settle all the issues of art and liturgy; what it can do, for those of us who find the framework acceptable, is move us beyond the point where we simply lunge at each other in the dark.

What Is Liturgy?

Our present-day controversies over the art of the church are due, in good measure, to the different understandings of liturgy and of art that we bring to the controversies. So I propose that, rather than plunging immediately into a discussion about the relation between liturgy and art, we talk first about how liturgy and art should be understood. Let me begin with liturgy.

Our word "liturgy" comes from the Greek *leitourgia*. The word was originally used for a contribution to the community made by a well-to-do individual—the outfitting of a warship, for example. Whereas we in modern times use public tax monies to outfit our navies, Greeks of classical times sometimes depended on the contributions of well-to-do individuals

---

1. This essay is a revision of the text of the keynote address for a conference sponsored by the journal *Image*, held in Houston, Texas, November 10–13, 2005. The title of the conference was "A Matter of Devotion: Art, Liturgy, and the Stuff of Worship."

to do so. Around a century ago Andrew Carnegie funded the construction of public libraries across the United States; the Greeks would have called that a *leitourgia*.

The early Christians borrowed this term to describe that they did in their assemblies. They performed a *leitourgia*, a service. Their calling it a *leitourgia* left open what they actually did in their assemblies; we cannot infer what they did from their borrowing of the term. Their borrowing tells us no more than that they understood what they did as a service of some sort. I find it interesting to recall that when I was growing up in an Americanized version of the Dutch Reformed tradition on the prairies of southwest Minnesota, we called what we did on Sundays "the service." We talked about when the service began, when it ended, and so forth. The Eastern Orthodox call their services the "divine liturgy." The idea is exactly the same.

So what I and all contemporary liturgical scholars mean when we speak of *liturgy* is simply what is done in the assemblies of Christians, particularly those on Sundays, the idea being that this is a service of some sort. What is done in the assemblies of a given group of Christians may or may not involve repetition from week to week and year to year; no matter, it is a liturgy. (Though let me observe parenthetically that, contrary to the self-perception of many congregations, there is always in fact a good deal of repetition in liturgy.) It may or may not involve the congregation reciting as well as singing words; no matter, it is a liturgy. It may or may not involve the congregation and its leader reciting words from printed texts; no matter, it is a liturgy.

A particular liturgy, then, is a sequence of actions, a sequence of things done. I think that it is of prime importance to go on to say that the actions in question are the actions of a social practice. Liturgy is not actions that a given group just up and does. Let me highlight just a few of the more important features of a social practice.

In the first place, a social practice is handed on from one person to another and from one generation to another; a social practice is thus a tradition. New participants are inducted into an on-going practice. What is handed on is knowledge of how to do certain things and, along with that, certain goals and norms for doing those things. Social practices are embodied norms. To learn the practice is to learn that this is the better or right way of doing something and that that other way is a worse or wrong way of doing it. What is also characteristic of a social practice is that it is open to alternative goals and norms, and to disputes over those alternatives. Social practices not only change over the years with respect to goals and norms, but are typically contested. All these things, I contend, are true of Christian liturgy; liturgy is a contested social practice.

Let me now enter, all too briefly, into a few of the contested issues. One of the most controverted issues over the centuries has been the purpose of the liturgy. Why do Christians do the things they do in their assemblies? Among present day liturgical scholars there is, so it appears to me, a near-consensus on one of the central purposes of liturgical enactments, namely, that the actions of the liturgy be performed: that the people praise God, confess their sins to God, and so forth.

This sounds like a dull truism: the liturgy of a congregation is what is done in its assemblies, and a central purpose of doing those things is simply that those things be done. In fact, it is not a truism. Liturgical scholars of the past have by no means always acknowledged this as a central purpose; so too, a great many laypeople of the present day do not acknowledge this as a central purpose. Let me explain.

Scholars of the past, and laypeople of the present day, often see the point of the liturgy as bringing about some effect in the members of the assembly. In present-day United States, traditional parishes have almost entirely disappeared and Christians shop around until they find an assembly that induces in them the effects they desire; churches are regarded as service organizations in the business of offering religious services to clients who want those services. The service desired is typically a religious experience of a certain sort; people shop around until they find an assembly whose actions produce in them a transporting religious experience. Or the service desired is assistance in sorting through the problems of daily life, especially the problems of family life; people shop around until they find an assembly which provides that service.

It would be a mistake to dismiss entirely this instrumentalist picture of the liturgy. In his letters Paul spoke of *edification* as one of the purposes of the assemblies—though let me add immediately that what he had in mind by "edification" was not a transporting religious experience but being built up in one's Christian existence. It would be even more mistaken, however, to think of the purpose of what is done in the assemblies exclusively in instrumentalist terms. Christians assemble to acknowledge God in praise, thanksgiving, confession, intercession, and the like. They do not perform these actions in order to produce some effect in themselves; they do so because it is right and proper to acknowledge God in these ways. This is the dimension of the liturgy that is in serious danger of being ignored amidst the marketplace mentality of present-day American Christians. The purpose of liturgy is not only *formative*; the purpose is *performative*: to perform actions of praise, thanksgiving, confession, intercession, and the like.

A related point of controversy down through the ages is the following: when we enter the assemblies, are we to put out of mind what we have experienced in our everyday lives so as to center on God, or are we to carry our everyday experiences along with us? And if one's answer is the former, how are we to think of the space in which the liturgy is performed? Is entering the space of the liturgy to be thought of as leaving secular space and entering sacred space?

Down through the ages, both liturgical scholars and laypeople have often thought along the former lines: to enter the space of the liturgy is to enter sacred space, and to perform the actions of the liturgy one must put out of mind the experiences of everyday life. It would be difficult, however, to find a prominent contemporary liturgical scholar who embraces that traditional view; here too a remarkable near-consensus has emerged. One might expect the Orthodox to think differently; in fact, the Russian Orthodox theologian Alexander Schmemann has been one of the most eloquent on the matter.

The secularist finds certain features of the world wondrous and awesome, and certain life-experiences good; that, for him, is the end of the matter. The believer, by contrast, perceives those same features not only as wondrous and awesome but as manifestations of God's glory, and those life-experiences not only as good but as God's grace to him. The secularist finds some actions right and some wrong, some just and some unjust; that, for him, is the end of the matter. The believer perceives those same actions not only as right and just but as obedient to God, and not only as wrong and unjust but as disobedient. The secularist finds our human existence filled with misfortune: diseases, hurricanes, tornados, earthquakes, floods, droughts; that, for him, is the end of the matter. The believer perceives those same events not merely as misfortunes but as something gone awry in God's world that God has the power to turn right.

When the believer enters the assemblies to engage in the enactment of the liturgy, she carries these experiences along with her in her acknowledgement of God. Her acknowledgement of God takes the form of presenting to God her life in the everyday. The praise and thanks she offers God includes praise for the divine glory she has perceived in her everyday life and the divine goodness she has experienced. The confession she addresses to God includes confession for the disobedience she has discerned in herself and others. The intercessions she places before God include intercession for deliverance from what has gone awry in God's world. The trumpets, the ashes, and the tears of the liturgy are trumpets, ashes, and tears for her experience of God in the everyday.

Let's pull it all together. Liturgy is the *presentation* to God of our lives in the everyday in the form of praise, confession, etc. And—a point I have not noted—liturgy is guide and energizer for our lives in the everyday.

Liturgy faces in two directions. The *telos* of liturgical action lies both inside and outside the liturgical enactment. Liturgy would not exist if we put out of mind our lives in the everyday when participating in the liturgy. We carry out everyday lives into the liturgy and we carry the liturgy into our everyday lives.

And as to space: to enter the space of the liturgy is not to leave behind secular space and to enter sacred space. There is no secular space—no space empty of God.

How to Think about Art

Let us move on to how to think about art. When I talk to students about art, I find that they assume without question that the basic contours of their way of thinking about the arts is simply the right way of thinking, the human way. It is how right thinking people have always thought about the arts. It consists simply of noticing how things are. What they want out of me as their professor in a course on philosophy of art is not that I will consider and evaluate different ways of thinking about art but that I will give depth and detail to the way of thinking that they take for granted.

The assumption is false. Our way of thinking about the arts does not consist simply of noticing how things are. Our way of thinking about the arts—I mean, that way of thinking about the arts shared by almost everybody who has been academically trained in art—emerged in eighteenth-century Europe as a way of legitimating and advancing some rather dramatic changes that were then taking place within the arts themselves.

At the core of our way of thinking about the arts is a narrative—I have called it the Grand Modern Narrative concerning the Arts. Let me present to you that narrative—first the way it is usually told, then the way I myself would now tell it.

In the eighteenth century in the West, so the story goes, art finally began to come into its own. Previously art had been in the service of values and interests outside art, these being imposed on artists by princes and prelates. Liturgical art is non-liberated art, art not yet come into its own; so too is art of the court, memorial art, and so forth. All such art is for a use. Art come into its own has no use; art is useless. Or as some preferred to put it: art come into its own is art for art's sake.

The idea was that finally, after millennia of preparation, artists were being liberated to pursue the value intrinsic to art, namely, aesthetic value, and the public was being liberated to practice the action peculiar to and distinctive of art, namely, disinterested perceptual contemplation of aesthetically excellent objects. A unique sphere of autonomous action was coming into existence, an art world, distinct from the world of business, of the university, and so forth, free to follow its own internal laws.

Beginning in the early nineteenth century, this eighteenth-century narrative concerning art coming into its own was caught up into a yet grander Romantic narrative concerning the nature and ills of modernity. It was the Romantics who first began to identify what was happening around them as not just recent but something new and distinct. A new age was coming to birth, call it modernity. The Romantic characterization of this new age was intertwined with critique. Modernity is fragmentation. Modernity shatters the old unities of society, religion, and mentality; in the resonant words of John Keats, it "unweaves the rainbow." What drives this fragmentation is the rejection of tradition in favor of what came to be called "instrumental reason"; that is to say, what drives modernization is the restless pursuit of better means to achieve our ends.

Art, so the story went, is the grand exception to these dynamics and ills of modernity. What accounts for art, some said, is not rationality but imagination; others said that what accounts for art is a unique form of rationality, interior rationality, as Kant called it, in contract to technical or purposive rationality. Either way, what emerges is not an assemblage of fragments but a work of organic unity. Art presents to us the image of an alternative to the fragmentation of modernity. Art is the social other. As such, it both launches a prophetic critique of modernity and sets before us an image of what could be instead.

From this picture of art as the social other it was but a short step for the Romantics to begin ascribing religious import to art. Some claimed the artist to be the prophet of the modern world, some claimed that works of art reveal the divine to us, some claimed that the works are themselves of religious significance. Here is an eloquent and unapologetic expression of this third point of view, from Wilhelm Wackenroder writing in the late 1700s:

> Art galleries . . . ought to be temples where, in still and silent humility and in heart-lifting solitude, we may admire great artists as the highest among mortals . . . with long, steadfast contemplation of their works. . . . I compare the enjoyment of nobler works of art to *prayer*. . . . Works of art, in their own way, no more fit into the common flow of life than does the thought of God. . . . That day is for me a sacred holiday which . . . I devote to the contemplation of noble works of art.[2]

---

2. Cited in Abrams, *Doing Things with Texts*, 157. Original reference: Wackenroder, *Herzensergieessungen eines kunstliebenden Klosterbruders,* 100–103.

This, in its main outlines, is what I call the Grand Modern Narrative of the Arts. I feel confident in saying that it is familiar to all of you. It is the taken-for-granted context of almost all theorizing about the arts over the past two centuries. What my students have wanted out of me is that I would develop it, articulate it, flesh it out. What exactly is aesthetic value? Wherein lies the worth of perceptual contemplation of objects of aesthetic value? And so forth.

My response is to argue, instead, for the rejection of the narrative and for its replacement by an alternative. Begin here: what is it for something to come into its own? I would say that something comes into its own when it is successfully used or engaged in the way that it was intended to be used or engaged. A chair comes into its own when someone sits on it and finds it comfortable. It is true that some chairs find their way into art museums where they are presented as aesthetically excellent sculptural objects and surrounded by signs saying, "do not sit on this chair." But they are not then coming into their own as chairs.

So now consider a piece of liturgical art—a hymn, say. Suppose the hymn is Martin Luther's hymn, "A Mighty Fortress"; and suppose that the members of a congregation join in singing the hymn as part of their liturgy some Sunday. I would say that this piece of music is then coming into its own; this is exactly how Luther meant his hymn to be used. The hymn can also be sung by a choir in a performance situation and admired by the audience for its aesthetic qualities; it may serve this mode of engagement very well. But it is not then coming into its own as a hymn.

Consider also the Romantic component of the Grand Narrative, the claim that art is socially other, high and lifted up above our social ills. Over the past quarter century or so critics have rubbed our noses in all the "isms" exhibited by art, not only of the past but of the modern period: racism, sexism, colonialism, Occidentalism, you name it. It has become impossible to think of art as the social innocent bearing salvific power.

Let me then suggest an alternative way of thinking. Whereas writing on the arts before the eighteenth century focused in great measure on the making of works of art, the eighteenth-century theorists began instead to focus on the work itself and on a certain way of engaging that work, namely, perceptual contemplation. This has remained the dominant orientation of art theory ever since. My first suggestion is that we move the central focus of our attention away from works of art to the social practices of art. More specifically, I suggest that we think of each of the arts as an interlocking cluster of three kinds of social practices: practices of composing works of art, practices of performing or displaying works of art, and practices of engaging works of art. The composition of works of art, for example, displays exactly the features of a social practice that I highlighted earlier: new practitioners are inducted into a practice that is handed down to them. Along with being taught how to do various things, they are taught goals and norms for what they do. Those goals and norms not only change over time but are typically contested at any given time. And so forth.

Second, I propose that when it comes to the social practice of engaging works of art, we take note of the fact that this practice comes in the form of many distinct modes of engagement. Not only is there art for aesthetic contemplation, but there are work songs, memorial sculptures, political art, icons, and so forth. And I at least find it impossible to say that to engage some work of art as memorial or liturgical art is inherently inferior to engaging it as an object of aesthetic contemplation.

You can see where this is going. I hold that we must reject telling the story of art in the modern world as the progressivist, Whiggish story of art finally coming into its own after millennia of preparation. Art did not have to come into its own. It was *already* in its own. Art intended for use in the liturgy comes into its own when it is in fact *used in the liturgy*; and art had been used in the liturgy for millennia. What happened in the eighteenth century was no more, though also no less, than a substantial alteration within the practices of art: the practice of art for perceptual contemplation acquired a prominence among the middle class of Europe that it had never enjoyed before.

Connecting Liturgy and Art

Let me now begin to connect the two, liturgy and art. In some of my previous writings I have said that just as aesthetic value calls the shots when it comes to art for perceptual contemplation, so too liturgy calls the shots when it comes to liturgical art. Some of the music that we listen to in concert halls is religious in one way or another; think, for example, of the music of Olivier Messiaen. But religious concert hall music is not liturgical music. Liturgical music is music composed and performed in the service of the liturgy.

I now think this picture of liturgical art is too simplistic and one-sided. What I wanted to oppose, in speaking as I did, was the attitude one hears expressed every now and then by artists and their supporters: the artist composes a painting in his studio and offers it to the church, the church rejects it on the ground that it cannot find a use for it or finds its style too inscrutable, whereupon the artist and his supporters become angry and charge the church with being a bunch of philistines who have no use for art, sometimes adding that, once upon a time, back in the Middle Ages or whenever, things were different. I still oppose this attitude. But I now think it is too simplistic to say that liturgy must call the shots for liturgical art.

It is true that liturgical art is *for* the liturgy in roughly the same way that museum art is *for* aesthetic contemplation. But when I say that liturgy calls the shots for liturgical art, the picture that comes to mind is that of minister or priest finding an artist, telling her what to do, and the artist then following orders. That is not how it goes. Or if it does go that way, we can be confident that the result will be dismal.

You will have noticed a congruence between my way of thinking of liturgy and my way of thinking of the arts. Both are social practices. The composition or use of liturgical art is an event within two distinct social practices: it is an event within the social practice of the Christian liturgy and an event within the social practice of the arts. If that event is to be successful, it must be a realization of the traditions and authentic norms and values of *both* practices. And for that happy congruence to occur, there must be a collaboration. Those who represent the liturgy cannot simply give orders to the artist, and the artist and her supporters cannot simply give a take-it-or-leave-it ultimatum to those who represent the liturgy. They must negotiate, each listening to the other. What emerges, at its best, will represent both a significant development within liturgy and a significant development within the arts. Both the history of liturgy and the history of art will have to take note.

The reason it will represent a significant development within liturgy is that liturgical art is unavoidably an *interpretation* of the liturgy. Sometimes in dramatic ways, sometimes in subtle ways, artistic interpretations of the liturgy change both the liturgy and our ways of understanding and experiencing the liturgy. A congregation explains its liturgy as part of the program it presents to an architect. But the building the architect then designs for the congregation not only respects its understanding of the liturgy but changes it.

My proposal, in short, is that we use an interactionist model for thinking about liturgical art. Liturgical art is that point at which the practice of the Christian liturgy and the practices of the arts interact with each other, engage each other. And in that engagement, each practice must honor the authentic norms and values of the other.

Principles for the Engagement

Are there principles for what should emerge from this interactive engagement? If I had to summarize how the various arts relate to the liturgy, I would say that some art serves as the *context* for liturgical action and that some serves as the *mode* of liturgical action. Architecture, quite obviously, belongs to the context within which liturgical actions take place; music and poetry belong to the mode, the "how," of confession, of praise, and so forth. A congregation confesses its sins with these words and this music; that is how it does it, that is its mode of confession.

I would say that the most fundamental principle for liturgical art, whether it belongs to the context of the liturgy or the mode, is that art must enable rather than obstruct the actions of the liturgy. This sounds bland and unexceptionable. But in fact the principle gets violated all the time. The building within which a congregation worships prevents it from doing what it thinks it really should be doing, or makes it difficult, or encourages some things and discourages others. The instrumental music is so loud, novel, self-conscious, tedious, or poorly performed that it distracts us from praise of God rather than enabling our praise. You know what I mean.

A more subtle, though equally important principle, is that liturgical art, whether it belong to the context or the mode of the liturgy, must *fit* the various liturgical actions, the liturgical season, and the nature of the liturgical assembly. What I mean by *fittingness* can best be explained with some simple examples. A jagged line fits agitation better than tranquility; an undulating line fits tranquility better than agitation. The interval of an octave fits better with rest; the interval of a second, better with restlessness. My view is that this phenomenon of fittingness pervades the arts. It accounts for why we find some music cheerful and some tragic, why we find some paintings joyful and some gloomy, and so forth.

Now for the application. Suppose that those responsible for a congregation's liturgy decide that, on a given Sunday, the confession will be sung—sung, that is, by the congregation. What this principle of fittingness tells us is that, in searching around for appropriate music, those responsible should look for music that fits the nature of this liturgical act. And what that requires, in turn, is that they understand the *nature* of this act—which brings us back, of course, to our discussion about liturgy and life.

Or take an example from architecture. When my congregation in Grand Rapids was getting ready to look for an architect to design a building for us, we visited a number of churches in the area that had been built within the prior ten or fifteen years. Eventually two things struck us about these buildings. Almost all of them were relatively dark inside. Some had light scoops. But the effect of these light scoops was only to alleviate the darkness at a certain point. We were also struck by how closed off these buildings were to the outside world. All of them were surrounded by large asphalt-covered parking lots; and most had small and inconspicuous entrances from the parking lot into the church.

The program we gave our architect specified that he had to achieve the opposite on both counts. For us, the proper metaphor for entering the liturgical space was coming into the light, not entering darkness; we asked our architect to design a building that would fit that self-understanding. And for us, entering the space of the liturgy was not leaving secular space and entering sacred space. We thought of the life of the church as a heartbeat, systolic and diastolic, entering and dispersing. So we asked the architect to impart a processional quality to the experience of entering and leaving, gathering and dispersing. The basic principle operative in both cases was fittingness. We were asking the architect to design a building that would fit the nature of the assembly, as we understood that, and that would fit our understanding of entering and leaving the assembly. Or to use other words for the same idea: we were asking him to design a building that would *express* the nature of the assembly, as we understood that, and would *express* that nature of entering and leaving.

Fittingness shades off into symbolism. In the case of symbols there will invariably be, I think, some sort of fittingness between the symbol and what it symbolizes. What is different about a symbol from ordinary fittingness is that a symbol has an established conventional meaning—a circle conventionally symbolizes eternity, a triangle conventionally symbolizes the Trinity, and so forth.

About symbols I have nothing to say other than to express my complete inability to understand why Protestants of certain sorts are so averse to the presence of symbols in their churches. Scripture is full of symbols; the buildings of the early church were full of symbols. What is the problem? It is true that in the course of history, churches have sometimes become a bewildering clutter of symbols. The thing to do in that situation is not to eliminate all symbols but to clean up the clutter.

In Conclusion

I close by raising a question that I will leave unanswered. I have been struck in recent years by how much of the art in our lives is memorial art—art meant to keep alive and honor the memory of some person or event from the past. Many of us, when we hear the phrase "memorial art," think immediately of Maya Lin's Viet Nam Memorial on the Mall in Washington, DC. But the Viet Nam Memorial was preceded by other memorial architecture and sculpture on the Mall in Washington. And those memorials were preceded, in turn, by a long and rich tradition of memorial art within Christianity. I have come to think that we should think of much, if not most, of the art produced by the church and her members down through the ages as memorial art. Paintings of Mary and Joseph on the flight into Egypt, paintings of Christ in the temple, paintings of the crucifixion—all these, and very many more of the same sort, are memorial art, art meant to keep alive and honor the memory of events in the life of our Lord.

No other religion, except perhaps Buddhism, can claim such a heritage of memorial art. The reason is not far to seek: more than Judaism, more than Islam, Christianity is a *historical* religion. What happened in history matters. Liberal Protestant theologians who have written about art in the twentieth century have been hostile to memorial art; they have preferred abstract art. I am thinking here especially of Paul Tillich. Their dislike of memorial art tells us something about their theology.

But suppose that you, along with me, believe that Christianity is a historical religion. What happened in history matters, and it matters that we remember what happened. Then will not memorial art have a significant place in the context of the liturgy? I mean, visual memorial art. We Protestants have no problem with keeping alive and honoring the memory of our Christian past in our hymns—and in our Sunday School papers. But we shy away when doing so with visual art in the church itself. Why is that?

We have something important to learn on this score from the Eastern Orthodox Church and its use of icons, and from the Catholic tradition. The standard way in the Western church of explaining the function of images in the church building was that images are pedagogues for the illiterate. That account is wide open to the Protestant objection that, as literacy increases, images lose their point. Already at the time of the iconoclast controversy the Orthodox thought differently of images. An icon, they said, is a memorial of the one it depicts; that is the word they used, *anamnesis*.

I leave it as a question that I have not fully thought through and that I dare say most of us have not fully thought through. If we do indeed believe that Christianity is a historical religion and that it is important to keep alive and honor the memory of decisive persons and events in the history of Israel and the church, then what is the proper place of memorial art within the visual context of the liturgy? Do we not run the danger of losing sight of the historical dimension of Christianity if, in the visual context of the liturgy, there are no memorials?

Afterword

Honor Everyone

> You are a chosen race, a royal priesthood, a holy nation, God's own people, that you may declare the wonderful deeds of him who called you out of darkness into his marvelous light. . . .
>
> I beseech you as aliens and exiles to abstain from the passions of the flesh that wage war against your soul. Maintain good conduct among the Gentiles, so that in case they speak against you as wrongdoers, they may see your good deeds and glorify God on the day of visitation.
>
> Be subject for the Lord's sake to every human institution, whether it be to the emperor as supreme, or to governors as sent by him to punish those who do wrong and to praise those who do right. For it is God's will that by doing right you should put to silence the ignorance of foolish men. Live as free persons, yet without using your freedom as a pretext for evil; but live as servants of God. Honor everyone. Love the brotherhood. Fear God. Honor the emperor. (1 Pet 2:11–17)

Honor was deep in the moral code of the ancient Mediterranean world. Everybody was not only to submit to those in authority over them but to honor them. The ancient Roman jurist Ulpian defined justice as "rendering to each what is due him or her." Honor is due those in authority over one. Persons were also to be honored for noble achievements—poets and philosophers, for example. But everybody is to honor and obey those who are over them.

It was by no means evident to the early Christians how they were to relate to this moral code of the surrounding pagan society. Going off into the wilderness somewhere and setting up their own society with its own authority-structures was never an option. So how should they relate to the extant authority-structures of the empire, of the household, of the family?

Should they act like revolutionaries and try to subvert these structures? Should they buckle under because they had no real alternative? Or should they submit and obey because they honored those in authority—honored them *because* they were in a position of authority?

At several places the letter writers of the New Testament address this question—in Romans 13, in Ephesians 5 and 6, in Colossians 3, and in 1 Peter 2. The counsel they give is always the same. As for the family: wives are to be subject to their husbands and children are to honor and obey their parents. As for the household, servants and slaves are to be subject to their masters. And as for the empire, political subjects are to honor and obey the emperor and his governors.

None of the New Testament writers imagined a democracy instead of an empire; none of them imagined households in which there were no servants or slaves; none of them imagined families in which there was joint-leadership rather than male headship. They spoke to what they knew. Christians were to live within the extant authority-structures. Paul makes clear in Romans 13 that the existence of authority-structures is not the result of the Evil One exercising his wiles but that it is God's will that society include authority-structures.

Children, wives, servants, political subjects—they are not just to buckle under to those who hold legitimate authority over them but to honor and obey them—that is the consistent counsel of the New Testament writers to the fledgling church wondering how it should relate to the extant authority-structures.

But immediately after giving this counsel to their readers, the New Testament writers throw in a "kicker." Yes, children are to honor and obey their parents; but parents must not provoke their children (Colossians 3). Yes, wives are to submit to their husbands; but husbands are to love their wives as Christ loved the church (Ephesians 5). Yes, servants and slaves are to submit to their masters; but their masters are to treat them justly and fairly, knowing that they themselves have a Master in heaven (Colossians 3). Yes, political subjects are to honor and obey governmental authorities; but governmental authorities must keep in mind that their task, in the words of First Peter, is "to punish those who do wrong and to praise those who do right" (1 Pet 2:14). Always what I called the "kicker" is added. Those in authority are not a law unto themselves. Authority does not stop with them. They too are under authority. Everybody is. They are under God's authority.

In Romans, in Ephesians, in Colossians, in First Peter—always it is the same pattern: those subject to some legitimate authority-structure are to honor and obey those in authority; and those who exercise authority are do so under God's authority and in accord with God's will.

But then, in the passage we read, the writer of First Peter throws in something that doesn't occur in any of the other New Testament passages that speak about living under authority-structures. "Honor the emperor," says the writer; that fits the pattern. But then he adds, "honor everybody." Not just those in authority; *everybody*. Don't just refrain from demeaning them, don't just tolerate them. *Honor* them. Honor everybody. Even criminals? Yes, even criminals.

What is going on here? What would lead the writer of First Peter to radicalize the scope of honoring beyond anything known in the ancient world—to democratize it, as it were? He doesn't say. But I think we can make a reliable guess. Every human being bears the image of God. Criminals too; there is nothing anybody can do to get rid of the image of God that they bear. And God loves all human beings—including criminals. We are to honor everybody because everybody bears the image of God and is beloved by God. We are to honor them *as* someone who bears the image of God and *as* someone who is beloved of God.

So not only are children to honor their parents; parents are to honor their children. Not only are wives to honor their husbands; husbands are to honor their wives. Not only are servants to honor their masters; masters are to honor their servants. Not only are citizens to honor their government; government is to honor the citizens.

This is explosive stuff. Eventually this democratizing of honoring undermined the authority-structures of the ancient world: undermined slavery, undermined authoritarian imperial government, undermined families in which children were treated as property, undermined marriages in which husband issued orders to wives. When emperors became Christians or Christians became emperors, they were enjoined by God to honor their subjects. When masters became Christians or Christians became masters, they were enjoined by God to honor their servants and slaves.

I am an American; until the first Tuesday in November, it will be impossible for me or any other American to put politics out of mind. As we live through the turmoil, we should constantly be asking ourselves, what is the Christian witness to our present-day American political order? You who are Canadians should be asking the same thing concerning the Canadian political order What, for example, is the application to our situations of the declaration by Paul and the writer of First Peter that those to whom they were writing were to honor the emperor and his governors? What is the application to our situations of their declaration that the God-given task of government is to curb wrongdoing and promote right-doing? What is the application to our situation of the declaration by the writer of First Peter to his readers that we were to honor everybody?

The Christian witness to our present-day American and Canadian political orders will include policy recommendations. But if we absorb what the writer of First Peter says, our Christian witness to the political order will go deeper than policy recommendations. It will speak to how we regard the government and it will speak to how we engage in political debate.

There is a great deal of bad-mouthing of government in my country nowadays, and a great deal of demeaning talk about those who hold positions in government. On the authority of Paul and Peter it will be the Christian witness to our fellow citizens that this is wrong, contrary to God's will. And not only will this be the Christian witness. Christians will go beyond this declaration to refuse to participate in such bad-mouthing and in such demeaning. They will indeed criticize their governmental officials, they will hold their feet to fire; but they will do while simultaneously honoring them *as* officials of their government.

It will likewise be the Christian witness to our present-day political orders that when we debate with each other, we are always to do so in such a way that we honor the person with whom are debating. And not only will this be the Christian witness. Christians will go beyond this declaration to conduct their own debates in such a way that they honor the one with whom they are debating.

An article on the front page of the *New York Times* of Friday, January 27 of 2012, included the following sentence about one of our American politicians: "in 1990, the political action committee that he ran, Gopac, [offered] Republican candidates . . . a list of words to describe Democrats—like decay, traitors, radical, sick, destroy, pathetic, corrupt and shame." If you honor the person with whom you are debating as someone who bears the image of God and is beloved of God, you will not use such language.

"You are a chosen race," wrote the writer of First Peter to his readers, "a royal priesthood, a holy nation, God's own people, that you may declare the wonderful deeds of him who called you out of darkness into his marvelous light. . . . Honor the emperor. Love the brotherhood. Fear God. Honor everyone." (1 Pet 2:9, 17)

Bibliography

Abrams, M. H. *Doing Things with Texts: Essays in Criticism and Critical Theory.* Edited by Michael Fisher. New York: Norton, 1989.
———. *Natural Supernaturalism.* New York: Norton, 1971.
Anselm. *Proslogion.* Translated by M. J. Charlesworth. South Bend, IN: Notre Dame University Press, 1965.
Aquinas, Thomas. *Summa Theologiae.* Translated by David Bourke. London: Eyre & Spottiswoode, 1975.
Augustine. *Confessions.* Translated by R. S. Pine-Coffin. 1961. Reprint, London: Penguin, 1984.
Austin, J. L. *How to Do Things with Words.* Oxford: Clarendon, 1962.
———. "Performative Utterances." In *Philosophical Papers,* edited by J. L. Austin, 133–252. Oxford: Clarendon, 1961.
Barnes, Jonathan, ed. *The Complete Works of Aristotle.* Princeton: Princeton University Press, 1984.
Barth, Karl. *The Christian Life.* Grand Rapids: Eerdmans, 1981.
———. *Church Dogmatics, Vol. I.1: The Doctrine of the Word of God.* Translated by G. W. Bromiley. Edinburgh: T. & T. Clark, 1975.
———. *Church Dogmatics, Vol. IV.2: The Doctrine of Reconciliation.* Edited by T. F. Torrance and Translated by G. W. Bromiley. Edinburgh: T. & T. Clark, 1958.
Bartholomew, Craig G., and Michael W. Goheen. *Christian Philosophy.* Grand Rapids: Baker, 2013.
Beardsley, Monroe. *Aesthetics: Problems in the Philosophy of Criticism.* New York: Harcourt, Brace, and Co., 1958.
Bell, Clive. *Art.* London: Chatto & Windus, 1914.
Bengson, John, and Marck Moffett. "Nonpropositional Intellectualism." In *Knowing How: Essays on Knowledge, Mind, and Action,* edited by John Bengson and Marc Moffett, 161–95. Oxford: Oxford University Press, 2011.
Benton, Matthew. "Epistemology Personalized." *The Philosophical Quarterly* 67 (2017) 813–34.
———. "God and Interpersonal Knowledge." *Res Philosophica* 95 (2018) 421–47.
Bonhoeffer, Dietrich. *Ethics.* New York: Macmillan, 1955.
Borger, Joyce, Martin Tel, and John D. Witvliet, eds. *Lift Up Your Hearts: Psalms, Hymns, and Spiritual Songs.* Grand Rapids: Faith Alive, 2013.
Braverman, Mark. *Fatal Embrace.* Austin, TX: Synergy, 2010.

Brunner, Emil. *Justice and the Social Order*. Translated by Mary Hottinger. New York: Harper, 1945.
Calvin, John. *Commentary on Genesis*. Translated by John King. Carlisle, PA: Banner of Truth Trust, 1965.
———. *Institutes of the Christian Religion*. Translated by Ford Lewis Battles. Philadelphia: Westminster, 1960.
———. *Isaiah 49–66*. Translated by William Pringle. North Charleston, SC: Createspace, 2017.
———. *John Calvin's Bible Commentaries on Habakkuk, Zephaniah, Haggai*. Translated by John Owen. North Charleston, SC: Createspace, 2017.
Coakley, Sarah. "Beyond 'Belief': Liturgy and the Cognitive Apprehension of God." In *The Vocation of Theology Today: A Festschrift for David Ford*, edited by Tom Greggs, Rachel Muers, and Simeon Zahl, 130–45. Eugene, OR: Wipf & Stock, 2013.
Cone, James H. *The Spirituals and the Blues: An Interpretation*. Maryknoll, NY: Orbis, 1992.
Crisp, Thomas M., Steve L. Porter, and Gregg A. Ten Elshof, eds. *Christian Scholarship in the Twenty-First Century*. Grand Rapids: Eerdmans, 2014.
Crossman, Matthew, Zoran Grozdanov, and Ryan McNally, eds. *Envisioning the Good Life: Essays on God, Christ, and Human Flourishing in Honor of Miroslav Volf*. Eugene, OR: Cascade, 2017.
Cuneo, Terence. *Ritualized Faith*. Oxford: Oxford University Press, 2016.
Deiss, Lucien. *The Springtime of the Liturgy*. Collegeville, MN: Liturgical, 1979.
Donahue, Charles, Jr., "*Ius* in Roman Law." In *Christianity and Human Rights: An Introduction*, edited by John Witte, Jr., and Frank S. Alexander, 64–80. Cambridge: Cambridge University Press, 2010.
Elkins, James. *What Painting Is*. London: Routledge, 1999.
Episcopal Church. *The Book of Common Prayer*. New York: The Church Hymnal Corporation, 1979.
Feinberg, J. "Noncomparative Justice." *The Philosophical Review* 83 (1974) 297–338.
Ford, David. *Self and Salvation: Being Transformed*. Cambridge: Cambridge University Press, 1999.
Gerrish, Brian A. *Grace and Gratitude: The Eucharistic Theology of John Calvin*. Minneapolis: Fortress, 1993.
Gioia, Ted. *Work Songs*. Durham, NC: Duke University Press, 2006.
Goldman, Alan H. *Aesthetic Value*. Boulder, CO: Westview, 1995.
Goodman, N. *Languages of Art: An Approach to a Theory of Symbols*. London: Oxford University Press, 1969.
Harris, Harriet, ed. *God, Goodness, and Philosophy*. Farnham, UK: Ashgate, 2011.
Hegel, G. W. F. *Introductory Lectures on Aesthetics*. Translated by B. Bosanquet. London: Penguin, 2004.
Horn, Stacy. *Imperfect Harmony: Finding Happiness Singing with Others*. Chapel Hill, NC: Algonquin, 2013.
Jasper, R. C. D., and G. J. Cuming. *Prayers of the Eucharist: Early and Reformed*. New York: Pueblo, 1987.
Kierkegaard, Søren. *Works of Love*. Edited and Translated by Howard V. Hong and Edna H. Hong. Princeton: Princeton University Press, 1995.
Lomax, Alan. *Prison Songs: Historical Recordings from Parchman Farm 1947–48, Volume One: Murderous Home*. 1997. CD.

Lovin, Robin. *Reinhold Niebuhr and Christian Realism*. Cambridge: Cambridge University Press. 1995.
Marcuse, Herbert. *The Aesthetic Dimension*. Boston: Beacon, 1978.
McDonnell, Kilian. *John Calvin, the Church and the Eucharist*. Princeton: Princeton University Press, 1967.
Niebuhr, Reinhold. *The Nature and Destiny of Man: A Christian Interpretation*. New York: Scribners, 1949.
Nussbaum, Martha. *Poetic Justice: The Literary Imagination and Public Life*. Boston: Beacon, 1995.
Nygren, Anders. *Agape and Eros*. Translated by Philip S. Watson. London: SPCK, 1953.
O'Donovan, Joan Lockwood. "The Concept of Rights in Moral Discourse." In *A Preserving Grace: Protestants, Catholics, and Natural Law*, edited by Michael Cromartie, 143–56. Grand Rapids: Eerdmans, 1997.
———. "Natural Law and Perfect Community: Contributions of Christian Platonism to Political Theory." *Modern Theology* 14 (1998) 19–42.
O'Donovan, Oliver. *The Desire of the Nations*. Cambridge: Cambridge University Press, 1996.
———. "The Language of Rights and Conceptual History." *Journal of Religious Ethics* 37 (2009) 193–207.
O'Siadhail, Micheal. *The Gossamer Wall: Poems in Witness to the Holocaust*. St Louis: Time Being, 2002.
Outka, Gene. *Agape*. New Haven, CT: Yale University Press. 1972.
Plato. *Plato, with an English Translation: Lysis, Symposium, Gorgias*. Translated by W. R. M. Lamb. Cambridge. Harvard University Press, 1946.
Ramsey, Paul. *Christian Ethics and the Sit-In*. New York: Association, 1961.
———. "Love and Law." In *Reinhold Niebuhr: His Religious, Social, and Political Thought*, edited by Charles W. Kegley and Robert W. Bretall, 143–88. New York: Macmillan, 1961.
The Reformed Church in America. *The Liturgy of the Reformed Church in America*. New York: The Board of Education of the RCA, 1979.
Reid, Thomas. *Essays on the Intellectual Powers of Man*. Edited by Derek R. Brookes. Edinburgh: University of Edinburgh Press, 2002.
———. *Inquiry into the Human Mind*. Edited by Derek R. Brookes. Edinburgh: University of Edinburgh Press, 1997.
Reynolds, David S. *Mightier Than the Sword: Uncle Tom's Cabin and the Battle for America*. New York: Norton, 2011.
Roberts, Robert C. *Emotions: An Essay in Aid of Moral Psychology*. Cambridge: Cambridge University Press, 2003.
Robertson, D. B., ed. *Love and Justice: Selections from the Shorter Writings of Reinhold Niebuhr*. Philadelphia: Westminster, 1957.
Scarry, Elaine. *On Beauty and Being Just*. Princeton: Princeton University Press, 1999.
Schaff, Philip. *The Creeds of the Evangelical Protestant Churches, Vol. 3*. London: Hodder & Stoughton, 1877.
Stackhouse, Max L. *Creeds, Society, and Human Rights: A Study in Three Cultures*. Grand Rapids: Eerdmans, 1964.
Stanley, Jason, and Timothy Williamson. "Knowing How." *Journal of Philosophy* 98 (2001) 411–44.
Strauss, Leo. *Natural Right and History*. Chicago: University of Chicago Press, 1953.

Stump, Eleonore. *Wandering in Darkness*. Oxford: Oxford University Press, 2010.
Sunday Missal. Totowa, NJ: Catholic Book Publishing Corp., 2011.
Tierney, Brian. *The Idea of Natural Rights: Studies on Natural Rights, Natural Law and Church Law: 1150–1625*. Atlanta: Scholars, 1997.
Torrance, T. F. *Calvin's Doctrine of Man*. Grand Rapids: Eerdmans, 1957.
Tuck, Richard. *Natural Rights Theories: Their Origin and Development*. Cambridge: Cambridge University Press, 1979.
The United Presbyterian Church in the United States. *The Worship Book: Services and Hymns*. Prepared by the Joint Committee on Worship for Cumberland Presbyterian Church. Philadelphia: Westminster, 1975.
Volf, Miroslav. *Free of Charge*. Grand Rapids: Zondervan, 2005.
Van Driel, Edwin. *What Is Jesus Doing? God's Activity in the Life and Work of the Church*. Downers Grove, IL: InterVarsity, 2020.
Von Allmen, J. J. *Worship: Its Theology and Practice*. Translated by Harold Knight and W. Fletcher Fleet. London: Lutterworth, 1965.
Wackenroder, Wilhelm Heinrich. *Herzensergieessungen eines kunstliebenden Klosterbruders*. Edited by Karl Detlev Jassen. Leipizig: Diederich, 1904.
Wallace, R. S. *Calvin's Doctrine of the Christian Life*. London: Oliver and Boyd, 1959.
Witte, John. *The Reformation of Rights: Law, Religion, and Human Rights in Early Modern Calvinism*. Cambridge: Cambridge University Press, 2007.
Wolterstorff, Nicholas. *Acting Liturgically: Philosophical Reflections on Religious Practice*. Oxford: Oxford University Press, 2018.
———. *Art in Action*. Grand Rapids: Eerdmans, 1980.
———. *Art Rethought*. Oxford: Oxford University Press, 2015.
———. *Divine Discourse*. Cambridge: Cambridge University Press, 1995.
———. *The God We Worship: An Exploration of Liturgical Theology*. Grand Rapids: Eerdmans, 2015.
———. *Justice in Love*. Grand Rapids: Eerdmans, 2011.
———. *Justice: Rights and Wrongs*. Princeton: Princeton University Press, 2008.
———. "Knowing God Liturgically." *Journal of Analytic Theology* 4 (2016) 1–16.
———. *Thomas Reid and the Story Epistemology*. Cambridge: Cambridge University Press, 2001.
———. "The Wounds of God: Calvin's Theology of Social Injustice." *The Reformed Journal* 37 (1987) 14–22.

Index

Abrams, M. H., 137, 159–60, 162
action, 72, 76–77, 92, 114, 123, 184–85, 188, 192, 230–32, 241–43, 249
   illocutionary actions, 184–85
   locutionary actions, 184–85
   perlocutionary actions, 184
addressee-specifications, 236
addressing God, 130, 214–17, 219–21, 227–33, 236–39
aestheticist tradition, 138, 142
aestheticizing gaze, 149–50
alethic tradition, 138
Alston, William, ix, xii, 217
   Perceiving God, 217
Anselm, 26
anti-Semitism, 80
appropriation, 156–58, 198
Aquinas, Thomas, xv, 103, 177–78, 182, 184, 188–90, 194–95
   sign-agency, 177–78, 180–81
Aristotelian principle, 40–41, 48
art, xiv-xv, 3, 5, 9, 12–15, 117, 119–73, 217–18, 240, 243–51
   fine art, 159
   functional art, 119, 142
   graphic art, 159, 169
   memorial art, 155, 244, 250–51
   representational art, 166
   social protest art, 159, 161, 163–66, 169–71, 173
attention, 12–15, 18, 63, 119, 134, 137, 146, 148–53, 209, 222
   absorbed, 12–15, 18, 119, 134, 173

disinterested contemplation, 14, 161
engrossed contemplation, 142, 145–47
attuned to God, 214, 221, 227, 235, 237–38
Augustine, 6, 83–86, 89–90, 96, 209
   Confessions, 83–85
   Of True Religion, 83
   On Christian Doctrine, 83
   the blissful apathy of God, 86
   The City of God, 83, 85
   use/enjoyment distinction, 89
aurora borealis, 8, 19, 128
Austin, J. L., 184
autonomy, 67–68
awesome, 20–21, 193, 195, 208, 243

baptism, 170, 189–91, 194
Barth, Karl, 27, 32, 52, 100, 111, 196, 201–3, 207
basis-specifications, 232–34
Beardsley, Monroe, 130–31, 138–39
beauty, 6–7, 21, 85, 89, 124, 148–54, 158, 161, 234
   nature of beauty, 150
Benton, Matthew A., 216–17, 221–25
   "God and Interpersonal Knowledge", 221–25
Book of Common Prayer, 196, 233
Brunner, Emil, 27, 29, 38, 102, 105–6
   Justice and the Social Order, 29, 38–39, 102, 105

Calvin, John, 83, 88, 91, 98, 177–88, 191–95, 207
   Commentary on Daniel, 96–97
   Commentary on Genesis, 86–87, 92
   Commentary on Habakkuk, 87–88
   Commentary on Isaiah, 94
   doctrine of patience, 96
   God-Agency, 177–81
   Institutes, 88–93, 95, 97, 177–78, 181, 185–88, 191–93, 207
Catholic, 99–100, 207, 236, 251
charity, 37, 42, 45, 50, 54–55, 59–61, 69, 76, 78, 84, 111–12
Christian(s), xi, xvi, 16–18, 29–30, 51–53, 56, 80–83, 88, 95, 97, 99–101, 104, 107, 110–12, 120, 129, 134, 155–56, 187–88, 195, 199–201, 204–5, 210, 216, 227–29, 240–42, 248, 251–55
Christianity, 7, 29, 32, 61, 83, 100, 107, 112, 194, 234, 251
Chrysostom, St. John, 236
Coakley, Sarah, 217
composers, 143–44
Cone, James, 133
   The Spirituals and the Blues, 133
consequentialist, 82

Dana, Richard Henry, 123
deconstructionist, 20
desire, 6–8, 19, 242
   dispositional, 7
   occurrent, 7
Dickens, Charles, 75
   Bleak House, 75
dignity, xiv, xvi, 11, 34, 61, 68, 82–83, 91, 93–94, 97, 107–9, 114, 121, 235
duty, 36, 49, 58, 60, 68–69, 92–94, 103, 109–12, 114–15, 123, 151, 153, 196, 211
   imperfect duty, 49, 68–69
   obligation, 31, 37, 46–47, 60, 65, 69, 92, 104, 110, 113, 115, 140, 211

edification, 242
Elkins, James, 217–20, 224
   What Painting Is, 217–20

emotivist tradition, 138
empathy, 153–54, 166–69, 172–73
Enlightenment, 80, 99, 103
equality, 39–40, 47, 106–9, 113, 150, 152
eudaimonia (eudaimonism), 68, 84
expressivist, 142, 184

faith, 31, 177, 179–81, 183, 186, 191–94, 206
Feinberg, Joel, 39–40, 42–43, 45, 47
fittingness, 122, 249–50
flourishing, xiv, 46, 119–20, 128, 134–35
   shalom, xiv, 120, 125–26, 133–34

generosity, xiv, 26–27, 29–31, 36–45, 47–50, 52–53, 55, 57, 102, 112
glory, 17, 90, 157, 181, 233–34, 237, 243
Goldman, Alan H., 139
good(s), 4–5, 10–19, 25, 27, 34, 36, 39–41, 43–45, 47–49, 52–53, 55–56, 58–60, 62–63, 65–72, 74–76, 78, 81–82, 93, 106, 114–15, 126, 153
   instrumental, 11, 13–14, 144–45
   intrinsic, xv, 4–5, 10, 12–15, 126, 131, 137–8, 144–47
grace, 178–82, 185, 188–91, 243
   instrumental cause of grace, 188–89
gratitude, 18, 54, 90, 232–33
grief, 83–85, 88–90, 96, 128

Hall, Donald, 12, 136–37, 142
Hegel, G.F., 138, 162
Hobbes, Thomas, 99, 103
Holocaust, 80, 155
Holy Spirit, 191–93, 204, 206–8, 238
honor, xiv, xvi, 11, 34, 61, 89, 91, 93, 95–97, 103, 116, 128, 154–56, 207, 211, 248, 250–55
Horn, Stacy, 132
   Imperfect Harmony, 132

iconicity, 92–93, 95
icons, 91, 247, 251
ideal observer theory, 140
   ideal critic, 140–42
ignorance, 77, 252
   willful ignorance, 77

image of God, xvi, 11, 17, 63, 86–87, 90–94, 98, 107–10, 235, 254–55
imago dei, xiv, 107, 109, 115–16
imagination, 20, 36, 57, 73, 143–44, 152, 163, 245
indifference, 75, 81
intentions, 71–72, 76–77
Israel, 16, 31–32, 79–80, 157, 234, 251

Jesus, 26–34, 36–38, 46, 49–52, 57–58, 61–63, 92, 101–2, 112, 125, 129, 134, 155, 170, 179, 183, 185–88, 191–95, 203, 206, 208, 211, 236
Jews, 37, 50, 79–80
Luther King Jr, Martin, 73
justice, xii–xvi, 3, 5, 8–9, 12, 16–18, 25–35, 38–40, 43–46, 48–50, 52–62, 64–80, 83–84, 86–90, 92–98, 101–2, 104–14, 150–58, 165–68, 252
  corrective justice, 26
  distributive justice, 8, 26
  first-order justice, 8–9
  primary justice, 26
  rectifying justice, 8
  retributive justice, 9, 26, 38
  second-order justice, 8–9
  social justice, 64–65, 70–78, 165, 168

Kierkegaard, Søren, 6–7, 27–28, 51, 102
  Works of Love, 7, 28, 51, 102
knowledge, 9, 138, 140, 146, 161, 199, 209, 213–39, 241
  de dicto knowledge, 215
  de re knowledge, 215–16, 218, 220–21, 225, 239
  doxastic knowledge, 215–17, 219–21, 230–32, 239
  knowledge-how, 216, 219
  objectual knowledge, 216–21, 230, 232
  person-knowledge, 216–17, 221–22, 225–29, 233–34, 237, 239
  practical knowledge, 216–17, 219–20, 228
  propositional knowledge, 215, 228

sub-doxastic knowledge, 219–20, 230

learning, 8, 18–19, 219–20, 222, 227, 234
listening, 7, 13, 119, 141, 145–46, 161, 207, 210–14, 227–29, 238, 248
  active listening, 212
  receptive listening, 211
liturgy, xi, xv–xvi, 3, 5, 9, 15, 17, 156–57, 178, 194, 196, 204–8, 211–12, 214, 217, 227–51
  acclamation, 200–3, 205
  formative, 239, 242
  liturgical action, 227, 231, 244, 249
  liturgical enactment, 200, 204, 214–15, 227–28, 232, 236, 242, 244
  liturgical singing, 120, 129, 133–34
  performative, 242
Locke, John, 99
Lomax, Alan, 122, 124, 126
  Prison Songs, 122–24
love, 3–21, 25–35, 38, 51–63, 84–96, 101–2, 111–13, 116, 128, 132–33, 145, 157–58, 170, 186, 206, 210–11, 216, 224–27, 232–36, 252–55
  activity-love, 4, 19
  agape, 27–28, 31–32, 51–52, 57, 62, 101
  eros, 4–7, 28, 38, 51, 57, 101, 145
  gratuitous generosity, xiv, 27, 31, 36–37, 41, 43–44
  love as attachment, 4–5, 52
  love as attraction, 4–6, 19, 26–28, 51, 145
  love as benevolence, 4–5, 27, 33–34, 52–53, 55, 57, 60
  love as care, 34–35, 63
  love as friendship, 4–5, 52
  mutual love, 52
  philia, 4
  self-love, 7–8, 28, 32

making and doing, 155
Marcuse, Herbert, 164
  The Aesthetic Dimension, 164
mercy, 25, 49, 111, 203

Mill, J. S., 81
Modernity, 103, 152, 162–63, 245
morality, 51, 58–63, 82
    actor-dimension, 60
    agent-dimension, 60, 115
    moral order, 60, 110, 112, 115
    patient-dimension, 60, 115
    recipient-dimension, 60, 115
Moritz, Karl Philipp, 137
music, 13, 46, 85, 119, 121, 123–24, 130–34, 143, 145–46, 160–61, 240, 246–47, 249
    folk music, 160
    song, 16, 119–26, 129–34, 142–44, 234, 237, 247
    work songs, 119–26, 129–30, 132–34, 247
musical composition, 143

New Testament, 4, 27–31, 53, 57–58, 113, 156, 199–200, 253–54
    books
        1 Peter, 253
        Colossians, 253
        Corinthians, 128
        Ephesians, 253
        Luke, 31, 36, 46, 57–58, 89
        Matthew, 31–32, 135, 209, 217, 221, 239
        Romans, 170, 253
        Thessalonians, 205–6
    parables
        Parable of the Laborers in the Vineyard, 26, 29–30, 36, 57, 102
        Parable of the Prodigal Son, 36, 46, 57
        Parable of the Good Samaritan, 49, 153
Niebuhr, Reinhold, 27, 29, 52, 56, 61, 100, 112
    The Nature and Destiny of Man, 56, 100
Nussbaum, Martha, 166
Nygren, Anders, 27–28, 38, 51, 57, 101

O'Donovan, Joan Lockwood, 104
O'Donovan, Oliver, 104–5, 108
occasionalism, 180–83
Old Testament, 16, 28, 57, 62, 70, 101, 120, 156, 199–200
    books
        Amos, 16
        Deuteronomy, 32
        Hebrew Bible, 16, 20, 120
        Isaiah, 58, 70–72, 94
        Leviticus, 32–33, 62
        Micah, 25
        Psalms, 129, 156–58, 200, 234
        Shema, 31
        Torah, 27, 32–33, 37, 51, 62
oppression, 54, 70, 154, 170
Orthodox, 17, 92, 130, 170, 214, 234, 236–37, 241, 243, 251

paint, 88, 149, 155, 217–20, 224
Palestinians, 79–80, 94, 154
participation, 156, 179, 214–16, 220, 227, 239
    fully compliant participation, 215
person, 4–7, 9, 11–12, 15, 17–18, 27, 29, 31–34, 36–37, 39–40, 43, 46–48, 50, 52, 54–56, 58–61, 63–65, 68–78, 80–82, 84, 87, 90–93, 97–98, 100, 102–3, 105–10, 114, 119, 127, 132–33, 138, 165–67, 169–70, 172, 179, 183, 188, 191–92, 207–8, 233–39, 241–42, 44, 250
    just persons, 149, 151, 153, 155, 157–60
    person-knowledge, 216–17, 221–30
Picasso, 155, 164, 169
Plato, 5–7, 26, 28, 145
    Symposium, 6, 26, 28, 145
poem, 12–15, 130–31, 136–37, 143, 152, 155, 198–99
postmodernist, 20
preaching, 185–86, 196–97, 199–201, 203–11, 213, 238
principle of correlatives, 58, 69, 115
principle of symmetry, 221

promise, 44, 48, 111–12, 177–82, 184–88, 191–92, 201, 203, 211
prophets, 70–73, 95, 227, 233
Protestant, 27, 56, 99–105, 107, 109–11, 113, 115, 179, 250–51
   Calvinist Protestantism, 100
   liberal Protestant, 56, 251
   modern Protestant, 99, 101, 103, 105, 107, 109, 111, 113, 115

Ramsey, Paul, 27, 52, 110
   "The Created Destination of Property Rights", 110
Reid, Thomas, 171, 232
   natural signs, 171–72
religion, 10, 80–83, 97–99, 162, 179, 217, 245, 251
rights, 3, 9–11, 30, 33–34, 48, 58–60, 64–70, 72, 74, 77–79, 82–83, 96, 99–16
   claim-right, 65–66, 113–14
   entitlement, 9, 103
   having a right to, 65–67
   human rights, 99–105, 107, 109–13, 115–16
   imperfect right, 69, 77–78
   natural right, 10, 67–68, 99, 101–5, 110–13
   perfect right, 69
   permission-right, 65, 113–14
   positive right, 10, 105
rituals, 15–16
Roberts, Robert C., 127
   concern-imbued construals, 127
Romanticism, 151
   Romantics, 151–52, 162–63, 170, 245
Rouault, Georges, 159, 161, 163, 165–67, 169–73
   Guerre, Miserere et, 159, 169, 171–72

sacrament, 95, 177–96, 210–11
Scarry, Elaine, 148
   On Beauty and Being Just, 148–51
Schmemann, Alexander, 243

Schubert, 4–5, 7, 19, 131
Seneca, 25
slavery, 77, 167, 169, 254
social justice organization, 72
Socrates, 6–7, 151
solidarity, 85, 125, 132–33
South Africa, 53–54, 74, 93, 153
   "Remember Sharpeville", 154
   Afrikaner, 53–54, 60–61, 74
   apartheid, 53–54, 61, 74–75, 153
Steinbeck, John, 164, 167
Stoicism, 89
Stowe, Harriet Beecher, 154
   Uncle Tom's Cabin, 154, 166–69, 173
Strauss, Leo, 103
   Natural Right and History, 103
Stravinsky, 141, 143
   Rite of Spring, 143
Stump, Eleonore, 217
   Wandering in Darkness, 217
symbol systems, 183–84

taste, 85, 89, 128, 140, 145
The Apostolic Tradition, 207
the grand narrative, 161–65, 169, 246
the Word of God, 185, 196–97, 199–13, 238
tolerance, 80–82
   nature of tolerance, 80–81
   religious intolerance, 79–83, 85, 87, 89, 91, 93, 95–97
transference, 168–69, 171–73

Ulpian, 9, 25, 59, 64–66, 252
utilitarianism, 34, 68

value, 33, 122, 139–40, 145, 161–62, 187, 244, 246–48
   aesthetic value, 139–40, 162, 244, 246–47
Viet Nam Memorial, 250
virtue, 9, 69, 93–94, 114–15, 133, 164, 171, 182, 189
Volf, Miroslav, 27

Weber, Max, 162

wellbeing, 29, 33–34, 128
William of Ockham, 103
wisdom, 17, 20–21, 208, 232, 236–37
Wolterstorff, Nicholas
    Acting Liturgically, 3, 196, 201, 227
    Art Rethought, 3, 119–20, 129, 155, 160, 165
    Divine Discourse, 156, 197–99, 201
    Justice in Love, 3, 5, 35, 112–13
    Justice: Rights and Wrongs, 3, 9, 30, 48, 64, 83, 112
    The God We Worship, 196, 207, 228

worship, 16–18, 97, 132, 155–57, 188, 196, 207, 212, 214–15, 227–29, 231–32, 234, 236, 238, 240, 249
    adoration, 17–18
    attitudinal stance, 17
    orientation, 4–5, 16, 103–4, 246
    reverence, 16, 18
    sung praise, 129–30
wronging God, 86, 95

Yoder, John Howard, 27

www.ingramcontent.com/pod-product-compliance
Lightning Source LLC
Chambersburg PA
CBHW022002220426
43663CB00007B/921